LAURA AND ME

A SEX OFFENDER AND VICTIM
SEARCH TOGETHER TO UNDERSTAND,
FORGIVE, AND HEAL

SYLVIA PETERSON

PRESS

DEDICATION

To my husband who has taught me how to
forgive quickly and love extravagantly, to
the "pocket people," my companions who
gave me a reason to remain steadfast, and to
Laura for courageously sharing her story.

TABLE OF CONTENTS

INTRODUCTION – WHY IS THIS A BOOK?

Have you ever wanted to know why adults sexually harm children? Perhaps you were a victim. Have you ever told anyone, or did you keep the secret all these years? Or maybe you have held someone you love while they cried and shook and told you their shocking and tragic story. You could be a professional who feels helplessly overwhelmed when you are told "what the problem is." It's possible you are related to someone convicted of a sexual crime against a child and wondering how your family arrived at this painful place.

Quite possibly you are none of these, yet hardly a night goes by without the news reporting another child has been harmed or is missing. We all ask the same question, "Why?"

In 2003 I had a unique opportunity. I was asked to see Laura Faye McCollum, the only woman in our state who is confined indefinitely as a violent sexual predator. Believing a man wouldn't answer my questions truthfully, I hoped Laura could. Until I understood, I would not forgive my own perpetrator. It wasn't very complicated. All I wanted to know was, *"Why did he do that to me?"*

A few months into my visits with Laura I realized three things. First, she wasn't likely to quickly blurt out the answers to my questions. She might not even know the answers. Or she might choose not to tell me. This was going to take time.

I had not anticipated the second issue. I became the recipient of contempt. Only my husband and Laura's chaplain supported my decision to see her. Virtually everyone else verbalized harsh judgments or abruptly changed the subject whenever it came up. Even in the Christian community, I was informed that the "worst of the worst" do not deserve to be recipients of the Fruits of the Spirit: love, joy, peace, patience, kindness, goodness, faithfulness, gentleness and self-control. Several people told me pedophiles had out-sinned their right to grace.

And third, my quest to understand, forgive and heal reached out beyond my own abuse. Some days I imagined my coat pockets filled with others who had the same questions as me. There were former victims, their friends and family, and professionals in the field of pedophilia. Also I included a sprinkling of offenders' family members. The crime wasn't theirs, but they were treated as though it was. We were all asking the same question, "Why?" I imagined them safely secured in the pockets of my raincoat and I gently carried them with me each visit.

I was on a psychological and spiritual scavenger hunt. During times of great discouragement the "pocket people" gave me a reason to keep going. "Sylvia, we cannot go there ourselves and we need the answers too. If you stop seeing Laura, we may never understand." I kept going, deliberately using my codependent tendencies as a motivational tool.

If you are a survivor of childhood abuse, parts of this book may profoundly disturb you. You could experience nightmares/ insomnia, sadness or hopelessness, forgetfulness, be more prone to accidents, have cravings for alcohol, drugs or food, or you may experience a deep rage that feels like it will destroy you and anyone else who gets in its way. Though uncomfortable and occasionally embarrassing in social situations, these are temporary. They aren't who you are today.

My own abuse memories are like cloying cologne. I don't like the smell, especially when it wafts into my life uninvited and unexpected. I've learned that God is bigger than anything I might remember. He knows exactly what happened and the effects it still has on my life today.

You aren't alone. Whenever we make a decision to heal into wholeness, we can trust God to walk beside us in new and tangible ways. He will unfold your path as you step onto it.

So, care for yourself. Take breaks. Go for a walk outside. Call someone you trust. See a professional. Pray "without ceasing." Listen to music. Journal your feelings.

You couldn't protect yourself as a child. Today you can.

So why do adults sexually abuse children? This book is my journey to find out *"Why?"*

Chapter One

OVERCOMING THE INITIAL REVULSION

Be strong and of good courage, do not fear or be afraid of them; for the Lord your God, He is the One who goes with you. He will not leave you nor forsake you. (Deut. 31:6)

While expertly rolling tobacco into a zigzag paper, Laura announced "I just got off suicide watch this morning. They'll be checkin' us more than usual today. Just thought you should know in case they give you the creeps."

I could feel her watching me while I concentrated on the perfect little cigarette she was carefully massaging into place. I deliberately paused. Was she testing my reaction?

Laura began to roll the paper back and forth gently, completely absorbed in the technical process. I watched her hands. She had thick, short fingers with rough, unkempt nails. There were numerous scars on her wrists and lower arms. They were the hands and arms of someone whose life had been rough and uncomforted. It was only our second visit, but I knew better than to interrupt her concentration. In less than a minute I followed the finished "smoke" up to her mouth as she licked the flap and eyed her work proudly.

"Why were you on suicide watch, Laura?" I took a deep breath in, letting it out slowly. Our first visit had been frustratingly benign.

She rolled cigarettes and I watched her smoke them while she sized me up. Looking back I was able to see that she had been testing me. Could I be scared away by uncomfortable silences and clouds of cigarette smoke?

My reason for seeing Laura was never articulated. In fact, I didn't want anyone to know. Embedded deep in my unforgiving secret shame were memories that never completely went away. Grandpa Ed molested me that summer. I intended to find out why. Many "experts" have researched and written about the perversity that causes a pedophile to prey on children, but I'd yet to find one that could answer my simple question. Why? Why do they do it? Would a male pedophile let me crawl into his head and extract the truth? Probably not, but I hoped a female would.

So, although I wanted others to see me as selflessly altruistic, Christian charity wasn't my driving force. Now I realized this wouldn't be as simple as asking Laura to tell me the answer and politely listening to her heartfelt reply. Whether it took three visits or three hundred, I wasn't going away until she told me the truth.

Those first two visits while Laura sized me up, I was doing the same to her. My plan was to build a rapport and slowly take her apart brick by brick until she answered me. "Why do people become monsters like you? How does this happen?"

On visit two there was no pretense, no superficial social conversation. Laura had either made the mental commitment to develop a relationship with me, or she intended to up the "ante" and see if I was tough enough to visit a sex offender. I should have been more grateful for the innocuousness of our first visit.

"Let's go outside so I can smoke this."

Laura and I left the six-by-seven foot room, the only place we were allowed to talk without being electronically monitored by both cameras and microphones. She crossed the adjacent "visiting room" quickly. Laura was a no-nonsense woman when it was cigarette time.

I tried to look back at the staff without being obvious. There were three men and a woman assigned to monitor our visit. They did give me the creeps. I couldn't tell for sure who they were protecting. Laura? Me? Maybe they were there just to make certain we both followed all the rules, some of which I didn't even know yet.

Or were they voyeurs, making barely more than minimum wage, but paid to watch for sexual behavior among people whose court files read like sleazy porn novels?

I also wondered— not for the last time— how I managed to get there as a middle-aged future pastor's wife and religious volunteer.

Laura pushed open the door to a small patio adjacent to the visiting room and propped it by pushing a huge can of sand into place with one foot. We sat side by side on a small concrete bench. I started to straddle it so that I could face her. Then I stopped. I didn't want my legs open, facing Laura. Even in jeans, I felt vulnerable.

The Special Commitment Center (SCC) is a societal anomaly of the prison corrections system. Washington State takes sexual crimes very seriously; in fact, prison time isn't considered sufficient deterrent for predators. In 1990 the State Legislature passed the Community Protection Act, which created a mental health treatment facility for sexual offenders. Initially this was located at The Monroe Reformatory and later moved within the walls of McNeil Island Correctional Center, the last island-bound prison in the United States. Finally the SCC moved into a new state-of-the-art facility on the north side of McNeil, surrounded by forest and unseen from the waters of Puget Sound.

At the end of their sentences perpetrators of sexual crimes are put through a battery of tests and mental health interviews. Their court transcripts are poured over by forensic psychologists. The End of Sentence Review Committee evaluates each case. Inmates are then assigned a "level" that is their label, essentially for the remainder of their lives. Level One is the least dangerous. Level Three indicates a likelihood that the offender will re-offend. Of the Level Threes, the files of those that are more likely than not to repeat their sexual crimes are sent to the prosecutor's office. There are still more consultations and experts with advice. Eventually three percent of Washington State's sexual offenders are civilly committed to the SCC and held indefinitely. They served their time, but are too dangerous to release into the community and are transferred from the Department of Corrections to the Department of Social and Health Services. By the time I began my journey into the Special Commitment Center in August of 2004, the offenders had moved into their new facility, separate from the prison and considerably more secure.

The DSHS bus transports staff, visitors, volunteers, and professionals from the ferry dock to The Special Commitment Center, dropping them off in front of a flat, concrete wall topped with four rows of curling concertina, razor wire. To one side is a ninety-foot tunnel leading to the front door. On my first visit I was too nervous to notice the extreme security measures. My second visit I discretely began to look around.

No one entered the tunnel without being seen by multiple electronic monitoring devices. Staff wore badges that allowed them to buzz through the front door. Everyone else rang a doorbell and waited to be escorted. From the area in front of the entry tunnel and throughout the entire complex, every move and word were being watched, heard, or both.

The State of Washington had promised the general public that the SCC would securely hold the "worst of the worst." And it did.

On this day 203 predatory men had been indefinitely, probably permanently, detained. And Laura.

I repeated my question while she smoked. "Why were you on suicide watch?"

Laura ran one hand through newly-cut brown hair. Her eyebrows were thick and wild. She wore no makeup. I tried to guess her age and decided early forties. Her thighs were short and thick, stuffed into gray sweatpants issued to her by the state. There were food stains down the front of her graying white T-shirt.

Laura tried to light her cigarette with her last match. It went out. After a stream of profanity she left to get more. I was the only SCC visitor on this day. I wondered if I was also the only personal visitor Laura had had in years. Family and friends don't remain in a predator's life for very long. Sexual shame is disturbingly contagious.

"It was just a misunderstandin'. No big deal," Laura continued when she returned with a new book of matches she'd secured from staff who loitered just out of earshot. "I wrote some stuff in my journal about how upset I was. My counselor, Rose, left. She's been with me four years. The staff freaked out that I might hurt myself, or put myself in a position where one of the men'll hurt me. That's always a worry here."

"Where'd she go, your counselor?"

Laura took a deep drag off her cigarette, creating a long snake of ash. "To work for CPS. (Child Protective Agency) I can't blame her. Better money and she won't have to take the boat to work every day. Everybody complains about that. She's tryin' to get a contract so she can keep workin' with me, if there's any money for it in the budget. Which there isn't."

I felt her drawing me to a place of non-emotion. It was easy to talk about budget cuts and our bankrupt state. I wasn't willing to waste our two hours on politics. "How does it feel to have Rose leave?"

"Rotten. And scary. The counselor who's takin' her place is very tiny, like a kid. I don't think she's a good match for me. She looks too much like my victims. When I talk to her I fight myself. I want to groom her, then other times I want to be just like her. There's a name for it."

"Transference."

"Yeah. That's it. Transference."

"Laura, that's a fairly normal part of the therapeutic relationship. Almost all clients go through some degree of transference." I crossed my heavy thighs self-consciously. I was suddenly grateful for a body that would never be tiny and petite.

"Still, she's not good for me." Laura threw the second half of the cigarette into the spindly bushes and stood, signaling we were going back inside until she rolled a new one.

One of the visiting room staff was a lanky Hispanic man in his twenties. George eyed us suspiciously as we crossed the empty visiting room and returned to the private interview area. I shut the door behind us. Laura and I sat down on the only two chairs and rested our arms on the small plastic table. Three walls were gray and bare. The fourth wall was shatterproof glass from floor to ceiling; I kept my back to the window so the staff couldn't see my face. I wasn't sure why that was important to me.

My husband had an altercation with George when we arrived that morning. John was a chapel intern finishing his Master's of Divinity degree; he frequently filled in for the full-time paid chaplain's vacation. George insisted John sign in as a volunteer even though he had a security badge that clearly labeled him as staff and had been coming out to the SCC for months. John balked, wanting to know when and why the rules had changed. George refused to explain and they had a verbal power struggle. George wouldn't back down; John finally signed in for the sake of peace. George felt his authority had been questioned and his anger was dark and brooding. Although none of it applied to me, I was clearly guilty by association in the festering mind of George. I guess I shouldn't have been surprised that he waited for John to leave the visiting area that morning and then retaliated on Laura and me.

After she had been escorted from her living area to the visiting room and patted down to assure security, George unlocked an adjacent room that was full of children's furniture and toys. Neither Laura nor I were small women. We would have been painfully uncomfortable sitting in toddler-sized chairs, if we could even squeeze into them without breaking the fragile plastic. But the issue was bigger than the size of the furniture. Laura argued with him. "I can't go in there. I'm not supposed to be around kids."

"No kids in here today, Laura." His eyes were cold and implacable. I wondered, not for the first time, why people choose to work at the SCC.

"Doesn't matter. It would put me in violation of my relapse prevention plan."

He didn't move, didn't speak.

Laura wouldn't budge. "My counselor'd be really upset if I let you put me in there. You wanna call and talk to her?" Her tone of voice was cautiously belligerent.

We waited, using up our finite time together with his infinite ego. "No." He looked at me as he answered. "I wouldn't want to get you in trouble, Laura. You can use the attorney visit room."

I wondered why it made a difference to him. Then I compared the location of the two rooms. He could see into the children's room without ever leaving his desk. To supervise the interview room he'd have to get up periodically and make the obvious effort to walk by our glass wall. That fifteen-foot journey was apparently tough for him. I knew when he passed by; the hairs stood up on the back of my neck. I felt stalked, not protected.

As soon as Laura and I came in from the smoking patio we continued.

"Were you feeling suicidal?"

"Nah. I'm not goin' to do anything stupid, but I was upset. Losin' Rose is big." Laura began the ritual of rolling a new cigarette. Her rapid switch of topics caught me off guard.

"I'd had a bad week in addition to Rose. There's this guy that lives here. He asked me for a pair of my underpants. Well, I didn't know just what to do. I could tell he liked me, but I like this other guy named Dave. I knew Dave wouldn't want me foolin' around with someone else."

I never considered Laura's romance potential and I certainly couldn't imagine giving away my underwear. I didn't know what to say.

"Uh, how often do you see Dave?"

"Not very often. But we found a way to spend a whole hour together a couple days ago. It was the first time we kissed." Laura's eyes momentarily sparkled with the light of infatuation. Her voice softened and became childlike. The change was dramatic and unsettling.

I suspected Dave was not part of Laura's treatment plan.

She jumped back to Mr. Underpants. "So he called me up and we decided to get together after I got him the underpants, which I gave him a couple days ago. But I went over to the gym where he works and he started yellin' at me and I lost my dignity right there by cryin' in front of some of the other guys, so I told him the whole thing was off. I wasn't his girlfriend and he better not ask me for nothin' again."

"So where are the underpants?" I couldn't think of anything else to say. It certainly wasn't a conversation I'd ever had previously.

"He still has 'em."

"Laura, could this ultimately get you in some trouble? Because I'm thinking that giving away your used underwear to an obviously sick man is not a really good idea. If the staff finds them, won't they know where he got them? You're the only woman here."

"Yeah, this could come right back on me. But they can't prove nothin'. Lots of stuff comes in here. Could'a been staff or a visitor or mailed here." She shrugged. "So Sylvia, why do you think

I did that, I mean, said I'd fool around with him and then changed my mind?"

I'm not a psychologist, but there were clues all over the place. "I think you were feeling a big, empty place inside you because Rose was leaving and you tried to fill that empty place with a new, sexy relationship. But then you realized that it wouldn't work. You'd still be empty and you'd feel bad inside because you cheated on Dave. So you backed out at the last minute."

I recognized my untrained analysis as a rescue from sicker possibilities. I was also giving her credit for integrity not evidenced so far.

She nodded while rolling still another cigarette. "Yeah, I like that.... but there's more. I'm in this class called "Sexual Deviancy Reprogramming." Everyone has to take it. The teacher wants me to make a collage of acceptable victims, you know, like adults. And then I'm suppose' to fantasize about them and talk into a tape recorder so they can analyze me. You know they make us do a lot of crazy stuff like that here, don't you?"

I nodded, more to keep her talking than to suggest I knew anything about sex offender treatment modalities. Before we were done, I'd probably know too much.

Laura continued without pause. "Isn't that just puttin' one victim in another victim's place? You and John are religious. I read the Bible and I know Jesus loves me, but I don't know what God would think about me fantasizin' on a recorder. But if I refuse, I won't pass the class. And if I don't pass the class I won't ever get out." Her voice had turned into a whine. "What would you do?"

My head was spinning. Dark, sick images crowded my brain, each fighting for prominence. I wanted to stand up, go to the restroom, and vomit. I wanted to flush everything I knew about Laura McCollum down the toilet and go home. I wanted to tell the chaplain I wouldn't be back. Instead, I plodded on.

"I have several things to say, Laura. First, I'm working on an assumption that you were sexually molested as a child. We haven't talked about it, but I think it's probably true." I watched her give me a slight nod. "As for your collage project, I can't advise you to be non-compliant with your treatment plan. I'm not qualified to give you clinical advice. I'm not even here to give you pastoral advice. What I am wondering is if you could make a collage that represents a healthy, godly husband. Not a victim, but someone you loved with every ounce of your being. What would it take for you to fantasize about being intimate within the safety and commitment of a blessed marriage? Maybe we could talk about what that would look like."

"Ya' mean I'd be dreamin' about my husband?" She sounded incredulous.

"Yes."

Laura's brow furrowed deeply. "I don't know. I don't think God wants me to fantasize about my husband."

"Why not? God created us male and female and He created us sexual. But His intent was that our sexuality would be confined to a blessed and holy marriage." I hoped my statement didn't come off as sanctimonious and condemning.

She was silent for several minutes while she considered this possibility. "Wow. This is goin' to really freak out the staff. It's too healthy. But I'm goin' to think on it awhile."

I'd made points. There was admiration in her voice.

She switched topics without pausing. "I'm unusual. I didn't start molestin' kids until I was thirty-two. I want to figure why that is. Most of the guys here started young, like before they were eighteen. Why'd I wait so long? The staff doesn't want to explore that with me because they don't believe me. They think I had other victims I'm just not talkin' about, but I swear I was thirty-two when I started."

I felt like I'd been sucker-punched; I didn't see it coming. This was the opening to the answers I wanted, but unexpectedly a surge of rage and shame made my questions inconsequential. Who was this woman? What horrible things had she done to end up in a prison with no exit doors except to the morgue? With great control of my voice and facial expression, I tried to hide my revulsion and kept the conversation moving.

"Did you have fantasies before that?"

"Oh, yeah, of course. I just didn't act on them. I kept it all together for a long time and then I just sort of lost it. I have fifteen victims."

Not had. Have. I wondered if in Laura's mind she still had some kind of relationship with the children she'd molested. I doubted the number fifteen. There was no way of knowing if she was exaggerating or minimizing; I just doubted she was telling me the truth.

Laura waited to see if I would react. My silence forced her to continue.

"The one that I feel really bad about is Annie. I didn't mean to hurt her. I loved her. Annie... Do you have any kids? Maybe I shouldn't ask."

I had to get away. Everything inside me screamed, "Run!" I excused myself to the restroom and splashed cold water over my face. It didn't matter that the make-up I had carefully applied in the morning was now melting onto my shirt. Leaning against the cold, tile wall I prayed, *"Lord, help me. How can I get answers if I can't even stand to be in her presence for a two-hour visit? I have to do this. There is no other way for me to forgive."*

When I felt color restore to my face I returned to the interview room.

Laura was waiting for an answer. "So what about it? Do you and John have any kids?"

"I don't have any children. My husband had two grown children when we married. I'm a stepmother."

"You have grandchildren?"

I hesitated. John's daughter had a gorgeous, bright, beloved two-year old son. I didn't want any part of his innocent essence to enter Laura's dark world. I recoiled at the thought of even saying his name out loud. Time slowed down while I searched for a protectively vague response. "Yes."

"Why didn't you have children? Maybe you could have some now."

"I'm fifty-two years old. It's too late. I didn't marry John until I was forty-five, and I specifically prayed for a husband who already had children. The desire of my heart was to be a wife and step-mother."

She read me with deadly perception. "What else? I mean, there's another reason you didn't have children. You coulda' had some before John."

Laura's steel grey eyes bored into my face. My chest constricted. I wanted to lie, not giving her the satisfaction of being right. Or I could use her technique and change topics, but I realized that she was either extremely intuitive or conversationally lucky. I wouldn't be able to hide for long behind incomplete truths and demand honesty from Laura.

I kept my answer simple. "I never had children because I was molested when I was a child. I didn't seek professional help until I was in my forties. Before that I was afraid." There, I'd said it out loud.

"Afraid that someone would do to them what they did to you?"

"Yes."

I felt naked and exposed. Maybe there was something about me that flashed strobe lights. Victim! Victim! Victim! Did perpetrators have some kind of extrasensory antennae that told them who was vulnerable and who wasn't? I didn't trust her with my private places. This was the first time I realized I was going to have to give up some personal information in hopes of luring Laura into doing the same.

Laura waited for me to disclose more. "I spent the first two decades of my adulthood trying to run away from myself. A husband and children are two of the things I avoided."

She smiled. "I want to talk about Annie."

My husband and I met while volunteering in the correctional system. Since then, McNeil Island had become part of our lives. A significant amount of time was spent preparing for and implementing programs for incarcerated offenders and their families, but not specifically with the sex offenders. We worked solely with "regular felons," murderers, robbers, drug dealers, and methamphetamine manufacturers. We never asked why the men were there. I assumed a few sex offenders were in the mix, but I didn't want to know who they were, and the institution screened most of them out of our programs.

That was before my husband started seminary. And before his mentor became the SCC chaplain. And before he began an internship there as part of his graduate degree in seminary. That was before he started talking to me about Laura.

21

Because of my childhood issues I said I would never go to the Special Commitment Center, but I began to wonder about her. What was life like for the only woman involuntarily committed as a sexual predator? Did she have exposure to other females? Did she have any "normal" women in her rigidly therapeutic life? With whom did she share her feelings, her life story, her fears and her dreams? Or did her crimes negate her right to have any of those things?

I prayed for several months before responding to the chaplain's invitation to meet with Laura.

"Sylvia, she needs a woman in her life who isn't an attorney, staff, or a psychologist. How else can she get healthier?"

Finally I agreed and called him back. "No agenda. No title. I will visit twice a month."

"Okay, Laura. What do you want to say about Annie?" I followed her back out to the patio to smoke another hand-rolled.

"Annie was eighteen months old. Her mother was an alcoholic. Her dad was a deadbeat. He never came around. Her mother used to leave her on my doorstep. I'd just hear her cryin' there and I'd open the door. There she was. So I'd take care of her until her mother came back."

"Was she your first victim?"

She paused. "No."

"So you knew you had a problem, but babysat little Annie anyway." It was a statement, not a question.

She continued. "Annie's mom had to know somethin' was up. But she was always drunk, so maybe she didn't care."

I deliberately made myself blink to stay present in the conversation. It was a therapy technique I'd learned to keep me from dissociating when I felt emotionally overwhelmed. All victims of childhood sexual abuse know how to mentally and emotionally disconnect when it begins to hurt.

"There was an older child, too. But she didn't stay with me like Annie did. I loved little Annie. She was born with fetal alcohol syndrome, so she was all messed up. But I loved her just the same as if she was normal. Part of why I'm here is because Annie was disabled. It's a bigger deal when you go to court."

"I didn't mean to hurt her. I couldn't help it. One time I even called my mental health caseworker and told her about Annie. She didn't believe me; thought I was makin' it up, like some freakin' fantasy or somethin'. So I took a bus and took Annie with me to the Mental Health Center. When I got there they called the police and took Annie to a foster home. Her mom eventually got her back."

I had time to respond while she paused to lick the flap of her tightly-rolled cigarette. "Were there consequences for what you did to Annie?"

"Not really. I told them there was somethin' wrong with me, but they didn't put me in jail or nothin'. They thought it was a mental health thing, so they increased my meds. That was in the early nineties. Things were different then.

"But that wasn't the end of it with Annie. I went into the hospital for awhile and then I got out. The next thing I know, I hear Annie back on my doorstep. I knew if I hurt her again, they'd really lock me up. So I called my caseworker again. Then I had a neighbor come and sit with me until someone could come get Annie."

"It sounds like you did the right thing." Her story didn't ring true.

Laura smiled. She took obvious pleasure in my answer. Then she jumped topic again, leaving me just a glimpse of logical progression. For an instant I saw myself as a middle-aged version of Spiderwoman, sliding down a fragile thread, chasing Laura through decades of diseased and twisted half-truths.

"I was on television. They interviewed me when I was locked up at Purdy. (The Washington Correction Center for Women located in Purdy, Washington.) I told them, 'If your kids don't want to go with some relative, don't make them. Parents got to listen to their kids if they want to keep 'em safe."

"Did Annie want to be with you?"

"Oh, yeah. She loved me. Right up until the end and in spite of everything' I did. Annie loved me.

"The last time I saw her was when I committed myself to Puget Sound Hospital. I knew I was losin' it and I needed somewhere safe to hang out. They can't keep people longer than twenty-one days, but I went anyway. Annie's mom gave me a lift to the hospital. I knew I wasn't suppose' to be around her. By then there was a restrainin' order. But she was drunk and I needed a ride. Annie's older sister was sittin' in the front seat and askin' all kinds of questions. She was five and talked all the time. Like she wanted to know where I was goin' and why I was sick and when I'd be home. You know, junk like that. I just wanted her to shut up. I even mouthed in the rearview mirror to her mom, 'Make her shut up.'

"When she asked me what kind of sickness I had, I wanted to say, 'I hurt little girls like you.'"

I felt the bile rise up in my throat again as the color drained from my face. I was dizzy and a buzzing noise had started in the back of my head, like a thousand cicadas on a hot summer afternoon. I swallowed and blinked. "Laura, that's a horrible thing to say to a little girl."

"Yeah, I know. That's why I kept quiet. Instead I gave her my Game Boy so she'd shut up. When we got to the parkin' lot, Annie crawled up onto my lap and hugged me. I told her good-bye. I told her I was going to get help and that no one would ever hurt her again. You know what she said back to me?"

"No."

"She said, 'No more hurt?' And I said, 'No more hurt, baby.'"

Sometime late in the night I awoke. The pounding in my head had not stopped. My mouth was dry and I could still smell Laura's acrid cigarette smoke in my nose and on my skin. John was softly snoring beside me. I slipped out of bed and settled downstairs on the sofa, pulling a blanket close around my feet and legs. I felt ill.

Laura. Who was she? A sexual psychopath? How does that happen? How was her childhood different from and the same as mine? Why did her molestation turn her into a perpetrator, while mine didn't?

Mentally, I looked through the darkened house, my comfortable life snuggled around me in a cocoon of safety. My husband and I both had respectable careers that kept us financially secure. We had close friends, a church, and a house, everything indicative of a solid middle class life. He was finishing seminary, a second career for him. He looked forward to graduation, ordination and a mid-life dream coming true: full-time ministry. To most people we looked pretty good. But how many people ever really look deeply into the lives of their friends? We both brought baggage into our marriage; everyone does. My history as a survivor sometimes complicated our roles and responses, negotiations and alliances. Our life together was not a lie; it was just a lot more complex than it appeared. Now it didn't feel safe.

Sitting alone in the dark, I was angry. I'd done my work. I'd graduated from therapy. I'd built my life the way I wanted it. But in two visits Laura had opened up the scar tissue and prodded old wounds. As though it had never left, I felt the raw, festering, angry flesh of my childhood abuse gushing from where I had been so certain it had healed.

My questions about Laura had me in an emotional stranglehold. I couldn't let go. They were the same questions I had about my own perpetrator.

Was she crazy and unable to prevent what she had done to Annie and the other children? Was she mentally deficient and didn't know the consequences of her actions? Did she even know right from wrong? Or was she merely ignorant because of her own pathological childhood? Was she treatable? Can humans really measure sexual psychopathology and accurately predict outcomes? Would a collage and fantasizing on tape really repair someone that broken? Should she ever be released back into society?

Was she evil?

And where was God in Laura's life? She'd mentioned Him a couple times, but I suspected she used the reference in a manipulative way. What was her actual relationship with God, if she even had one? Could Laura ever reach a place of redemption? Was she already there?

I hated to even ask myself. If Laura realized that she had sinned and repented of those sins, did that make us equal at the foot of the cross? I didn't want that to be the case. My theology had hit a brick wall. When it came to Laura I didn't want to apply what I knew to be true about redemption, forgiveness and grace.

Sexual wounds feel insane. They hold terror and shame of overwhelming proportions. It is indescribable to people who have never had that experience. I had believed, needed to believe that

25

complete healing was possible, at least in my own case. Now I wasn't so sure.

As the night plodded slowly through the clock and headed into light, I thought of Annie. Where was she now? Who was she now? I began to quietly cry. I didn't want to awaken my husband. I didn't want him to know Laura had triggered all my fears and shame. John was fiercely protective; he'd try to talk me out of continuing the visits.

Fifteen victims. Fifteen shattered lives. Fifteen potential perpetrators if the statistics were right about the abused eventually becoming the abusers.

Where was God when Annie was being abused? Where was He when Grandpa Ed was climbing the stairs to my bedroom at the farmhouse? If He was really sovereign, how could He just stand there and allow things like this happen to innocent children?

My prayer that night was flippant and laced with bitterness. "How can You fall asleep on the job just when children need You the most? How can You justify such severe neglect and expect to be trusted? Laura's on the hook. Grandpa Ed is definitely on the hook. But you are hanging there with them."

Like an intrusive snapshot, I flashed to Calvary. God was hanging on the cross. He came to save sinners, which is a really good deal for a pedophile. It was little comfort to me at that moment.

Even now in the safety of my silent house, I felt unsafe. A deep, malignant relationship was beginning to form between Laura and me. Was it possible for victims and perpetrators to know each other in some dark, immeasurable part of their brains? Were they two sides of the same coin, unable to ever be completely free from each other? I didn't know how to articulate my feelings to someone sweet and "normal" like my husband.

I thought about Laura's collage project. If I were to make a collage of Laura and me, what would it look like? I involuntarily shivered and pulled the blanket tighter around myself.

My collage would be dark, lots of deep blue and black. There would be two figures, one on each side of the paper, joined by a pitch black, winding and dangerous road. Each figure would carry the light and goodness instilled when God made man in His image.

Each would also have dark places. Initiated in the garden, darkness has rolled downhill ever since.

I stared at the imaginary collage I had created. Through extraordinary circumstances Laura and I were now walking slowly towards each other.

I had never forgiven my grandfather. Not only him, I'd never forgiven my grandmother and my parents for failing to protect me. My unwillingness to forgive was an embarrassment. I knew what scripture commanded me to do. I steadfastly refused to do it. As soon as I figured out why the terrible things had happened, I would forgive. "Really, God. I promise."

Suddenly a familiar friend popped into my awareness. More than anything in the world, I wanted the comfort that only large amounts of sugar could bring me. I'd spent a lifetime using it to medicate myself.

I thought back to the end of my visit to Laura.

John retrieved me from the interview room. His loving presence and intrinsic kindness were like a balm. Laura liked John. She immediately stood up and shook his hand. I'd almost forgotten what she said to him as we left.

"Take good care of her," referring to me with a slight nod of the head. "She's been through enough."

No more hurt? I quickly did the math. She was arrested five years after the date she said her goodbye to Annie. Either she had continued to abuse Annie, or there were more Annies in Laura's history. I didn't believe anything she had told me so far. What kind of a monster could molest fifteen children? Maybe more?

"No baby, no more hurt."

Toward the end of our second visit eye blinking no longer worked. I must have "zoned out" because I didn't recall giving Laura our address until a packet of papers arrived from her three days later. Not my home address, I didn't want her to ever know where John and I lived. However, we also kept a box at the post office for mail from inmates. She probably told me she'd write; I didn't remember.

Inside the envelope she sent me her autobiography, an assignment from the therapist who had replaced Rose. I didn't want to

27

read it, but I couldn't stop myself. This could be "the mother lode" of clues to the answers I sought. It started:

This is the story of my life. This is drawn from what memories I have and what has been told to me by family members and child protective services. To my knowledge it is accurate. I write this in honor of the child that was me.

My name is Laura Faye McCollum; I was born December 21, 1957 in Memphis, Tennessee, at John Gaston Hospital. I was two months premature. It is believed my early arrival was due to my mother's use of alcohol while pregnant with me. I was otherwise a healthy newborn.

When I was released from the hospital to my birth parents I went to live with them and eight other siblings. I have four brothers and four sisters. I am the youngest child. I have one brother who is mentally delayed that I call my baby brother, although he is chronologically older than I am.

My dad's name is Clarence Orlando McCollum who is now deceased. He died in 1970. He was fifty-seven years old when I was born. He was born in Corinth, Mississippi. I do not know the date of his birth or the date he married my mother. He had one brother; his name was Jonathon and he married a woman named Pearl. I never met my grandparents on my father's side of the family. They lived in Sacramento, California.

My father had beautiful striking blue eyes, a big belly and he dipped snuff that always seemed to be dribbled and dried in his beard. I don't like the smell of snuff. I don't remember a whole lot about my father since he was not around much as he and my mother were always out drinking. I don't remember ever seeing my father and mother show affection for each other. My father was a street peddler and sold his wares to make money.

I am unsure what my father's relationship was with my mother. If I go by what I have been told and the few memories I have of them, I would have to say it was dysfunctional in every way. Both my parents were chronic alcoholics. They gave little time to me as a child. My mother and father lived together for many years. I have no idea how long they were married or if they divorced or only separated.

My parents loved their alcohol and were not capable of loving each other or their children. Their alcoholism impeded them from even the simplest of tasks such as paying bills, buying food, or providing medical care for the children they brought into the world. I don't believe my parents needed children nor should they have conceived any children since they were irresponsible as parents.

My father and mother suffered from chronic depression and mood swings; they would be fine one minute and ranting the next. My father had no hobbies other than drinking and fighting with my mother. My father also suffered from hypertension, diabetes, and cirrhosis of the liver. Even with his health issues he drank. I don't believe my father ever used drugs, but then I was never told if he did.

No, my father was not supportive. He was neglectful as a father in every sense. I don't remember ever spending any quality time with my father as a young child. I have no memories of my father ever picking me up or comforting me as a baby. I have no memories of him ever reading me a story or playing with me as a young child. My father was never around much that I can remember.

I put Laura's autobiography down and then picked it up again. Then I set it down a second time. All this was fine and well, but it didn't get me anywhere. I scanned the document to see if Annie's name appeared. It didn't. Frustrated, I threw the whole thing in my desk drawer.

Chapter Two

COMPASSION? NOT IN A PIG'S EYE

Behold, the wicked brings forth iniquity; Yes, he conceives trouble and brings forth falsehood. He made a pit and dug it out, And has fallen into the ditch which he made. His trouble shall return on his own head. (Psa. 7:14-16)

Apparently many people knew Laura's name. I did not when I began meeting with her. The chaplain could not tell me very much. The law of confidentiality is extremely restricting. Her admission to the SCC meant there were multiple victims and violence. That's all I knew.

After session two I decided to search the Internet. I wasn't disappointed.

In less than a minute I had printed two articles related to her apparently controversial move to the SCC. The first one was sympathetic of housing Laura with male sexual predators. The article said this:

For the past six years, convicted child rapist Laura Faye McCollum has lived a lonely existence inside the state's women's prison. On Monday, she is scheduled to move to the new Special Commitment Center on McNeil Island to live among 190 other dangerous sex offenders—all of them men.

McCollum, 46, is one of only three female sex offenders in the nation considered dangerous enough to be civilly committed–a process by which offenders are sent indefinitely to tightly controlled treatment programs after they have completed their criminal sentences.

The other women–one in California and one in Minnesota–are housed and treated apart from the men.

In the early 1980's, the Minnesota Department of Corrections attempted coed treatment of sex offenders, but abandoned the program after less than a year. Ruth Mathews, a psychologist who helped develop a program specifically for the women in Minnesota, said the coed effort there "was pretty disastrous."

"The women were actually getting worse," Mathews said.

Women are more likely to be sex abuse victims themselves, Mathews said, so placing female sex offenders into groups with men can be harmful and leave them feeling revictimized.[1]

The article went on to report that through 1997, while housed alongside the forty-two male predators at Monroe Correctional Complex, Laura had reported that the men touched her, exposed themselves to her, and verbally taunted her. If she was a survivor of sexual abuse as a precursor to her role as predator, I could see how abusive it would be for her to live with men who sexually objectified her. I also couldn't help wondering if any of them had ever requested her dirty underwear.

This first article raised some valid and humane points in regard to Laura's housing arrangements.

The second writer had none.

Popular Seattle news critic, Ken Schram wrote "Don't Shed a Tear for Laura McCollum" and said this:

There are people who'd have me feel sorry for Laura McCollum. I don't.

Not even a little.

Laura McCollum is whining about being sent off to the Special Commitment Center on McNeil Island. She doesn't want to be the only woman living with almost 200 men.

All of them sex offenders.

All of them considered dangerous.

Same as her.

31

McCollum has been convicted of repeatedly raping an 18-month-old girl and then trying to smother the life out of the baby with a pillow.

I stood up, walked around the room and sat back down. Was this Laura's Annie, the little girl with fetal alcohol syndrome that she professed to love? Tears welled up in my eyes and began to slowly drip down both cheeks.

She's admitted to molesting more than a dozen other children, mostly girls, no older than three.

One psychologist has said that placing female offenders, like McCollum, into groups with men could be psychologically dangerous for her.

Well isn't that just too (blank) bad.

Public safety is the issue here, not McCollum's potentially fragile psyche.

McCollum is being shipped off to McNeil Island because she's a predator who is too dangerous to be free. She'll be housed in a separate wing from her perverted brethren; be under constant supervision, and have group therapy with men who pose no direct threat to her.

Feel sorry for her?

Not in a pig's eye.[2]

Laura would never, maybe should never be accepted by society. The often acerbic author was in the majority. I wanted to believe I could have more compassion than that, but at the moment I didn't.

Sunday night I returned to The Special Commitment Center with my husband who continued to fill the vacationing Chaplain's job. Laura knew I would be coming in at the same time as the SCC families and she had promised to join us for the Protestant Family Worship Service John was leading. I told her, "I will be your family if you come to the visiting room and join us for church." My curiosity had propelled me into anticipation and I was looking forward to seeing her again.

John and I had volunteered in the prison at McNeil for many years. We made the trip out there at least once a week and sometimes as many as nine times a month. We knew many of the staff and were treated with respect and even a degree of affection. We had worked hard to develop a reputation for being fair, following the rules, supporting the staff's decisions and still remaining unswervingly committed to the prison programs that kept families together. We often worked with offenders' relatives and had developed lasting friendships with a few.

My experiences within the prison system did not adequately prepare me for my first encounter with the SCC families and the way they were treated by the staff. Because the chaplain listed me as "a religious volunteer" I bypassed most of the visit procedures. Family members had a daunting list of steps they followed in order to visit their civilly committed loved one. It was not for the impatient or proud.

First they reported to Western State Hospital (Western Washington's Mental Hospital) to assure they were on that resident's visit list. Photo ID was required. Then they were scanned for metal and their personal carry-on articles were searched (which often included sanitary supplies and baby diapers). A strictly enforced contraband list included such items as pens, lipstick, chewing gum, breath mints, and lighters. The SCC contraband list changed frequently.

The dress code forbade sleeveless blouses, shorts, bare feet, cleavage, and leggings. It didn't matter how far someone traveled to get there or how infrequent the visits were. Sometimes family members drove hours from Eastern Washington, waited in line for another hour in the pouring rain, and then were told to go buy something else to wear or the visit would be denied. Some of them could barely afford the gas to drive there, much less a new outfit.

Next the family members were escorted by staff onto a bus that drove them to the dock, where they waited until cleared to load onto the walk-on Department of Corrections ferry. It was a twenty-minute ride to the island. They were required to sit inside the ferry on the first floor. Only staff and volunteers were allowed to ride in the open air on the second floor where the view was spectacular. The class distinction was obvious.

After disembarking, the families were lined up single file by staff who attentively kept them all in view. Regardless of the weather, which is raining and cold more often than not, they walked down the 200-foot dock to a waiting bus. After the ten-minute drive to the North side of the island, everyone disembarked and moved again in a supervised group. They traversed the tunnel, cleared through one door and into the lobby area, and went through the same doors as I had as a volunteer. The difference was this: family visitors had to line up single file along one wall until they reached the visiting area. Then they waited. Staff had to confirm that their loved one was permitted to see them. Sickness or discipline or misfiled visitation paperwork could squelch the visit after a family member spent hours getting there. I'm not sure why this information wasn't obtained prior to the intense security procedures. It wasn't unusual for visitation to take an entire day. For families living outside the Tacoma area, tack on driving time.

Several things struck me that Sunday night. The first was the incredible lack of emotion from the thirteen people making the trip with us. I was curious. Who were they and what kept them visiting when most families had stopped eons ago? I couldn't ask. They were silent and unapproachable. I imagined them with impenetrable walls of sadness, yet going through the robotic motions of obligatory visits. When I searched their faces, I couldn't find any sign that my assessment was wrong.

From where I was seated on the ferry, I could see George who was their escort on Sunday nights. He was staring at John and me. His eyes were dark and menacing. It perplexed me. Between glares at us he barked out orders to the family members, reminding them where to sit and the necessity of staying in a group. And then his entire demeanor suddenly changed and he was chiding first one family member and then another, teasing with barbs of humor that had a bite and left no doubt that he was in control. I found his banter annoying. He made comments as though they were friends and equals, but then when they attempted to return the quips he bristled and quickly reestablished professional boundaries. To me it was an abuse of power, something he should have known.

One African-American woman had especially beautiful facial features. She was also so large she could hardly walk. There is a strong connection between obesity and childhood sexual trauma.[3] I wondered if she had been a victim of the person she came to visit. I hoped not. I watched in dismay as George flirted with her and then walked quickly away when she responded.

An elderly woman reminded me of my mother, clean-cut and proper, with tiny bone structure and delicate features. She looked like a retired librarian or perhaps a schoolteacher, but sat alone and spoke to no one. Once I caught her eye and smiled. She quickly looked away.

Two older ladies were sitting off to the side. They didn't talk to each other or make eye contact with anyone until we were waiting for the bus at the end of the dock. One of them, dressed in shabby pants and a misshapen blouse walked over until she was standing directly in front of me. Slowly her eyes met mine. They were cold and vacant. She had long, gray facial whiskers on her chin and a jaw tremor that caused them to rhythmically bob up and down.

I introduced myself. "Hi, I'm Sylvia Peterson. I am here to attend the Family Worship Service." I held out my hand. Hers was cold and limp.

"I'm Clara."

I wanted to talk, but I was speechless. The more she stared, the less I could think of anything to say. Superficial social conversation would have been trite. Deep, probing questions were inappropriate. I smiled and stalled for time.

Clara took a small step forward, still staring at me. I felt uncomfortable. I was leaning against a freestanding metal handrail. There was nowhere to go. She was standing so close that I could smell her breath, a combination of tooth decay and garlic. There was something almost predatory about her movements. And then it struck me. Clara was mentally ill. Her face was expressionless and the facial tremor was typical of the side effects of psychoactive medications. It wasn't hard for me to imagine her family tree included sexual perversion. Was she also a victim, or a genetically corrupted relative?

Clara didn't say another word, but stood there staring into my face until the bus arrived. No one else seemed to notice, except for George, who watched my discomfort with a sarcastic smirk.

One extremely beautiful, impeccably dressed woman was there to visit her son. John and I knew her family around the time her son was arrested. He went to SCC on a plea bargain to avoid a nasty court case that would have shamed his parents. Soon after, they were asked to leave the Catholic Church, an apparent disgrace

35

to the "Family of God." This was a not uncommon example of the impact sexual shame has on families. That was before the Catholic Church was forced to "fess up" about its priests' sexual deviancies. It struck me that the hypocrisy of their experience could easily have driven them away from God and Christian community. But it had not. John and I held them in extremely high esteem. Many, many Sunday services included only the Chaplain, their son, and his still-grieving parents.

One woman in her late thirties was there with her obese grade school age son. They were dressed in jeans and comfortable shirts. I wondered about bringing children into the Special Commitment Center. Could there be emotional harm from repeated exposure to men who fantasized fondling them or worse? What could a mother do to prepare a child for visitation? Or would this boy have to find his own means of protecting himself—like overeating?

In all there were thirteen family members with us that evening. As they filed in, John went to the chapel to prepare for the service. I was looking for Laura when George motioned me over to the desk.

"If your husband behaves like he did on Friday, I will permanently kick his *(deleted)* out of here. Do you understand me?"

I was speechless. I nodded.

"His behavior was illegal. I could have him arrested."

For a moment I couldn't remember what had happened on Friday. Then it struck me. In addition to their disagreement about signing him in as a volunteer, they had had a second disagreement. Laura brought me two CD's of her friend, Dave's music. We tried to get George to loan us a CD player from the chapel so we could listen to them while we talked. He refused. I asked if she could go get hers from the living unit. He said no. Finally, as we were leaving she gave the CD's to John so I could listen to them on the weekend and return them to her on the Sunday visit.

As a chapel intern he could carry occasional personal items in and out of the institution without search and seizure. As a volunteer I could not. When George realized John had Laura's CD's he stopped us and demanded they be given to him as contraband. George was again asserting his authority and control, lowering John's status to that of a volunteer rather than that of staff. John gave George the CD's and apologized; we left, making a note to discuss it with the full-time paid chaplain when he returned from vacation. Apparently the issue wasn't resolved.

George berated me in front of the three other visit staff. I felt my face flush. "You better tell him that I can get both of you permanently kicked out if he tries anymore tricks like that. Do you understand me?"

I nodded. Then I turned away and began to cry hot tears of frustration similar to my family role as a naughty child, even though I'd done nothing wrong. George was supposed to call Laura's unit to let her know I was there. Under the circumstances I was afraid to ask for such a huge favor. Instead I walked down the hallway off the visiting room.

A small, but pleasant chapel was at the end and I ducked inside, glad to be away from George while I collected myself. Then I looked up. A camera was pointed directly at me; I imagined George watching my flushed face and watery eyes with smug condemnation.

I was angry, not just with George, but with myself. There were lots of things I wish I had the courage to say, but my fear was that a power struggle with staff could keep me from seeing Laura. The paradox infuriated me. Did I have to be victimized in the present in order to heal from my victimization in the past? Under my breath I prayed for God to find me a healthier was to deal with George. After sliding into a chair where my back was to the ever-watching camera, I shut my eyes and took several deep breaths. I wasn't that child anymore.

In 2 Samuel the Bible tells a brief story about King David moving the Ark of the Covenant to Jerusalem. The Ark was so sacred that human hands were forbidden to touch it for any reason. Sometime during the journey the oxen stumbled and the cart transporting the Ark began to tip, threatening to toss the Holy of Holies into the mud. Uzzah, one of the privileged priests who had been guiding the cart, reached out his hand to keep it from falling, a reflex action any of us would have taken. But we are told, "Then the anger of the Lord was aroused against Uzzah, and God struck him there for his error, and he died there by the Ark of God."[4]

I'd always found the story disturbing. Wasn't God extremely harsh? Uzzah forgot that God made the dirt and the dirt never deliberately disobeyed Him. Dirt never sins. It is cleaner than any well-intentioned priest called to transport the Holy of Holies. Touching the Ark was an act of arrogance. God had warned them of the consequences. Now He followed through.

I doubted George knew the story, but he certainly treated the families and me as though we were of less value than dirt. I was guilty because I was married to a man who had challenged his authority; the family members of the residents were guilty for their association and loyalty to the men held at the SCC. I had expected to have moments where I felt afraid of the residents. I never expected to feel afraid of the staff. I was.

Only four of the family members who traveled with us came to the Protestant Family Worship Service. So did the three residents to whom they were related. They represented a meager representation of the SCC population. It was a powerful statement for the spiritual health, or lack thereof, of civilly committed sex offenders.

Laura didn't show up. Did she remember I was coming? I doubted that George had called her unit to tell her I was there. I never asked.

Later that night when John and I stopped for gas we saw two of the family members at the local mini-mart. It was the mom with her young son. While John pumped gas I approached her. In the brash lighting of the grocery aisle her skin was tobacco-yellow and her eyes were underscored by dark circles of tiredness. It was almost nine o'clock. She had cold drink bottles stuffed under her arms and a large bag of chips clutched in her hand.

I decided to talk with her now that we were away from the constant eyes of George and too many electronic monitoring devices.

"Hi, it looks like you got off the island." I hoped she remembered me, but she didn't act like it. "I met you today going in for a visit," I clarified. I felt the need to protect her anonymity and the exact location of our meeting, even though we were essentially alone in the little store.

"Yes," was all she said, but she made a slight attempt at a smile.

"Would you mind if I asked you a question?" I saw her shoulders tense although she didn't walk away. "How are you treated by the staff when you visit? I've been going into the prison for years,"

I offered in explanation. "I felt very uncomfortable tonight. Does it ever feel like that to you?"

The visit had left me irritable and frustrated. I knew I was leading her, but I didn't care. Were families also the "worst of the worst"?

We stood in silence a moment too long. Then she began to silently weep. "It's a very sad place," she offered in explanation.

I strained to understand. "You mean because of the despair of the situation, being held indefinitely?"

She shook her head. "Not exactly. It's just sad. And there's more to it than that." Suddenly she furtively looked away. "I'm sorry. I can't really talk right now."

I wanted to understand. Lacking the ability to do that, I wanted to encourage her. Before I could think of something to say she walked away, then stopped and turned back. "I like your shirt and pants." Maybe this was the only social conversation she could handle at that point... a superficial compliment for my plain red T-shirt and faded old pants.

I bought a half gallon of ice cream and three chocolate bars.

A few days later I received another letter from Laura.

Dear Sylvia

Hi. Thank you for your visits and willingness to visit and get to know me and for accepting me for myself. Sorry I missed Sunday. I forgot. I hope you will be allowed to send some makeup. Will you pierce my ears on one of our visits? Will you take a photo w/me? Chaplain is gonna get me some free clothes for winter. Maybe he will let you go with him. I go to court in January for my LRA hearing. Dave is fine. I love him so much. Do you think that you may like to call me sometime? Here's the number just in case. Well, write if you like. Mail is good.

Love in Christ, Laura

I carried her letter with me for several days. It was a classic example of offender manipulation: say a few nice things about the recipient, insert God, claim the recipient is the only one who cares, ask for whatever you want. However, I was willing to put that aside for now and move to the telephone issue. It already took several days to recover from our visits. Between my secular job and ministry obligations, I didn't have more time for our conversations. If phone calls affected me similarly, I wasn't willing to talk on the phone.

My second concern was that I needed to be able to look Laura in the eye when we talked about sexual abuse. It would be easier to fabricate, minimize and deceive on the phone. I decided to stall and see if she brought the issue up again.

This was the first time she had mentioned going to court for a LRA hearing.

In spite of a statewide public outcry that sex offenders be held permanently so that there is no chance of them re-offending, the legislature determined that the SCC could not violate their constitutional rights by keeping them locked up for life. The courts determined that offenders must have a reasonable chance to succeed in treatment and an opportunity to earn an eventual release to a less restrictive facility. Thus the concept for a "Less Restrictive Alternative" (LRA) was born. However, the movement from concept to reality had been slow and controversial.

Finding sites for LRA's was extremely difficult. The State Legislature also concluded that the six counties that had five or more sex offenders in the SCC as of April 1, 2001 must allow the "siting" of LRA's to house them when they are released. There was public outrage! "Not in My Back Yard" became the battle cry of a huge cross-section of the general population who collectively became known as the "NIMBY's". The legislature countered with assurance of stringent and extreme security requirements for the still un-sited facilities.

Two problems remained. The first was financial. In 2004 it costs about $25,000 a year to house an offender in the prison system, slightly more for females because their health care costs are higher than those of incarcerated men. It costs about $100,000 to keep the same offender at the SCC. Under the legislated security requirements it would cost $400,000 a year per offender in the LRA. The current Washington State budget cannot afford such expensive safety. The legislature had boxed itself into a legal and financial dead end.

The second problem was related to security. Hearing after hearing ended in fear-fueled shouting matches. Local "NIMBY's" threatened to prevent buildings from being purchased or built that would house transitioning Level Three sex offenders. Some even threatened to burn down the houses, populated or not. Community hysteria had effectively blocked every proposed site.

The legislature's intent was to move offenders into the community and reintegrate them to grocery stores, jobs, school, and other "normal" activities. But that wasn't going to happen until the communities were willing to accept them. Finally the state built several little cottages on McNeil Island just outside the razor wire and concrete, but still on the SCC grounds. These would have to temporarily represent the state's intention to provide Less Restrictive Alternative facilities.

Laura anticipated completing the requirements so she could appear before the court and request a transfer to one of the cottages. For her this was the first big step to an eventual life of freedom. As much as she wanted to move on with her life, I did not support her transfer. I kept remembering the way she looked when she smiled and said, "I want to talk about Annie." Maybe I was reading too much into her at this point, but I thought I saw pleasure on her face as she recounted her abuse of the baby with fetal alcohol syndrome. And even if it wasn't pleasure, I didn't recall any expression of remorse at the pain she had caused. Remorse at being caught? Yes. Remorse at abusing and almost killing a child? No.

I decided to take a few minutes, read more of her autobiography. Maybe there was a correlation between Laura's childhood and her crimes.

My father did not love me or want the responsibilities of yet another child. He was the adult. He and my mother were supposed to care for my siblings and me. My father's love for alcohol was all that mattered to him. My father and I never went anywhere together or did any activities together that I remember. My father and I had no common ground even when I got older.

He did however teach me a lesson I have never forgotten. When I was five years old my father and mother were permitted to take us home for a day visit. We ate lunch and played. Later he sat me up on a fence and told me to jump into his arms. He would catch me. He did not catch me. Instead he stepped back and allowed me to fall hitting the ground. I began to cry. My father looked down at me and he told me that when you cannot trust your father, you cannot trust anyone.

I loved my father. Even though I knew it was one-sided, it did not stop me from loving him. I wanted nothing more as a child than my father's and mother's love. I would have done anything to have them love me and not be sent away.

Doesn't every child love their father? A little girl's first love is her father. I was no different. I loved him even though he was not there for me. I still love him. Even though there was no love or trust, my dad gave me life. Giving me away was a gift. It was the one unselfish thing he and my mother did.

I believe my father never wanted me. This knowledge is painful. My life could have been different had my parents only wanted it to be. What does it say about me when my father and mother did not want me? My brother and sister took care of me even though they could not have been very old themselves. It was nothing uncommon to not have my parents around. I was used to them never being home or around me.

I have four brothers and four sisters. (I am choosing to delete the names of Laura's siblings, friends, and victims to protect their privacy.) I do not know their dates of birth.

My mother and father's lack of love presented many problems for me as a young child. I still wear the scars. When I was little there never seemed to be enough food or milk to eat and drink. It seemed like I was always hungry. I was always dirty and covered with sores and head lice. I remember the house was always dark and very cold.

My Uncle Jonathan and Aunt Pearl owned a small grocery store. They gave us food and milk to eat so we ate. They would come over to our house while my parents were out drinking and take us home with them. They would give us kids a bath, clean clothes and feed us a hot meal. Afterwards they would place us in warm dry beds for some sleep. They loved us and gave us all the things we were so desperately in need of. I loved them. When I would go back to my parent's house I would sometimes sit by the window wishing Uncle Jonathan and Aunt Pearl would come back. I learned that their visits meant food, milk and best of all was a bath and clean clothes. Eventually Uncle Jonathan had to call CPS to intervene in our home situation.

I was two years old when the CPS was called and took me away from my home. My parents were gone constantly, sometimes for days. When I was two years old I along with my siblings was taken from my birth parents and we all became wards of the state. We were all placed in receiving homes, orphanages and foster homes. I remember we all slept in the same room on the same mattress to stay warm. There was a dresser in the corner of the room.

I was told we were removed from my parents due to malnutrition and severe neglect. There were also accusations my father molested my oldest sister and there were two children born. I don't know if he did or not. We were all dirty and unkempt. We were covered in sores and lice. The situation with my parents was not improving.

The police and CPS came out and took all of us. I cried so much that I threw up. I was terrified. I had no idea what was happening or why we were all being separated into different cars. I wanted my brother. He was the only one who made sure I ate and was taken care of. He was still young himself. He had the worry of taking care of me and my brother who was retarded. My older sister helped him out. They were the only idea of parents that I had and now what would happen to me?

I had expected to feel compassion for Laura as I continued to read her autobiography. I didn't. Sadly there are lots of children in the world who weren't wanted or loved. They didn't all become child molesters. So far I hadn't read anything that justified the life choices she had made. Not only did I not feel empathy, I felt angry without knowing exactly why.

It was only a couple of days later that the next letter arrived. Like her conversational style the letter jumped from topic to topic.

Dear Sylvia,

Hi I received your letter. I was glad and very surprised to get mail. I don't get mail unless it is legal mail. I am happy Chaplin is going to allow you to bring in makeup for me. This is very exciting. I am writing this on my computer and hoping it don't go out before I finish this thank you and appreciation letter to you. Thank you for being my friend and accepting me for the person the Lord is shaping and changing me to be. I love you for this and for the visits. You are a kind and special lady. I believe the Lord sent you to me to be my sister and friend. I thank Him for you.

I hope to purchase a new computer and monitor for myself. I just have to get more work hours first. Hopefully, I will have enough to do so by next year some time.

Will you consider bringing some eye shadow and mascara? I hope to get some clothes from the thrift store soon. I need some tee shirts and a sweat jacket with a hood for the chilly mornings. Hopefully they will have these things. I cannot afford clothing at this time and I want to save for my computer first. I am not picky. Second hand is good and it is nice of the store to do this.

Have you ordered Dave's CD's yet? I'm enclosing the address in case you are having trouble finding them. I sure love Dave. He is my heart and life. I pray Jesus will work this out for us. We spent the last few days together; it was great. I love him so much. I have nothing but my heart and love to offer him. I pray it is enough.

My PlayStation broke so I donated it to Toys for Tots. They will fix it. I miss it. I am an adult so I will learn to do without it. Some child will enjoy it if it can be fixed. I hope it can.

Christmas will be here soon and my birthday. I will be forty-seven. I am getting better, not older. Ha ha! Will you pray for me that I pass my polygraph that is coming up soon? Pray for my future LRA. I go to court Jan 2005. Would you write me when I go there? I would like this very much.

Dave may be going to the same LRA as me. He has a third CD coming out 2005. Tell me what you think when you hear them. I will tell you something strange. For the past few years I have dreamed about someone who plays music and singing with them. I believe this is what I have been dreaming about. The Lord will bless us. I just know He will. I am excited about our next visit. I get very depressed and lonely here. Mail and visits are special. They give me hope that others do care.

This letter is becoming a book so I will close for now. Write when you can. God bless you.

Love, Your friend Laura.

I was relieved that she hadn't mentioned the possibility of phone calls, so I went on-line and bought Dave's CDs.

Laura was gradually spreading through my life like a slow-growing, persistent toxic mold. Hardly an hour of the day went by without my thoughts being drawn to her and her life in the SCC. I was severely conflicted. I wanted to stop our visits and run back to my "pre-Laura" life. It was safe and predictable there. But I couldn't go back. I was obsessed. I had to know who she was and how she got that way.

Her letters made it sound like I was doing this for her. I still wasn't. My list of questions wasn't getting smaller. In fact, it grew with each visit. What was wrong with my grandfather? What possessed him to do that to me? And why did my grandmother permit it to happen under her own roof, over and over again? And where were my parents? Like Annie's mom, they had to know something was going on. What is the pathology that permits pedophiles to offend? How can it be healed? Is there forgiveness for them at the foot of the cross, because I still didn't think there should be. What would happen if I got to heaven, and through some incomprehensible miracle, Grandpa Ed was there? That wouldn't be heaven for me. It would be hell. Maybe heaven had separate spots for the repentant pedophiles that transferred there. I doubted it would need to be a large piece of real estate.

The Special Commitment Center was the most secretive, evil and non-therapeutic place I had ever experienced. How could collages and fantasizing on cassette tapes heal predators who had once been somebody else's victim? And what about the families I had met? Were the staff and system punishing them too? What exactly was their crime? Loving someone who was sick didn't sound like a criminal action to me. It sounded like an admirable combination of commitment and compassion, although there could be a certain amount of dysfunction there also.

I wanted Laura to give me the answers to all my questions. The possibility she couldn't or wouldn't was inconceivable. So as much as I wanted to run, I didn't. Where else could I go to get the answers? Besides, imaginary people were in my pockets, people just like me who couldn't interview Laura. They deserved answers also. I couldn't let them down.

My husband has always been kind and patient, but I began to feel an edge of tension between us. All the work I'd done on sexual abuse recovery occurred years before he and I met. He'd never seen me when I felt crazy. He couldn't imagine the depth of rage a survivor is capable of feeling. He'd never spent a single night in our bed when I didn't want him to touch me, so what could I say to warn him that things were changing? I wasn't certain how to articulate my concerns, but I knew it was time for us to talk. I began to construct the conversation in my head at some future time when we were both relaxed and he could hear me. If I was honest about my feelings, would it scare him? And if I minimized my inner conflicts, could he really be a support to me? I began to cry. What if I was honest and he couldn't understand? What if he advised me to stop seeing Laura, turn back and keep our life together stable and on course?

I couldn't stand the idea of tension escalating between us, but I didn't want to talk to him yet. My only recourse was to make sure my visits to Laura didn't go on too long. That urgency was elevated by the sugar addiction already showing on my hips.

I also started a file to keep notes of my visits. Maybe in time they could help me find the truth.

Chapter Three

TRUTH OR FICTION?

The beloved of the Lord shall dwell in safety by Him, Who shelters him all day long; and he shall dwell between His shoulders. (Deut. 33:12)

Laura wasn't an advocate for small talk. My next visit started abruptly, and then stampeded like a bucking horse stirring up all sorts of mud and dirt.

"I wanna ask you some questions, but I don't know if I should."

Her ice blue eyes softened slightly. I couldn't tell if her concern was manipulatively contrived or honest and protective. This was only our third meeting and Laura McCollum was much more intelligent and complex than I had anticipated.

"Then I guess we need some ground rules, Laura." She waited for me to continue. "I think the rules need to be the same for both of us. If you ask me a question, I have three choices. I can answer it honestly. I can defer my answer by saying something like 'I don't have an answer for that right now. Can we come back to this later?' Or third, I can tell you that I'm not comfortable sharing that information. And if I ask you a question, you have the same three choices."

I looked at her. Today she was in her favorite gray sweat pants and stained white T-shirt. Her nails were shorter and more jagged than I remembered; they looked like she'd been both chewing and ripping them. Whoever paid for her latest haircut should get their money back.

I wondered if Laura had any idea how many questions were running around in my head and how few answers. "Does that sound like something we could both agree to?"

She nodded. "Yeah, I like that, 'cause I have some questions but I don't wanna upset you."

I took a deep breath. "What do you want to ask me?"

She didn't answer. She just stood up and pulled a hand-rolled cigarette out of her pocket. It was my signal to walk outside.

The weather had jumped from summer to autumn with no transition. There was a cool breeze on the small patio. We were the only people in the visit area except for five staff assigned to watch us. I watched storm clouds roll in from the coast. Other than the sky, there wasn't anything else to look at from the patio.

Laura sat down on the concrete bench next to me and crossed her legs "Indian Style" in front of her. She had trouble lighting her cigarette because of the combined wind and damp air.

"I don't want you to tell anyone, but I had sex with L. L. Cool. That's his nickname. You know— the guy that wanted my panties?" She waited long enough to check my face for a reaction. When she didn't read one she continued. "Now I don't know what to do. Should I tell Dave about it?"

"Maybe before you make that decision we should talk about why you had sex with this guy."

"I don't know. I just wanted to, I guess." Laura sucked a long, deep breath of her cigarette, leaving an amazing four-inch piece of ash dangling off the end. When it broke off and scattered down the front of her, she didn't seem to notice.

"How did you feel about it at the time? How do you feel about it now?"

"I knew it was the wrong thing to do. I won't do it again with him." She looked at me shyly and giggled. "It was kinda fun. I can't lie about that. Do you think I should tell Dave?"

I looked up at the two patio cameras watching us and wondered where two people could meet that wasn't monitored. Additionally, Laura had a staff escort everywhere she went. The SCC was trying to protect her from the sexual harassment she experienced at the Monroe Complex. Their tryst had to have been difficult to arrange. The part of my character that wants to rebel against authority was inappropriately pleased, even though what she had done was wrong. The paradox of the SCC was that all the cameras and monitoring equipment were meant to prevent secrets, and yet it was a dark and secretive place where residents were fiercely protective of one another. If it wasn't captured on camera it would be hard to prove and punish. They'd probably get away with breaking the rules.

"Laura, I wonder if sometimes you do things because you feel bored, lonely, angry, frustrated, or manipulated."

Her eyes flew open. "Why do ya' think that?"

"You live in an artificial environment. Life isn't real here. And I'm just telling you that's how I'd feel locked up here. Now, about confessing to Dave... what is your motive?"

"What do ya' mean?"

"What do you want to accomplish if you tell him?"

She thought for a minute. "I think honesty is important in a relationship. I should be truthful?" It was a question, not a statement.

"Would you feel better if you told Dave? Got it off your chest and came clean?" I waited while she thought about the question. Eventually she nodded. "Then your motive for telling Dave is so you feel better. Also, if he is upset or angry, it reinforces that Dave cares deeply about you, right?" She nodded again. "And if you tell him, you think it will probably hurt or upset him. Right?"

She sighed deeply and dramatically. "Are you sayin' that my reason isn't very good? It's selfish."

"Yes. It means you're willing to hurt Dave in order to feel better yourself. Telling him may be honest, but it isn't very kind. I'm suggesting you check your motive." I waited for her to think about it, and then started to continue, but the patio door opened abruptly. One of the male staff called Laura over to him. I waited. She came back in two or three minutes, looking unconcerned.

"I just got in trouble for sittin' with my legs up. It exposes my... my... It exposes me too much. I have to sit with my legs down even though they barely touch the ground and it isn't very comfortable."

I felt myself blush uncontrollably. Was the staff reading sexual possibilities into us sitting on a concrete bench talking?

Laura switched gears without a breath. "So I guess I won't tell Dave. I don't wanna' hurt him. Instead I think I better confess it to God because it was sin." She watched me for a reaction.

Because I was fairly sure Laura was saying what she thought I wanted to hear, I chose not to react.

"I'd like to see you find some healthy ways to deal with the feelings you tried to change by having sex with someone you don't even care about."

"I get lonely. I go to work. I go to group. I eat. I sleep. If it wasn't for Dave I'd go nuts."

I believed her. Infatuation is a powerful distraction from life; I'd had a few diversionary relationships in my younger days. What must existence be like for Laura? "I still don't quite understand this place. Is it a prison? Is it a mental hospital? What is it?"

Her answer was cold and mechanical. "It's a maximum security prison that pretends to be a treatment center."

"Do you think people are getting well here?"

She laughed without humor. "What do ya' think?"

"I think I want to learn more about the treatment modalities. What you've shared with me so far is discouraging and disturbing. Is this the best that mental health services have to offer sex offenders?"

Laura stood up, flung her cigarette butt on the ground and looked at both the cameras that were watching us. Then she deliberately turned her back to them and faced me. Her voice dropped to a whisper. "Nobody knows of a way for therapy to fix evil. Most therapists don't even believe in demons. I pretty much have to deal with mine on my own. Or at least I did when I got here. I'm OK now. I jus' have to control 'em better when I get out."

She led me back into the visiting room. I didn't believe her demons were under control. Like most of the two hundred men also held in the SCC, she was allowed absolutely no interaction with people who met her victim profile. It seemed to me Laura's demons had very little to work with at the moment.

We returned to the small interview room. I sat down, grateful to be inside where it was warmer. She grabbed the doorknob. "Is it okay if I close this? If it makes you nervous to be in here alone with me we can leave it open. I understand."

"You can close it. I'd like to show you what I brought today."

"OK, but I gotta use the bathroom first."

While I waited for Laura to return I looked at the items. Bringing Laura the makeup she requested was no minor feat. The chaplain had to shoot memos all over the institution describing the items. I pictured someone in security thinking, "Hmmm, what could Laura McCollum use mascara for? A bomb? Door lock jamming? A disguise for escape?" After the memo went out I still had to wait for various people to approve or disprove the items.

If I had attempted to bring the same items to a male offender, it would have been disallowed as contraband. Cosmetics could be used as a tool in deviant fantasies.

After the makeup was approved, I still couldn't bring it to her. Instead, I was required to buy the items, leave them in their tamper-proof packaging and give them to the chaplain. He was allowed to hand them back to me once I was in the institution. After all that, I was anxious to see if she liked them.

When Laura returned I gave her the makeup and watched her gently take out the items one at a time and look at them.

"So what do I do next? I mean, how do I put this stuff on?"

"Do you want me to put it on you the first time?"

She jumped like she's been shot. "They're not goin' to let you touch my face! Maybe you could talk me through it and I'll put it on myself."

I felt immediately stupid. Touching someone's face is very intimate. Of course the staff wouldn't let me put makeup on her. Along with stupid, I felt sad. I couldn't imagine living my life completely devoid of any intimacy, no matter how innocent. I wondered if Mr. Underpants had taken the time to stroke her face and make her feel beautiful. I hoped so.

Laura's reaction reminded me that everything I did was observed and analyzed. Every touch, facial expression, and overheard word was suspect and checked. There were two reasons I refrained from touching her. First, the risk of an innocuous touch being misread as a sexual advance. And second, my persistent dislike.

We moved on with her cosmetic instruction. A few minutes later the change was remarkable. With foundation, mascara and lip gloss her face softened. Suddenly her eyes were huge and luminous and her dimples came to life. She was surprisingly pretty and feminine.

"I only brought these items this time because I don't want the men making fun of you. In a month or so I'll bring you some eye liner and something to hide the dark circles under your eyes."

She was smiling. "I really look good?"

"Do you want to see for yourself? Look in the mirror?"

"No!" She jumped back from the table a second time. "I don't like mirrors. I can probably use one to put on the makeup, but I don't wanna look at myself."

I didn't ask why. "You look beautiful," I assured her.

Laura sat back in the chair, switching topics without segue. "Is it hard for you to visit me, knowin' that I'm a pedophile and you was molested as a little girl?"

"Yes. It is hard."

"Why are you doin' it? Why are you willin' to visit me and be my friend?" Her voice took on an odd quality, flirtatious and childlike. "Why're you here?"

I thought of the sleepless nights I'd had after our first two visits and the protective warnings of my husband and friends. Laura watched me through her new mascara-lengthened lashes. She looked surprisingly benign.

"I'm here because I believe you are part of my healing. Through you I have an opportunity to understand what was done to me — what is done to thousands of children every day. My hope is that understanding you will help me forgive and heal. I don't know exactly how it's going to work, Laura, but I believe it will happen. And maybe it will help you heal, too."

Suddenly Laura had a mission, maybe even a redemptive one with which to mitigate her destructive life. "Is there anything you wanna ask me? Anything that will help you heal?" Despite the sincerity of her words, she wasn't looking me in the eye. She was focused on my chest.

"Yes." I leaned forward and rested my chin on my hands, which caused her to look up. "I want to understand how you became a pedophile. You weren't born that way. What happened to you, Laura? And I want to understand how it feels to be you. I've been asked to talk to a civic organization that works to make the world a safe place for children. It's not until January, but maybe you could help me plan what to tell them."

"I'd like to. I could tell people how to keep their kids away from people like me. One thing is, if their kids don't like someone, they need to jus' go with it. There's a reason. Parents shouldn't ever make their kids go with people the kids don't like. I could give ya' some pointers like that." Laura excused herself to ask the staff for more matches.

While she was gone I remembered the times I had begged to stay home from the obligatory trips to my grandparents' farm. I don't remember anyone ever noticing my reluctance, but I wouldn't have disclosed the real truth. My memories remained sketchy. Maybe Grandpa Ed gave me a reason not to tell. Maybe I was protecting the fun grandpa who also let me ride on the tractor and watch kittens being born. Maybe I was protecting myself; what we did was wrong and I didn't want to be punished. Maybe I made up a reason not to tell because I didn't know what else to do.

My parents rented our house from my grandparents. I was convinced that if I told anyone, we would be homeless and it would all be my fault. Perpetrators convince children they have the power to do great harm if they disclose their abuse to anyone.

I was interested to hear Laura's tips on keeping children safe from her.

She stood up without further comment and we went back outside. This time she leaned forward to keep her feet on the ground. "Sylvia, what does your abuse feel like to you?"

A large bumblebee settled on her shoulder and I chased him away. I hoped the camera could see the bee so it didn't look like I was trying to hit her. The paranoid life of a resident sex offender was beginning to interfere with my usual reactions.

I answered honestly and without detail. "I spent almost ten years in therapy. A lot of healing took place. But it feels like there is scar tissue, or speed bumps in my emotions. I can be going through life and suddenly something will happen that hits that scar tissue and I feel the pain again."

Laura lit a fresh cigarette. She had apparently rolled several ahead of time. "Mine feels a little like that. But it's more like a wound that has a scab on it. And then somethin' happens and the scab gets knocked loose and is just hangin' there. And it hurts and is bleedin' again. I guess I'm still tryin' to get to the scar tissue stage."

"What is the relationship between that scab and your crimes, Laura?" I asked the question in my gentlest tone of voice.

"There's a relationship. I don't know if I can explain it. I want you to read a couple of books that explain it better than I can. I'll get paper and a pencil from my staff and write down the titles before you leave. I don't remember the authors, but you'll figure out how to find them. What they kinda say is that there are these things called neurons." She held up her hands with both index fingers pointed at one another. "And there's an electrical charge that goes from one to the other and that's how information gets passed."

I nodded. I'd taken enough college biology to know a little about what she was saying, but was surprised Laura did.

"Well, the theory is that in a pedophile like me there is a misfire." Her fingers stabbed at each other in the air and missed.

"Are you saying that the misfire is caused by a chemical imbalance or by childhood trauma?"

"I think it's trauma. I think it messed up my wiring."

I thought about what she as saying. If that were true, then all abused children would become perpetrators. They don't.

"Laura, I'd like to do some research on this. I'll find the books and start there. But I have to tell you, long ago I figured out that just because something is published doesn't make it the truth."

Laura laughed. Then she was serious again. "What sets you off? I mean, what things bump your scar tissue and remind you of your abuse?" she asked.

"Spiders."

She looked at me suspiciously. "What do spiders have to do with it?"

"My grandparents lived on a farm on the southern Oregon Coast. Part of Grandpa Ed's 'play' was to pretend to lock me in the cellar. There were spiders in there. When my abuse memories have been triggered I feel the spiders crawling on me. Sometimes I even break out into welts that look like spider bites."

She looked impressed, then sympathetic, but momentarily speechless. Whatever she had expected for an answer, this wasn't it.

I followed her back inside. After we sat down it was my turn. "Are there differences between men who molest children and women who molest children?"

She thought for a moment. I could tell she was nervous because she had unconsciously started groping her coat pockets for a cigarette in spite of the fact she had just smoked one.

"Yeah. There's the obvious, of course. Women are rare. But there's more to it than that. Men who hurt kids are into it for the power and control and..."

"And physical enjoyment?"

Laura chuckled. "I was thinkin' that, but I didn't know if I should say it out loud. It's different with women. We are more nurturin' of our victims. I loved the children and I didn't wanna hurt them. It just got out of control. One minute everything was good and I was takin' care of them and then... the bad stuff happened." Her face turned red underneath her new Clinique foundation. She began to diligently search her coat pockets, avoiding eye contact with me.

"I want to know about the first few years of your life. By the way, thank you for sending me your autobiography, but I'd also like to hear it from your own mouth. When you tell me, I can visualize the story better. Where were you born? How many siblings do you have?"

I didn't tell her this was a "truth test." If the autobiography was honest, her answers would be consistent. If any part of her story was fabricated, it would be hard for her to remember what she wrote.

"Tennessee. I was born in Tennessee. My parents had eight children."

"What number were you?"

"Number Nine."

I stopped for a moment and wondered at her answer. She was not including herself in the number of children her parents brought into the world. It sounded like an unconscious discounting of her very existence. I chose not to dwell on it.

"Tell me about your parents."

"They was poor. And they was drunk all the time. We lived in a two-bedroom house, with all us kids in one big bed at night. There wasn't much to eat and they weren't ever home. I was only two when the authorities took us away from 'em. But I remember. We were split up and put in foster care."

"Do you know where any of them are now?"

"One sister. She has one of my kids living with her. But neither of them wanna have any contact with me. I have four kids. All girls. I gave them all up."

This was the first time I'd considered that Laura might have children. I was surprised. Did she actually give them up or had they been taken from her? Of her fifteen victims all of them were girls except two. Were her own daughters on the list?

"That sounds very hard, Laura."

"Oh, that wasn't the hard stuff. The hard stuff is what happened to me in foster care. That's where my wires really got messed up. We kids would a been better off if they'd left us with our parents. They was drunks and all that, but they didn't beat us or hurt us or nothin'. I was little, but I can still remember the day they took us away. If they'd a just left us there I wouldn't be sittin' here today. It wasn't too bad until I was six. That's when it started."

I was so engrossed in her story I lost track of the time. The door opened abruptly and the chaplain entered with my husband in tow. "Time for us to go now, Laura," he announced.

I had no choice but to say goodbye and leave. Two weeks felt like a long time until our next scheduled visit. I'd have to wait to hear what happened to her in foster care, but at least we'd broken the ice. I was moving toward my goal.

By the time I got home exhaustion was slowing my speech, my walking and my ability to think. It was an unnatural kind of tiredness, the consistent emotional, mental and spiritual toll for visiting Laura.

I crawled onto the bed fully clothed and pulled the quilt over me. It didn't matter if my husband was expecting me to fix dinner. He wouldn't starve to death if I couldn't find the energy to cook. I began to silently cry. My head pounded and I wished I could fall asleep so I wouldn't have to think about anything.

The last awareness I had before drifting off was the unmistakable sensation of a large spider crawling up my neck. When I batted it away I realized it was just a strand of my hair.

For the next few days I was tired and irritable. Every night I awoke around two o'clock and slipped downstairs to sit alone in the dark and eat ice cream. It took the edge off. Sometimes I prayed, but usually I just tried to understand Laura and the Special Commitment Center. During the fourteen days between visits I reviewed each detail in my mind and waited eagerly for snippets of information my husband brought back to me. He was still doing his internship under the tutelage of the chaplain.

One thing he reported was that after all the cosmetic memos had been signed and approved, Laura still wasn't allowed to keep her new makeup. The facility policies were written for male offenders. New policies would have to be written and approved for a female to have cosmetics in her room. Until then, the chaplain would keep them in his office and she'd have to apply them there.

John talked briefly with one of the staff about Laura wearing makeup. "We can't even get her to take showers, so why would she wear makeup?" I could think of a couple reasons why she might not feel safe taking her clothes off and standing in the shower. It made me even more intent on getting her a few things to address the feminine adult part of her personality. I also requested that I be allowed to pierce her ears.

I had already gathered some clothing catalogs for our next visit. I didn't want to do any shopping for her until I knew what styles and colors she felt comfortable wearing. How we dress is a reflection of who we are and who we want others to think we are. Laura was too complex and nebulous for me to guess. Although I had special permission to bring in catalogs, again I wouldn't be allowed to actually carry them myself. The chaplain would have to transport them and hand them to us during the visit with full knowledge of the visiting room staff. Otherwise George would confiscate them like he did Dave's CD's and Laura could be infracted, i.e. written up for disciplinary action.

One day I cleaned my closets and found a few items I thought she might like: a pair of brand new jeans that were too big for me, red sweat pants with a matching vest, and a blue plaid shirt. John agreed to give them to the chaplain who could then deliver them to Laura. It would give me an idea of her size when I started shopping. I'd already figured out the institution wouldn't let me take in a tape measure and get actual numbers to work with. I visualized the hysteria that we'd create if I tried to measure her chest, hips, and inseam. Trial and error would take longer, but we had no choice. If she was really going to court in a few months I wanted to find something suitable for her to wear, something other than grey sweatpants and stained T-shirts.

A few days later another letter came in the mail. I was beginning to feel overwhelmed.

Dear Sylvia,

Hi. I was so happy with the makeup. Thank you very much. You made me feel special and pretty. It was very kind of you to purchase makeup for me.

I want you to know how good your doing this makes me feel inside and about myself. I like the makeup and cologne very much thank you. I have wanted my ears pierced for awhile now, so the sooner you can do this I would be happy. I feel like I have a big sister now. I miss having one so it is cool that you came in my life. I know the Lord brought us together. He blessed me with you for a friend.

As far as looking at catalogs for clothes, it would be nice. I like sweat pants and jeans, tee shirts for every day, but some dress slacks and blouses would be nice too. I don't want the men here commenting about how I look, so one dress for court is plenty. Hey, do you happen to have some extra sheets and a comforter I can have for my bed? I get cold and the state blankets are not real warm.

Do me a favor. If I ask for something and it is too much, tell me ok? I am looking forward to getting my makeup from chaplain and my ears pierced. I hoped you would call this weekend, but I guess you are relaxing for your next work week. I think the best way to do our phone calls is to have a set day and time so that I am here. You pick the day and time.

I am really sorry that you had to live through such abuse by your grandfather and that your innocence was stolen. You were a little girl and you did not deserve that. I was seven when my foster dad started with me. At seven years old it lasted until I was thirteen years old. I understand this affected us both and I would be honored to help you in any way I can. I will gladly help you with your speech just let me know when. Sylvia I am glad we met and it was not by chance. I am sure the Lord has His hand in this friendship.

I love you. Take care and I will see you soon.

Love you, Laura

I couldn't avoid the topic of phone calls much longer. There needed to be some boundaries. I would not be giving her my phone number; I needed to be able to control the time since I probably couldn't control the content. I didn't want to be triggered so badly that I wasn't completely present in the rest of my life.

Sunday, John and I visited a friend's church. Laura had sent me her picture and I put it in my Bible. Despite occasional references to God, I didn't know what she believed about sin and redemption. I made a mental note to add it to my list of questions. God's forgiveness of Laura was between Him and her. I wanted to know Laura's comprehension of that forgiveness, and what about her forgiveness of herself? Sometimes she was so emotionless talking about sexual abuse that I wasn't convinced she was remorseful. But maybe her lack of sorrow meant she had dealt with her own forgiveness and chose to move on. Sackcloth and ashes might make her victims and their families feel better, but at some point we all need to heal beyond the shame of our sins. Had Laura?

When the worship music began we sang a beautiful song about crawling up into God's lap, resting our head on His chest, letting him hold our hands in His, and experiencing the peace of looking at Him face to face. A goose bump of desire ran down my spine and then I began to cry. Once the tears started, I was unable to shut them off.

I realized with profound clarity that since meeting Laura my whole world had changed. Before her, I lived in a relatively safe place with sanctuaries carved out for myself at work, at home and in my personal friendships with the people who loved me. In a few short weeks I found myself psychologically outside of those places, hurled back into my childhood where the perverted clouds of abuse continually threatened rain. Buried deep inside me those places still festered and they still hurt. Food medicated them for awhile, but now I was throwing huge amounts of sugar at the pain.

When did I quit feeling safe in my own life? I couldn't identify an exact date. But I knew the only safe place for any of us was in the lap of God. I cried and cried. *Where was God's lap anyway?*

"Are you okay?" John was looking at me with concern and intent. I nodded and turned my face away. The service continued, but I had emotionally and mentally exited the building. Only my physical body was left to participate.

It was time to try to explain a few things to my husband, but I felt mentally lethargic. I didn't want to talk about abuse, especially my abuse. I'd shared a little bit about my childhood with him before we were married. It was the responsible thing to do. But he let me know he didn't want the details. It was upsetting to him. I honored his boundary and we didn't talk about it again. If some life event rubbed against my scar tissue, I took responsibility for it. I simply told him I had been "triggered" and he knew to give me a little space. Now I felt resentful that we might have to go back and review my past. How much did he need to know in order to support me while I worked with Laura? I felt very awkwardly "little." I was seven emotionally and fifty-two-years-old physically. I couldn't figure out what to do.

The next day I returned to Laura's life story. What happened to her after CPS became involved? Shouldn't things have improved?

The social worker was very kind. Her name was Mrs. Norton. She took me to the county hospital where (deleted) and the rest were already at. I did not like this place with all its strange smells and bright lights. I was terrified. I wanted (deleted.) I was not allowed to see my siblings until I had been seen by the doctor. He was an older man. He had kind eyes.

I was bathed and fed before I saw him. He gave me a purple with pink ribbon that was on his neck.

I was finally allowed to see my brother. I was crying so hard I threw up again. I crawled onto his lap where I fell asleep.

When I woke up I was in a strange house in a bed that was not filled with my siblings. I was very frightened. I went to see who was around. I don't remember much about this house other than there was an older woman who lived there. She took care of me for awhile. She used to leave pennies around the house. I would find them and try to give them back. She gave me a green, antique fruit jar to keep the pennies in. I did not stay long at this home. I don't even remember the lady's name.

Even though I was very young I knew my brother loved me. I was always safe with him. I was unable to express with words all that I saw and felt. It was all new and very scary. I was not sure what was happening to me. My family was gone. This was certain and it caused me great distress and confusion. I had never been without my siblings. We had always been together from day one. I don't remember them not ever being there with me. Now they were gone. I was alone and felt lost.

I knew that whatever was happening was not right. I loved my siblings.

Shortly after I was removed from my birth family many of the people I met and the places I lived gave me a clear understanding that I was broken. There was something wrong with me. I did not understand or like going to so many homes or having so many parents that always sent me away.

I did not understand the entire situation. I just knew I did not like it. I did not understand why I never stayed in a home for very long or why I always had to leave to go to yet another home and family who would eventually send me away too. Why was I so different? Why would no one love me or keep me?

I was told some years later that my anger and behavior made it difficult to find a family who would keep me. It has been said that I was a hard child to place. I don't remember every single home I lived in. I was much too young.

I do remember one foster home well. It was the home of Mr. and Mrs. McCurly. They had four other foster children living there with them. They also had a maid. Her name was Esther. She had a grandson named (deleted) who came to work with her everyday because the McCurlys both worked outside the home. She watched me while the older kids went to school. (Deleted) was about a year older than me.

I set her writing down. Maybe it was because I expected Laura to be abused beyond the neglect of her birth parents, but I felt knots of anger pulsing in my shoulders and upper back. Was the entire document fiction? I certainly couldn't remember my first few years of life with that attention to detail. How could Laura? Did she make it all up, or had someone told her these things later? Either way I had to keep going. What if the answer was somewhere in her history? What possible events in a life could create a desire for sexual intimacy with young children? What kind of abuse could begin to explain such behavior? I was more determined than ever to find out.

One of the most common effects of childhood abuse is amnesia. The mind cannot process what is happening, so it builds a wall and puts the abuse memories behind it. Later the child really can't remember with any clarity what happened to him or her. This amnesia is one of the biggest challenges in children reporting their crimes, being believed, and obtaining enough proof to prosecute. Serial sex offenders know this. In fact, they count on it.

I had very sketchy memories of my childhood. I didn't just forget a majority of the abuse, my need to protect myself had also taken huge pieces of my good memories. Sometimes the details that cannot be retrieved are the most painful. What a child forgets is as significant as what they remember.

Consequently, I was suspicious of the detail Laura put into her autobiography. I didn't want to think she remembered with that degree of precision because she was brighter than me.

I took a stretch break and made myself a cup of tea. While I waited for the water to boil I closed my eyes. My weight was creeping up and I felt powerless to intervene. Sugar was the only thing that gave me even temporary emotional relief. I felt embarrassed. Shouldn't I be such an outstanding spiritual icon that none of this bothered me? Could my reactions be a failure of faith?

Tucking my legs under me on the sofa, I carefully balanced the tea and Laura's autobiography. I wasn't expecting John to be home for at least another hour, which should be enough time to find out why the McCurleys stood out in her memories of foster care. But I couldn't read it. Suddenly I was completely exhausted. I set the teacup where it wouldn't spill and that's where my husband found me an hour later, deep in sleep.

By our sixth visit I no longer looked for small talk to create the illusion of a safe emotional place. We had less than two hours each session and didn't waste much time. It was my turn to ask some questions.

"You shared with me that you went into foster care at age two. What happened there, Laura?" I was curious. This could reveal whether or not she was being honest with me. I didn't think she was.

"You really wanna hear this?" Her words had the effect of a warning shot across the bow of a boat. Today she was wearing the jeans I sent her and a long-sleeved purple T-shirt. Her makeup was artfully applied and she looked much softer, but she tensed before she answered. Under the mask of make-up she looked masculine and predatory. I was shocked at how quickly she could assume an entirely different persona.

"Yes. I want to know what happened to you..." I wasn't sure how to word my request without sounding overly clinical and insensitive. She watched me struggle and waited patiently. There was no nice way to say it. "I want to know how and why you became a sexual predator. I'm not sure I can understand without hearing about your own abuse."

If the question bothered her, it didn't show. "OK." I could see her deciding what to say. "My first few years in foster care weren't that bad. Then when I turned seven, on my seventh birthday my foster dad got in my bed and put his hand over my mouth. That was the first time he did it to me."

I forced myself to remain silent. This man should have been her protector, her safe place. "Happy Birthday," I sarcastically whispered under my breath.

We were both silent for a few minutes while the staff checked on us. We'd left the door ajar. The weather was insistently cramming one more summer-like day into autumn and the air was unseasonably warm. When the staff moved away she continued.

"That's when I remember it startin'. My foster mother was there too. I don't think they were havin' much sex with each other at that point. I had two foster sisters, their born children. I don't think they were molestin' either of them."

"Did your foster father force his wife to participate, or did she choose to be involved?"

Laura had started to perspire. "It's hot in here. Let's go outside." She stood up without waiting for me to reply.

I followed her out to the visit patio. Despite the deceptively warm temperature, dark clouds were blowing in from Puget Sound. Thunderstorms would arrive later, hopefully not until I was home. The ferry dock was a brutal walk during wind and rain.

I expected Laura to pull out a cigarette and looked at her quizzically when she didn't. She apparently read my mind. "I quit. Two weeks ago, right after your visit. I got pneumonia and decided I'd better stop while I could still breathe."

I waited for Laura to pick up where she left off and was disappointed when she didn't. "Dave's movin' on Monday."

"Moving where?"

"Into one of the duplexes."

"I don't understand the significance of that. Tell me about it." I knew they were Less Restrictive Alternative housing, but I wanted to hear Laura's explanation.

She seemed relieved to move to her favorite topic, Dave. "He's graduatin'." Suddenly her face and voice entirely changed; she was talking "baby talk." It was disturbing.

"The cottages are kinda like a group home where several guys live. They have to cook and clean and do normal stuff for themselves. I guess they don't really grocery shop, but they do make a list and the groceries are brought to 'em. The idea is that they'll learn to live more like you normal people. Then they can move out."

"Where are the cottages in relation to where we are?"

"If you look over the wall on the other side of the smoking patio, you can see them from here. They're suppose' to be really nice inside. He doesn't wanna go. And I don't want him to go." Her voice continued to be childlike.

"Will you be able to continue seeing him?"

"Not as much. He can still come in for yard, but Dave's not much of an outdoor person."

I wondered, not for the first time, if their relationship was as mutual as Laura wanted to believe. If Dave loved her the way she professed to love him, wouldn't he make the effort to see her even if he wasn't "an outdoor person?"

Laura continued with a seemingly shy smile. "I love him so much. He said we could spend this weekend together. I know he's really worryin' about what it will be like for him after he moves. He thinks he'll kinda stay to himself so no one picks on him. He don't want trouble. This will be a big adjustment."

"How long has Dave been down?"

"A long time. He was arrested when he was nineteen. Then he did fifteen years in DOC. He transferred here on the day he should 'a been released. Now he's forty-four. How many years is that?"

I quickly did the math. "Twenty-five years." Dave had missed the years when young adults learn and practice their life skills. Had he ever had a checking account? Owned a car? Figured and filed his taxes? Gone on a real date?

"That's a long time, Laura," I said gently.

"Yeah, I know. I think it's good that they put the guys somewhere so they can begin adjustin' to normal life. Dave knows he has stuff to learn, like getting' along with people."

"Will you ever go to one of the cottages? Isn't that why you're going to court in January?"

Laura ignored my reference to her court date. "No. They can't put me there with the guys because there's only one bathroom and less supervision. I guess they could move a refrigerator and stove into where I am and let me start cookin' for myself, but I already know how to do that, so what's the point? Some of these men don't even know how to boil water. Believe me, I don't need to practice cookin' and cleanin'. My attorney wants me to go to a halfway house in Spokane. She's told me a little 'bout the place and I don't think it's a good idea."

"Why?"

"It's a big house where everyone has their own bedroom and there's a central kitchen. I don't know how many people stay there at a time. I thought it sounded like a good idea, but the more I think about it, it sounds kinda cheap and dirty."

"Is it co-ed?" I remembered the article on housing male and female offenders separately. Was Laura being victimized? It sounded to me like Mr. Underpants had been successfully manipulative. Would she have to go through the same thing at a halfway house where there was much less supervision?

"Yeah, there are men there. I don't think I want to go, but I don't have a lot of choices. Not too many places will take an SVP like me."

"What's an SVP?"

Laura got up and motioned that we were going back inside. "A sexually violent predator. There aren't that many of us and nobody wants us to move next door."

I stood up to follow her. Just for a moment I thought I saw a spider crawling down the wall and I jumped back. Then I realized it was just a trick of the lighting and felt silly.

Apparently Laura changed her mind about not smoking. She abruptly turned back to the patio and dug deep into her pocket until she found one mangled cigarette. She waited for me before she lit it and sat down again.

I watched her smoke in silence.

Chapter Four

SWAPPING ABUSE STORIES

*I am in great distress. Please let me fall into the hand of the
Lord, for His mercies are very great... (1 Chron. 21:13)*

I n my mind there was a distinction between a sexual predator
and a sexually *violent* predator. While I watched Laura, the
muscles in my neck and shoulders tightened. She had my full
attention. I wasn't sure why it made a difference, but it did. In a
sense all molestations are violent, if not of the body, certainly of
the mind, emotions, and soul of a child. But what had she done to
the children in addition to molestation?

Of course the "NIMBY's" didn't want a Laura moving into
their neighborhood, labeled violent or not. I thought of the story
she told me about Annie, and then of the children who lived across
the street from John and me. My neighbor kids were older, in
grade school. They weren't typical of Laura's tiny victims, but my
grandson was. How would I feel if a Laura moved onto our block?

We remained silent. If she was expecting me to criticize her
return to tobacco, she must have been disappointed.

Part of me didn't want to believe that child molesters could be
cured. Life was easier, more black and white if once identified they
remained locked up forever. Unacceptable shades of gray only
materialized when I tried to visualize varied degrees of healing.

How could that be reliably determined? And if Laura couldn't give up cigarettes, I doubted she'd ever be able to quit molesting children. So, in a strange way her tobacco relapse was comforting to me. It was black and white. Measurable. No need for conjecture.

Suddenly she stood up and motioned toward the door back into the visit room. I started to walk behind her; then I looked up at the camera and imagined George staring down at me. For just a moment I felt dizzy, but kept walking. As soon as we were safely behind the closed door of the interview room I took the topic back to Laura's childhood.

"How long did your foster parents abuse you?"

She thought for a moment. I was certain she was withholding information.

"Until I was thirteen. How old were ya' when your abuse started?"

I didn't want to talk about my abuse. This was supposed to be about Laura, not me. Would she answer the same questions I wasn't willing to answer? "I was seven or eight."

"How old were ya' when it stopped?"

"Eleven. Grandpa Ed quite molesting me around the time my periods started. Pretty clever of him, wouldn't you say?" I couldn't keep the sarcasm out of my voice. "It just stopped and that was that."

"Did ya' ever tell anyone, I mean, when it was goin' on?" She was visibly warming to the topic and it made me uncomfortable. I didn't want to provide her with a sexual thrill hearing about my own abuse. Her motives weren't trustworthy. I continued cautiously.

"When I was sixteen I had a big fight with my mother and walked across town to our family doctor's house. I told him, but he didn't believe me. He called my mother to come and get me and told her that I was upset because she didn't like my boyfriend."

I reversed the object of the conversation before she could ask me anything more. "What about you? Did you ever tell anyone? If you were in the foster care system there must have been a caseworker or someone who checked on you?"

"Of course I told. But do ya' think anyone would believe a little kid? When I was about eight I started actin' out. I wouldn't let anyone touch me. I was sent to Mental Health and I told the therapist, but she didn't believe me neither. Things were different in the sixties than they are now."

I nodded in agreement. People didn't talk about the sexual abuse of children back then. Society believed it was rare and only occurred in low-class families that lived deep in the rural areas of the country. In the fifties and sixties children learned to "put up" and "shut up."

The statistics varied slightly from study to study, but the numbers were staggering. I had recently done some research in "A Minister's Handbook of Mental Disorders" by Joseph Ciarrocchi.

Some pervasive myths about child sexual abuse foster a traumatizing impact on its victims. The first myth is that the children make up stories of abuse. In fact 10–20 percent of children have experienced sexual abuse (Kaplan and Sadock, 1988). Kinsey's original report of interviews with 1,200 women revealed an astonishingly high rate of abuse. Twenty-eight percent of the women interviewed reported that they had some sexual experience with an adult before age 13. Even if we keep in mind the many criticisms of Kinsey's sampling methods, one may sadly conclude that in too many instances there has existed a sexual open season on little girls. Lower class girls reported more intimate sexual contacts than middle class ones. As is also typical, few victims reported the abuse to legal authorities.

The second myth is that children provoke the sexual contact or are responsible for its continuation. Some pedophiles do create a warm, nurturing relationship with their victims so that children may respond with intense ambivalence toward the sexual abuse. At one level fear and anger may result, yet the pedophile may represent a nurturing caretaker in an emotionally deprived environment. This ambivalence often presents the child from revealing the abuse. This may also interfere with recovery since it involves coming to terms with pleasant aspects of the abusive relationship.

Long term affects measured in adulthood indicate greater depression in abused adults compared to non-abused ones by a margin of 2–1 (17 percent versus 9 percent). They also are more likely to engage in self-destructive behavior, have poor self-esteem, feel anxious and isolated, have higher rates of substance

*abuse, avoid sexual activity, have more sexual dysfunction, and
tend toward revictimization. This last feature means that some victims manifest a learned helplessness during interpersonal relationships which prevents them from exiting subsequent abusive
relationships.*[5]

Laura continued. "I don't think they believed me because
Damon—his name was Damon, was old. They didn't think
someone his age coulda' been all that interested in sex," Laura
continued.

"How old was he?"

"Fifty-seven."

I spontaneously burst out the first genuine laugh I'd had at
the SCC. Laura flinched. I had startled her and immediately apologized. "I'm sorry. It's just that my husband is fifty-seven. Back
then we thought people were old in their fifties. Now we don't."

Laura chuckled and began searching in the pocket of her jacket.
I expected her to emerge with a hand-rolled cigarette and was
pleased when she pulled out two small packets of graham crackers.
She handed me one unceremoniously and we began breaking off
pieces and chomping in unison.

Laura continued. "The mental health lady told my foster
mother what I said and when she got me home I was really in
trouble. She said that if I ever told anyone again she'd kill me.
I believed her. That's the last time I told anyone 'til long after I
moved out."

"How old were you then?"

"Nineteen. I started actin' out when I was eight or nine and
everyone said I was just overly sexual. Nobody asked where a
little girl would learn that stuff. Gladys, my foster mother put me
on birth control pills when I was eight."

That would have been 1965. I wasn't sure the pill had even
been invented then. I didn't have any way to verify the information Laura gave me. She was an expert liar. I made a mental note
to look up the date birth control pills became available.

Whether it was true or not, the pain of her childhood sexual
trauma was very real to Laura. And who would ever put a little girl
on "the pill?" I was also curious as to what constituted "acting out"
in Laura's world. Had she started molesting her peers? I thought

she didn't start until she was in her thirties. The only issue where I could genuinely support her was in regards to birth control at age eight.

"I think that is terrible, Laura! Girls don't need contraception until they begin menstruating and are sexually active. That was absurd. And you deserved to be believed. We both did. Things are different today. There's more awareness of the issues involved. Teachers and caseworkers watch children for signs of abuse. Society is learning to pay attention to what children say, both verbally and behaviorally."

As soon as the words were out of mouth I wondered if they were offensive. Somewhere in Laura's history fifteen or more children had either been believed or their behaviors had pointed caseworkers, parents, and doctors to their abuser, Laura. How many others might there be who weren't believed?

If she noticed the correlation, it didn't show. She continued to probe my childhood.

"Shouldn't your family doctor have known somethin' was going on with you, Sylvia? Weren't there signs that ya' were being abused?"

I didn't act out sexually at the time. No one sent me to a Mental Health Clinic. I'm not even sure our little town of four thousand people had one. There were some subtle signs, but I didn't want to share the details of my childhood with this woman. We were in an odd game of counterintelligence, two women tip-toeing into a secret life neither of us wanted to admit.

The room was beginning to spin again and the crackers tasted rancid in my mouth. Maybe Laura's story was worth the few things I had to share.

"Our doctor had to have known. In fact, there's no way he could not have known." Laura was watching me intently now and she nodded, encouraging me to go on. "My mother took me to see him one time and demanded he do a pelvic and a pap smear. I was only eleven years old. He tried to talk her out of it, but she refused to leave the office until he had examined me."

Laura looked aghast. "What did he say?"

"I don't know. I don't remember anything except feeling ashamed, like I had done something wrong. I didn't know why

72

the doctor and my mother were arguing. A few years ago I talked to my gynecologist about it. He said he would never do a pap on a little girl that age, no matter what the parent said. I felt the shame all over again. He also said because of my mother's insistence, he would have called Child Protective Services and I could have been removed from my home."

Even now, over forty years later it comforted me to think that someone might have believed me. But Laura was right. In the sixties no one believed little girls. No one paid attention.

We stood up simultaneously and moved toward the door. The air had become fetid with secrets. When we were outside, Laura changed the subject and I was grateful.

"I got written up yesterday. There's these arcade games in the gym." She looked at me to see if I was listening. "You know what those are?"

"Yes." I took a couple deep breaths and blinked hard to force myself to leave our earlier conversation and move to the present one.

"Well, me and this guy was playin' games in the arcade, but the machines are real close together so we had to stand close. After about a half hour one of the staff yelled, 'Hey, Laura, you aren't suppose' to be that close to any of the guys. Step away.' Well, that... that..."

I watched her word-search to avoid profanity.

"It really made me mad. So I went over and said, 'Listen. If ya' have somethin' to say to me, I'd appreciate it if you'd respect me enough to come over and say it without disrespectin' me in front of my friends.' The staff person got mad and wrote me up for bein' belligerent. It's no big deal, really. But I didn't appreciate bein' treated like that."

"I'm glad they watch you, Laura. This isn't a healthy environment for a woman. The men do try to take advantage of you, like the underpants guy."

Laura laughed with genuine humor. "Oh, so you still remember that, do you?"

I nodded. It wasn't something I was likely to forget. She was pleased whenever I showed genuine interest in her, even more so when I took her side.

"Sylvia, you have no idea what goes on here. For instance, you'd be amazed if ya' saw the stuff these guys have mailed into 'em. It's really gross. And then there's the stuff the staff brings in. Drugs. Pornography. Lighters. Come on, everyone knows we aren't suppose' to have lighters. They can be made into bombs. But a lot of guys have them... I'll never rat out my friends."

"So what's the pay-off for the staff? There has to be a reason they bring contraband in."

Laura shrugged. "I don't know." She looked at me through her mascara-lengthened lashes. "Okay, I kinda know. But I don't want to say and I don't know for sure."

I prompted her anyway. "In exchange for sex? You and I have talked previously about the Special Commitment Center's sickeningly sexual environment."

"Yeah, everythin' here is about sex. Every gesture is analyzed. Every action has sexual motives."

"Laura, how can people get healthy in an environment that is this unhealthy?"

"They can't. Do ya' really think we're here to get healthy? This isn't a treatment center. It's a prison where the sentences have no real end. They can hold us for as long as they want and there isn't nothin' we can do about it. The only reason I'll probably get out is because of the liability I create. If even one of the men hurt me or anything like that, the state is goin' to have trouble explainin' why they didn't keep me safe." Her voice had a tinge of skepticism. "That's why I can't be more than three to five feet away from staff at any given time."

This announcement startled me. "What are you talking about? Staff aren't that close to us when I'm here." Now I was really wondering how Laura and Mr. Underpants, aka L.L. Cool found a way to get together.

"Yeah, because you aren't a male pervert." She pronounced it "pre-vert."

"But they're watchin' the rest of the time, and ya' don't sit where you see staff walkin' back and forth just outside our room. When I go to the cafeteria I have to sit with staff next to me for my own protection. Same when I'm in the yard or the gym. The only time I get to be alone is in the bathroom, the shower and after I

74

go to bed at night. The rest of the time I am court-ordered to have staff with me.

I was troubled. What would life be like in Laura's world? No privacy was one issue. The other was the daily reality of living in a situation where she was unsafe all the time.

"Are there other residents here with one-to-one protection?"

"Yeah, of course. There's guys here who are so violent they're kept locked up twenty-three hours a day and come out in handcuffs and shackles to shower and walk the yard. And there's one guy who is retarded."

"Mentally retarded?" I explained, "Today we call it developmentally delayed or developmentally disabled."

"Well, he's jus' like a little kid. He's real sweet, though, and he trusts just about everybody. I don't go around him. Can't because of my crimes. It's in my relapse prevention plan."

"Is he safe here, Laura? Locked up with pedophiles?"

She shot me a look that validated the naiveté of my question. "He's not even as safe as I am! I can at least tell these guys to go hose themselves. He can't. He's everybody's toy. The saddest thing is this is the only home he'll ever have. The guys use him like he's a child. Ya' know what I mean."

I nodded for her to continue.

"Suddenly they assigned extra protection for the little guy. I sure hope it works. He seems sweet."

I couldn't let go of her liaison with Mr. Underpants. My curiosity finally peaked. I had to ask. "How could you be guarded every minute and still find a way to not only negotiate sex, but have it?"

Laura laughed and her blue eyes sparkled in a mischievous way. "I told you, I have my ways. Besides, me and L. L., we set it up on the phone. So that was easy. And think about it. I still have the right to go pee by myself."

Her adaptation to institutional life spoke to her cleverness, creativity and determination in a sick kind of way, but the environment sounded sicker than the people it housed.

Laura broke into my reverie. "I wish they'd send me to Arizona or Minnesota. Somewhere else. I did five years in prison and now I've been civilly committed for seven more. And there's no end in sight. I could be here the rest of my life. One of the problems is that I don't want to do the stuff they're askin' me to do in therapy. In fact, I quit group this morning. I'm not getting' anything positive sittin' there listening to a bunch of sicko guys talk about their sexual fantasies. How is that suppose' to make me better? And I'm not doin' that stupid collage assignment. I don't want to fantasize about new victims, old victims or more acceptable victims. What difference does it make? They're all victims!" Her voice rose with emotion. She lowered it to keep from drawing the staff's attention.

"The deal is this. If we don't do what the state says we have to do in therapy, then we never get out. If we don't agree to a lot of sick... you know, stuff, we'll be locked up forever. And do ya' really think anyone cares? Of course they don't!"

My voice was deliberately calm and quiet when I responded. I couldn't think of a way to kindly sugar-coat my response. "No, society doesn't care. Sex offenders are 'throw-away' people. It's not right. God doesn't think anyone is a throw-away. But it's the truth, Laura. Once you are here, the people who could change things for you don't want to know what goes on here. Are your civil rights violated? Yes, they probably are. Are the therapy models they use re-victimizing you? Yes, they probably are.

"Every time I come in here I realize that something is very wrong. No one deserves to be abused, even if they have been convicted of abusing others. The system that keeps you here looks evil to me, evil masquerading as therapy. Laura, I am so very sorry this is your life experience. I don't really know what else to say."

It was the longest speech I'd delivered since visiting her and my words expressed more compassion than I actually felt. We sat in silence for several minutes. Tears welled up in Laura's eyes. I wanted to soften my words by reaching out and touching her hand, but if the staff saw us, even for just a moment, they would interpret our actions as sexual.

So we sat in silence. There wasn't anything else to say.

By the time John came to retrieve me from the visit room I had a pounding headache and my stomach was churning. He knows me well and could tell I needed his gentle attentiveness. I wanted to run into his safe arms, but even husband and wife cannot touch in the SCC without sexual appropriateness being called into question.

On the boat back to Steilacoom I was silent, listening to little snippets of conversation between employees of both the Department of Corrections and the Special Commitment Center. The two groups generally did not like each other. Two entirely different cultures worked side by side on a very small island.

Then I heard one conversation that piqued my interest. One of the SCC staff was talking about a problem the administration was having. Apparently they had discovered one SCC resident had been there for years and was never committed through the courts. The significance was enormous. If it was true, he was unlawfully detained, denied his civil rights and because of his crimes, probably forgotten by anyone who could actually help him.

The second issue I overheard raised the hair on the back of my neck. Suddenly I was fully alert. There was another resident who was developmentally disabled. The SCC employee said that not only had he never been civilly committed, he had never even been convicted of a sexual crime. After his arrest he was moved into residence with the state's most dangerous sexual predators and forgotten. Somehow he had slipped off the Department of Developmental Disabilities radarscope. In a state that prides itself on being ahead of the other states in its treatment of individuals with disabilities, he had been discarded and tossed into a secretive world of violent pedophiles.

The man who was doing most of the talking looked around furtively. I shut my eyes and pretended to doze.

He continued by saying that the administration had not offered any extraordinary protection. Now, however, there was a new superintendent who had inherited a number of potentially litigious problems. The new "sup" received a letter from a resident named Frederick, himself a convicted child rapist, who reported that the men were routinely preying upon the nineteen year-old. Records were pulled and reviewed. Nobody was sure how this young man had come to live unprotected, unconvicted, and uncommitted.

Staff was immediately assigned one-to-one for his protection.

The two men continued talking in hushed conspiratorial tones. The administration realized that they had at least two legal time bombs in their midst. And there could be others they didn't even know about. How could they resolve the issues without admitting that they had violated both men's civil rights up until now? How could they fix the problem and still avoid litigation? They laughed. Was it really such a big deal? After all, sex offenders are throwaway people. Right? Besides, they mused, the reports of sexual inappropriateness were probably exaggerated. The offenders were under constant surveillance.

I wanted to interrupt them. I wanted to shout at them. I wanted to stick my index finger in their smug, self-righteous faces and tell them he wasn't safe. He would never be safe there. I thought of Laura. I wanted to scream, *Don't you know anything? Several times a day he is going to have to use the bathroom!*

As soon as we got home I crawled into bed for a couple of hours. When I awoke it was dark out. I heard the television news on downstairs and my husband talking back to it with irritation at the pre-election rhetoric. Just the sound of his deep voice comforted me.

I laid there and thought about Laura. Something had irritated me. I reviewed the entire visit in an attempt to find it.

Several weeks prior in a conversation with the chaplain, he indicated that Laura's childhood sexual abuse was a horrific story. And yet, what she had chosen to share with me didn't sound all that bad. In fact, it was pretty lame. Had she withheld the traumatic details, or had the chaplain been horrified by a story that to me was ordinary?

Also, on an earlier visit she had indicated that she began victimizing others when she was in her early thirties. If that was true, what was the sexual acting out she was doing at age eight that led her into the mental health system? And when was oral contraception available? What year?

I struggled to disprove the details Laura shared with me. I wanted to discredit her. I wanted her to be a liar. It was more comfortable than believing her.

But that wasn't really what annoyed me.

I didn't want to deliberately minimize her sexual abuse, but based on what we had shared thus far, I was convinced mine was at least equal, if not worse than Laura's. If I put arbitrary numerical values on abuse, hers and mine, I was pretty sure mine would score higher. That left me with the resurfacing of an earlier question.

Why did Laura McCollum become a violent serial pedophile? Why wasn't I one also?

When I compared our stories, the result was this: my empathy plummeted. I didn't deny that she fit the category of female offenders whose "own abuse had a mitigating effect on their level of responsibility,"[6] as author Michele Elliott put it. Unfortunately, it wasn't mitigating enough. I was mad.

I got up and went to my computer, ready to make some notes from the visit. I knew I'd experience a degree of relief after I remembered everything into print. But first I did a little research.

Mass distribution of oral contraceptives began around 1965. Laura might have been prescribed birth control pills at age eight. I just couldn't imagine what physician would do such a thing, even for a little girl who was "acting out."

Later that night I pulled out her autobiography and read about one of her early foster families, the McCurleys.

> I was about four years old. They would leave a light on in my room at night because I was afraid of the dark. Even though I liked this family a lot (they were very kind and loving and they took good care of me) I still missed my mother and father. I dreamed of going home to my parents.
>
> When I would get to go to the CPS office to see my family I would spend all my time with (deleted) and (deleted.) I don't remember ever seeing (deleted) until many years later when she was married. I would beg to go home. They were always promising to take us home again. My dad and mom would tell me when they were leaving to be good and the bad people would let me come back home to live with them.
>
> I was very lost and sad without my siblings. I felt I was the cause that we were split up. I was not supposed to be born. I was told my mother tried to abort me by using a clothes hanger.
>
> It was hard for me as a child to understand why my family was gone and I had been placed with strangers. I did not care much for these intruders

that took away my stability and family. I was considered a behavioral problem and a hard to place child so I went from home to home. When I was three I went to live at St. Peter's Orphanage. I stayed till I was about four years old. They found another home for me. I don't remember a lot about Saint Peter's. I did get into gymnastics and was good at the tumbling and balance beam or the horse as it is called. I would see my real family two times a month and my parents brought us candy and a toy most times. I loved my dad and mom very much and I did not understand why I could not go home. I would misbehave and cry when they would leave, clinging to my mom and dad. Eventually the contact stopped all together. Again, I felt it was because I was bad.

Esther worked every day for the McCurleys and she always brought (deleted) with her. We were the best of friends. We were inseparable, thicker than thieves we were. We went everywhere and did everything together. He was my constant friend and I loved him. Esther was like a second mother to me. She never showed favorites between (deleted) and I. Often she would bake cookies and homemade biscuits for us with syrup. She would bathe us and would grease and plait both our hair. She was beautiful and she had very dark skin with the biggest brown eyes, the softest skin and the very best arms for hugging me and (deleted).

I was a very happy child here. I would have liked if they had been given permission to adopt me however their application was denied. My parents were not willing to sign the papers.

I had been with the McCurly family a short time when Esther became ill. She moved in with us and (deleted) I would keep her company and lie in bed with her while she was so sick. As time went by Esther slept more. When she died I felt alone and lost. We all went to her funeral. While standing there

I cried. I broke free from Mrs. McCurly's grip. I ran and laid on Esther's casket crying, begging her to wake up and not leave me and we were her babies. Who would love and take care of us?

She didn't wake up, she did leave us.

I don't remember a lot about afterwards or why I had to leave the McCurly home. I had to leave (deleted) behind. I never saw him again. Even at this young age I understood that I didn't belong or fit in anywhere. I felt I had no say in any part of my life or what was being done. It was as if only the adults' wants and needs were considered. It seemed like everyone knew something I didn't.

I was about five years old when I went to live at Portaleaf Orphanage. When I got settled in I went out to play and found out that (deleted) and (deleted) were both here as well. I was glad. We used to play and have meals together. They used to protect me from some of the bigger kids because I would not fight and got beat up a few times. I had hoped that I would be able to remain here with. However, shortly after my arrival was moved to a new place. He went to Western State Hospital in Bolivar, Tennessee for mental health issues. I remained here for a few months. Then I had a visit from my social worker saying she had possibly found a family for me.

I don't remember how long I wanted a home with my own mother and father. I felt unwanted, unloved and all alone. I was very confused. I am not sure my dream for a real family will ever come my way. I hope it will someday.

I was six years old when I went to the Purvis home. That's when things got really bad.

I set down Laura's autobiography. It was late and my husband was interrupting me every few minutes to remind me I had to get up and go to work the next morning. I put Laura's life back in the desk drawer and went to bed, but I was awake most of the night listening to his gentle, rhythmic snoring.

Laura and I hadn't talked about God except for a couple passing comments. Laura knew I tried to live a life of faith, but I experienced a "check in my spirit" when I considered exploring whether or not she was saved. There was another possibility. I didn't want her to tell me she and God had reconciled.

If Laura had given her life to Jesus Christ and received his redemptive grace, I had a problem. Would that make us equals at the foot of the cross? Intellectually I knew there was no grading system for sin. In God's eyes they are all bad. But Laura's were extreme. I didn't want us to be spiritual equals. I didn't want us to be "sinners in the Lord," or worse yet, "sisters in the Lord". The idea was nauseating.

And if Laura wasn't saved, did I have a responsibility to present the gospel to her? Not too many people were in a position to do that. I was.

There was an applicable Biblical precedent that provided me with no comfort. God instructed Jonah to go to the Ninevites and tell them what would happen if they didn't repent. He refused. Jonah hated the wicked people of Nineveh. If they repented God would mercifully bless them. Jonah deliberately headed in the opposite direction, went aboard a boat and was thrown overboard because the crew thought he was responsible for the stormy weather. That's how he came to be swallowed by "a great fish." God got Jonah's attention; for three days he was inside the fish. After he was spit out on dry land, Jonah went to Nineveh, though reluctantly. In fact, he had no intention of convincing his enemies to change and ask for God's forgiveness. When Jonah got there he only spoke one word. "Repent!" And the people did.[7]

Was there a big fat fish belly in my future?

Beyond salvation, I had one more issue. What if Laura expected me to know why God allows abuse in the lives of innocent children? Where was He when she moved in with Damon and Gladys? Where was He when I was at the farm? I hate it when people ask me questions and I should know the answer, but don't.

Did it reveal a lack of faith on my part if I couldn't completely exonerate God? If He was sovereign and didn't protect us, He was malevolent. If He was truly kind and loving, but couldn't protect us, He wasn't really sovereign at all. I was sure there was more to it than that; I just didn't know what. Either way, God had some explaining to do.

Laura proved to be a much more prolific writer than me. A card came with the mail a few days later. Her list of requests followed every visit. She was a bottomless pit of needs. I wondered how long it had been since anyone was willing to give to her without making sexual counter demands. I guessed it was probably close to forever. I shopped and sent her some print sheets and a warm, colorful comforter, also some yarn so she could crochet hats and blankets in her free time. I knew I could find people somewhere in the homeless community where it wouldn't matter if they were crafted by "the worst of the worst."

Dear Sylvia

I enjoyed our visit very much. I was glad to see you. I thank you for the quilt and sheets. I am glad to have you for a friend. Can you still send me some Goldfish food? I hope you have a good time with (John's daughter) in Oregon. I look forward to hearing about your stay. I am almost done with the blanket. I will start making hats soon. I am enclosing the address to the place I am supposed to go.

Hey, guess what? I am going to get to go to Redwood. (Less restrictive housing on the SCC campus.) I found out today. They have to build me a restroom shower. Hopefully that will be soon.

Dave lost your CD order. It will take about six weeks. I am happy I will be over there with him. Pray for us.

I love you, Sylvia. I am glad God blessed me with you. God bless you and watch over you.

Write soon.

Love, Laura.

John woke me the next morning. "Come on, Sweet Pea. Time to get up. I have two dozen fresh donuts and brought you a latte."

I rolled over and groaned. The last thing I wanted to do was go back out to the Special Commitment Center. I wouldn't see Laura. Instead John and I had agreed to teach a parenting class for the few men who still had contact with their children. I had carefully screened the material we were going to present. Anything that could be effectively used to "groom victims" was left out.

"Sweetest Pea! Your coffee's getting cold!"

"Coming, Dear," I muttered under my breath. On mornings like this, my husband's consistent cheerfulness and boundless energy didn't strike me as character assets. However, the triple-shot latte did.

We rode the ferry with three busloads of visitors. Most went to the prison; a handful transferred to the SCC bus with us. I saw Clara, but she didn't acknowledge me. The woman I'd tried to talk to in the mini-mart wasn't there. I was disappointed even though I wouldn't have much time to talk.

John and I had appropriately low attendance goals for this first parenting class. Of the more than two hundred men incarcerated at SCC, less than five percent had knowingly fathered children. Most of the residents were either homosexual, pedophiles, or had no experience in committed heterosexual relationships. Seven dads had been notified we were inaugurating the program. Our expectations were exceeded when four initially showed up.

As the dads began to share their stories, I was struck by how different they were from the incarcerated fathers we'd worked with in the prison. I had expected most sex offenders to be Caucasian, but we had only one. The other dads were an African-American, a Pacific Islander and a Native American. In the prison four men from four different races wouldn't have spoken to each other. Here in the SCC they were level-set by their crimes. They knew each other and were immediately at ease.

As they began to share stories, their candor and humility struck me. These dads were able to articulate great insight into their crimes, victims and their own psychological and emotional disabilities. They'd had lots and lots of therapy and it showed. I experienced them as more openly disclosing than Laura.

The men talked about their wives, ex-wives and children. It was one thing to have a dad in prison. It was something entirely different to have a dad doing time indefinitely for a sex crime.

They talked about their shame. They laughed as they had mock-fights over the donuts. They cried openly when they talked about the effect of their crimes on their children's lives. The starving souls of these four dads latched onto my husband and me, feeding hungrily on our kind attention. At the first break they all stood up and left.

John read my mind. "Do you think they'll come back?" We knew from our experience presenting similar programs for the Department of Corrections that when a program is too emotional, men leave when they've had all they can absorb.

I looked at the table we'd been sitting around. "They'll be back."

"How can you sound so confident?"

I smiled. "There are still donuts left."

As if on cue one of the dads returned, but not alone. Three new men were with him. As they lunged toward the food, one of them announced, "Hey, I have a wife and kids. How come nobody told me about this class?"

I watched him curiously. He was African-American and very handsome, about six feet two with a medium build and enough shoulders to indicate he lifted weights. His skin was the color of mahogany. He had gray-blue eyes and an easy smile. His graying hair had been straightened and was stylishly cut. His clothes were expensive. He looked more like a tennis instructor than a sexual predator. Why would a man like him need to commit a sexual crime to satiate his appetite? I didn't have trouble imagining him as a husband and father; I couldn't picture him as a rapist or child molester.

John responded first. "The class was posted in all the units. Didn't you see it?"

He smiled. "Nope." Slowly and carefully he licked the sugar icing off his fingers. Then he looked up and caught me watching him. He flashed a perfect pair of dimples. I blushed.

"I didn't see the flyer, but I think this is a great idea. My wife and our kids live in Alaska and it is really hard on them having me here. You have no idea what it's like for our families. I need some new ideas about how to stay connected to my kids. When you live here and you're blessed enough to have family who still love you, you realize it's critical to maintain those relationships. That's the only thing that matters."

The other dads rejoined the table and a fresh wave of donuts disappeared.

"Do you want to join us for the remainder of the class? We'll be here until three o'clock," I offered.

He thought for a moment. "I'd sure like to. But I promised I'd be at the Seventh Day Adventist church service today."

I wasn't willing to let him off the hook. "That service is held every Saturday. We're only planning to do this class quarterly."

"Good point. I'll watch for the flier next time. Like I said, being a good dad and a good husband is a big priority for me." He smiled and stood up to go.

I checked the clock. We were running late. John and I had a lot of material to cover in the hour remaining until lunch. I stood up also. "By the way, I don't think we've met before. My name is Sylvia Peterson and this is my husband John."

He stepped forward and shook both our hands warmly. "Hey, you guys are great to come out and do this. Most people don't care a bit about us or our kids. You can count me in for next time. Oh, sorry, I should've introduced myself. My name's Leroy, but everyone calls me L.L. Cool."

He said good bye to the other men and left.

I was momentarily speechless. I had just met Mr. Underpants.

Chapter Five

THE ART OF
MANIPULATION

*I can do all things through Christ who strengthens me.
(Phil 4:13)*

I made the trip to the Special Commitment Center every other week. As autumn slipped into winter the weather turned cold and the rain was unrelenting. Most days I dreaded the trip and worked to stay emotionally distant. I watched myself protectively from the perspective of a third person, ever aware of the "pocket people" who traveled with me. That technique helped the intolerable to be a little more tolerable.

Laura continued to have a long list of things she wanted me to do or obtain for her. John and I called them the "I-wanna-do-fer-me's;" some crossed the line and could have gotten me permanently expelled. A few could have gotten me arrested.

The residents at SCC were not allowed to write each other letters or give each other gifts. To a small extent this was over-looked by the staff. Gifts, money, stamps and cigarettes were often used as currency for sexual favors. Sex offenders are highly skilled manipulators. Laura was a professional.

On one visit she skillfully persuaded me to buy a Sony PlayStation II as a combined birthday/Christmas present. Of course she would also need games and explained in great detail the challenge I would have finding appropriate ones.

"We're not suppose' to have anything marked 'Mature' or 'Adult'. Even games rated 'Teen' might not be okay. And make sure there's no sex and no violence. Better make sure nobody's naked too. Oh yeah, and no sexy talkin'. And I can't have games with kids in 'em. Not even cartoon kids. Games rated 'Everyone' would be best."

As I listened I became angry. Buying her all this stuff was one thing. I had the money. But did she really think I was going to personally play all the games and screen them? And what if I found a cartoon child? Was I expected to return the game and say, "Gosh, I'm sorry. I'm looking for an appropriate game for a woman who is sexually attracted to very young children."

In the end she recommended I stick with "Pac Man."

"Laura, what do you do to stay busy here?" I had innocently asked on that visit.

"Not much. That's why I want a new PlayStation. I have a TV, and I crochet. Sometimes I hang out with the guys and watch 'em play sports. Boredom's the worst part of bein' here. Well, maybe not the worst, but it's pretty high on the list."

Technically the State of Washington considers incarceration in the prison system to be more limiting than the SCC. Once inmates are civilly committed, they are supposedly given better living quarters, better food and fewer restrictions. After all, this was a treatment center, not a correctional facility. Although Laura was allowed to work forty hours a month at $1.35 an hour, she rarely did. The money she earned would have bought toiletries and cigarettes. But in most ways Laura was more incarcerated and restricted than she had ever been at the Washington Correctional Center for Women. At least there she had a few female friends.

John and I had been trained on inmate manipulation while volunteering in the prison system. We usually knew when offenders were attempting to take advantage of us. Laura was playing me like a fiddle and I knew it. I began setting limits on how much money I spent on her each month and how many favors I did. Knowing I was her only bridge to the real world of shopping malls and specialty shops, I determined to stay on a budget. Or, more honestly,

I began budgeting after I realized how much the PlayStation and games were going to cost me.

But there was one more element to her manipulation. One of the best ways to get someone to like you is to ask them for help. Somewhere in the back of our brains there's a little voice that says, "You must like this person or you wouldn't be doing these things." Sometimes the technique is a game changer.

Laura's hook was this: if I do what she asks of me, she feels loved, and I will feel more affectionately committed towards her. There was a problem. Except for an occasional random moment, I didn't feel loving towards her. I felt repulsed. As soon as I got the information I'd come for, these visits were over. If that was difficult for Laura, well, there are consequences to her crimes. It wasn't my job to mitigate them.

Meanwhile her letters kept coming.

Dear Sylvia

Hi. How are you? How's John? I was glad to see you the other day at church. I can hardly wait to get my Play Station 2 and games. I get so bored and depressed because I have nothing to do. I get tired of being around the men.

You know if you find a robe you like it doesn't have to be purple. I can hardly wait to see you on the 3rd. Bring change so we can have goodies, OK? When I move to Spokane will you write me? Maybe you can visit at least 1 X a year. I don't want to lose your friendship. I love you, Sylvia. You are my best friend, like a big sister to me.

You didn't feel good on your last visit. Are you feeling better?

Sylvia a friend here is going to send some money to you for me for my birthday. I want to know if you can cash the check and put it in a money order form and send it to me. We are not supposed to give each other things, but we do anyway. I thank you. If you choose not to, let me know asap. I love you and will see you soon.

Love, Laura

Was she completely nuts? I could lose my volunteer credentials if I laundered money for her. Did Laura think she was important enough for me to risk that?

I found pen and paper and made of list of her requests over the previous two weeks:

The "I wants"	The "will you do for me"
1. Play Station	1. Shop for her
2. Games/Joy stick	2. Bring change in coins & small bills
3. Purple bathrobe	3. Write/visit when she moved to Spokane
4. Money to order extra snacks	4. Convert the birthday money
5. Winter coat	5. Change visits from Friday to Monday
6. Underwear in a bigger size	6. Call her attorney for her

I wasn't motivated to fulfill any of them.

On my next visit Laura crossed the visiting room with a shuffling gait and hunched shoulders. No make-up today. Her now-favorite purple shirt was wrinkled and she'd started cutting her own hair because she was out of money. She looked older than her forty-eight years. There was a dark masculinity about her that put me immediately on guard.

"Dave broke up with me," she groaned as she plopped into the plastic chair in "our" interview room.

"What happened?"

She started going through her coat pockets as though looking for cigarettes, then gave up and reached for the Coke Classic and Reece's candy I'd already purchased for her.

"I don't know what's goin' on. He told me he didn't want to be with me anymore. One of his friends got involved and started tellin' him that since he already has a wife it's not right for him to be talkin' about being with me. I think Dave gave in to a big case of the guilts."

This was the first time Laura had mentioned he was married. "So what's the deal with the wife?"

"I don't think she counts." Laura looked up at me quickly, trying to gauge whether or not that line was effective. I struggled to look expressionless. She continued. "After all, they've never had sex." She looked hopeful. "Maybe they aren't even legally married since the marriage has never been consummated. They were married after he came to the SCC. But she quit comin' to visit. She doesn't write or call anymore."

What kind of woman would marry an incarcerated sex offender? What was the motive? What was the possible payoff? I couldn't think of any.

"So why are they married, Laura? I don't get it."

She shrugged, licking the chocolate candy from her fingers. "I don't think she wants anything to do with him. But they're married and so he feels like he should break up with me."

There was something incredibly sophomoric about Laura's social life. The emotional games that she and the men played reminded me of junior high school when my friends and I had huge crushes that flashed hot and bright like comets in the night sky. But in truth they came and went without so much as a serious conversation or a kiss on the cheek from "the real true love" of our lives. However worthwhile these do-or-die romances made us feel, in retrospect they were pathetic imaginings that barely hinted at the flavor, complexity, depth, joy, and commitment of an adult Christian marriage. Laura's relationship with Dave was the stuff of cheap, sleazy romance novels. It was all she had.

I searched to find words that would help her feel supported without giving the impression I approved. "I'm really sorry Dave hurt you, Laura. What do you need to help you get through this?"

She shook her head miserably and sighed with profound emphasis. "Nothin'. I'll just have to live through it. Maybe he'll change his mind. Or come to his senses. I know he knows that I love him, and I know he loves me too."

"Why don't we sit outside before it starts to rain?" I wanted to break up the conversation as quickly as I could without seeming rude. My face was starting to ache. I couldn't look neutral much longer.

We walked outside to the concrete benches and looked up at the gray clouds rolling in from the coast. The air felt crisp and the wind biting. It was late October and the autumn storms were lining up across the Pacific Ocean, each waiting its turn to attack Puget Sound.

"Sylvia, what did you find out about...?" Laura looked at the cameras and audio monitoring equipment. "You know, about our friend that shouldn't be here," she whispered.

I knew who she meant and I felt myself tense up. I didn't want her to share my information with anyone who could use it against me. Then I decided I was being uncharacteristically paranoid. The SCC was causing me to experience a common post-molestation fear; I would be punished for telling the truth. This is a serious issue for people who were sexually abused as children. I pressed through.

"After a little research, I can't find records that he was ever convicted of a sex crime. It's possible he hasn't been court ordered to be here. I don't know how he got here and I don't have a clue how to get him out. Want to help me figure it out?"

Laura's face brightened, her romantic devastation momentarily forgotten. "Yea. What do you need?"

"I know someone who works for Washington State Department of Developmental Disabilities (DDD). They tried to look him up. He was never in their system, so they have no jurisdiction." She wrinkled up her face, a signal that she didn't understand why that was significant. I continued. "If he was born mentally disabled or became disabled before age eighteen, and had deficits in his ability to take care of himself, and was not expected to significantly improve, he should have been referred to the DDD who would do an intake and assign him a caseworker. But he doesn't show in their files. So I am trying to find out how he got here."

"I think he went to 'juvy' (juvenile detention) first, either Green Hill or Echo Glen and then came here."

"Well, he probably has a heck of a case right now. His civil rights appear to have been violated. Laura, I don't know how to help him. Are his parents still living and if so, where? Or does he have a guardian? An attorney? And where did he last go to court, when and for what?"

"I see him in the gym on weekends. I can ask 'im. I'm pretty sure he'd know the answers to some of those questions. What else?" Laura was warming up to her mission.

"I can't figure out who has oversight here. If this were a hospital or a nursing home there would be licensing agencies and ombudsmen who were authorized to investigate complaints. I can't find any such entity for the SCC."

"Oh, there is." Laura looked up at the cameras focused on us. "Let's go inside. I'm feelin' cold."

Once inside the relative security of our little room she continued. "There is somethin' called the IIOC that is located at Western State Hospital. They investigate complaints here. Also, there's a Resident Advocate who investigates complaints and reports directly to the court. She's a really nice lady. She might be able to help."

I appreciated Laura's trust in the system, but I didn't share it. The people who investigated issues at SCC were on the same payroll as the people they investigated, the Department of Social and Health Services. It seemed to me that the fox's crafty brother was in charge of making sure the fox didn't harm any of the chickens.

"Since I can't take any notes when I visit, could you write me a letter with information about who you think has oversight? And try to talk to DD Guy. Maybe there's a parent or a guardian somewhere out there. But like I said, I think he may have fallen completely through the cracks of the system."

Laura nodded. "I'll see what I can find out. I know what it feels like to fall through the cracks..." For a moment I pictured her as a small child who was not believed by her caseworker, or anyone else for that matter.

And what about me? I grew up in a family with two parents who loved me and I still felt like I'd fallen through the cracks. But I couldn't afford to let my mind roll around in pity. My goal was to explore Laura, the key to my abuser. I hoped we'd get around to continuing our discussion of her life. I didn't want to appear voyeuristic, but if I couldn't figure out Laura, my visits were for nothing. If God brought me here to learn what I needed to know so I could forgive and heal, what would it mean if none of that occurred? Conversations with Laura were costing me too much to buy me nothing at all.

"Did you feel like you fell through the foster care cracks?"

Laura nodded. "I gotta go to the bathroom," she announced and motioned to one of the staff to escort her. While she was gone I had time to think about the disturbing piece of her autobiography I'd read the previous night. I wished now that I hadn't read it so close to our visit.

I was six years old when I went to the Purvis home. I was scared to death when we arrived. Sheila told me she would come back in a week to see how things were going. I said ok and she left. I was given a bath, my hair shampooed and cut very short. I was given clean clothes. I noticed they were boy's clothes except for the underpants. They had obviously been expecting or at least wanting a boy. I must have been a surprise as well as a disappointment.

I was scared. Even I knew I wasn't a boy.

After my bath Gladys unpacked all my toys and clothing. She then repacked my clothes along with the baby clothes that the McCurly family had bought for my dolls and she threw it all out. I was confused by this. I did not like it however I did not question her. My toys were replaced with cars, trucks, toy guns and a train set.

Damon was fifty-seven years old, tall thin with gray hair and pale eyes. He smoked non-filter camel cigarettes. He always smelled of tobacco. He was a carpenter by trade. Gladys was forty-five years old and a stay home mother. They lived in a small white duplex. They owned a black tom cat named Halloween. They occupied only one side of the duplex. Damon's older brother and his wife lived on the other side.

My room was in the back of the house off the kitchen. There was a door that locked that led to the bathroom in the hallway where they stored junk. I was afraid to go to the bathroom at night. I was scared someone would grab me. So there was always a pot kept in my room that I used at night if I didn't wet the bed. It was my job to dump it each morning.

I was not expecting to stay in this for long. When I went to live with the Purvis family the first year was not so bad, then things changed rapidly.

My seventh birthday arrived and I was so excited. I wanted a bike so much I just knew I would get one. Instead of a bike I got a little red pajama doll with her pants pulled down. I was embarrassed. I asked the family why they laughed at this. I laughed too, but I am not sure why.

I went to bed. I must have fallen asleep. When I woke up Damon was sitting on my bed. His hands were heavy, rough and calloused. He reeked of sweat, cigarettes and stale booze. He told me to be quiet or he would kill me. I was so afraid. I thought I would die. I lay there crying and wishing my mother was there. I was numb after awhile. It was like floating high on a cloud above the pain. I saw Esther come to me. She held out her arms to me and called me to her that she would care for me. I don't know if I was dreaming or not. When things were at their worst I would see her. She would stand at the foot of my bed with her arms stretched out to me beckoning me to her. I would be in bed awake as far as I know. Then she left like she came and never came back.

The next morning when I woke up I started to cry. I was very afraid. I wanted a bath. I could not ask for one because I had had one the night before. I hid my pajamas and panties. I then washed myself. I wanted to tell Gladys, but I knew if I did she would not believe me. She would beat me thinking I was lying.

At breakfast the next morning Damon acted like nothing had happened. I began to suffer nightmares and wetting my bed even more.

While Laura was gone I checked all the corners of the room in case there were spiders and made a decision to talk with her about the autobiography.

She returned quickly.

"I've been reading the story of your life. It's very hard for me to hear about your abuse. I've just started the section about you and the Purvis family." Although a part of me wanted to hear the details of her abuse, I was relieved when she didn't tell me.

"I ran away when I was thirteen. When I told the case worker what had been goin' on, no one believed me. In fact, they sent me to a mental hospital for awhile. And you'll never guess who I ran into?"

"Who?"

"My real dad."

This was new information. But it didn't stop there.

"And my sister."

"All three of you were in the mental hospital at the same time?" At last, a detail that I was pretty sure wasn't true. Inside me lived a critical moderator who was committed to ferreting out the truth. That part of me wanted to shout, "Ah, ha. Caught you! That is statistically almost impossible."

Laura insisted they were there together. "I walked up to my dad and guess what he said. 'Hey, Laura, want a Pall Mall? How ya' been?' That's what he said. He offered me a cigarette and we sat down and talked. Just like that."

I watched her face. There was no evidence in her expression that this was fabricated, but it didn't sound like a true story to me. At the age she was separated from her parents, how would she even recognize her father? More to the point, how would he recognize her?

And which sister was there? Was the whole family insane? And where was her mother? I think I would have expected more than the offer of a cigarette.

I let Laura continue and tried to follow her random thoughts. I tend to be a chronological, systematic thinker. Laura wasn't.

"We kids should'a never been taken from our parents. My dad felt real bad about it. I didn't tell him what my foster dad did to me.

I didn't wanna upset him. He was old by then. That's the last time I saw him. Years later I heard he'd died and I felt real bad about it."

I decided to steer the conversation away from her birth father. "What role did your foster mother play in your abuse?" I couldn't remember if I'd asked this already. Sometimes I couldn't recall parts of our conversations because I had disassociated; other times I was testing her for consistency.

"She didn't really participate. It was her job to take their two kids and leave the house so he could have his way with me. I know she knew what he was doin'… messin' with me and all. It's funny, but I hate her even more than I do him. She shoulda' protected me. That's a woman's job."

Laura stopped abruptly. We both heard the hypocrisy in her words. "That's a woman's job." Wasn't it also Laura's job to protect the children placed in her care? Instead she had done to them the very things Damon had done to her, maybe worse.

Finally she spoke. Her voice was quieter and I felt like she'd been reading my mind. "I guess that sounds kinda weird coming from me. Maybe I shoulda' protected the children better."

Children like Annie? I didn't feel like letting her off the hook. I was certain Jesus would have handled this conversation with a puddle of grace. I had none, but managed to speak with more gentleness than I felt. "Maybe you couldn't, Laura. Maybe your own abuse made it impossible for you to protect anyone."

She thought about that for a moment before continuing. "I still guess I coulda' done better than I did."

That was an understatement of the facts.

"So you stayed with your foster parents from ages six to nineteen?"

Laura didn't answer me. "When the mental hospital released me I was sent back to my foster parents and that's when my mom beat me and told me I'd better not try to tell any lies like that again. But he stopped, probably because by then I was getting too old to be appealin'."

I felt the familiar wave of nausea wash over me and I swallowed to manage the bile rising up in my throat. What kind of a monster considered a thirteen-year-old girl too old to be desirable? I also wondered what those first few nights were like after she was returned to the home. Did she lie in bed, awake and waiting to be punished, waiting to be abused, and somehow also waiting to be loved?

The mental hospital had been a more loving home to Laura than her middle class house with two parents, two older sisters and a cat named Halloween.

"I ran away again at age nineteen. That's when I went to the Salvation Army Mission. I met a guy there who'd jus' lost his job. He had three kids and no way to feed 'em. After a couple of weeks we left and went to Texas together. He got a job there and we found a place to live. It didn't work out. I didn't like the way he treated his kids. He acted like the fourteen-year old daughter ought to take care of the younger kids and do all the stuff a mom shoulda' done."

I wanted to ask Laura if that included sex. Instead I let her continue. "But I thought takin' care of the kids was my job, so we started fightin' a lot."

Was she really interested in the dad, or in the kids? Maybe the dad had figured out his children were in danger. Even if she really didn't start her crimes until more than a decade later, Laura had admittedly been attracted to children many years earlier. And she still hadn't clarified what constituted "acting out" when she was grade school age.

I had so many questions that I didn't know where to begin. In my mind I was writing each one on a note card and I kept shuffling the deck trying to prioritize what to ask next. But by the time I made a decision and opened my mouth, Laura had moved on to a new topic and I was scrambling to write on more mental note cards.

As if reading my mind, Laura made a chronological jump. "I was only convicted of molesting one child, and that's just because I almost killed her."

"Annie." It was a statement, not a question.

"Yes. Annie. I didn't mean it to get that out of control. Scared me. 'Specially because of how much I loved her."

I didn't want to hear about her great love. The idea made me ill. "How did you get caught?"

"Annie's dad eventually got custody of her. One day she had a doll and she started doin' stuff to the doll that I'd done to her. I don't know why. Maybe because that was normal for her and it felt good, or maybe because she was tryin' to let someone know what was goin' on."

Because it *felt* good? Was she completely nuts?

"They took out an arrest warrant for me. I didn't even know until a few months later. I was livin' with some guys and they got in a fight. I called the cops. They came out and took everyone's information. Later they came back and arrested me for abusin' Annie."

"How did they know you almost killed her?"

Laura shrugged as if she didn't know the answer. "After I'd been in treatment for awhile I started feelin' the guilts about the other kids. So I wrote a letter and slid it under my therapist's door and admitted to the others. I included dates and names and who their parents were, but I was never convicted because they couldn't find any of my victims."

I listened to Laura tell this version of her story, but parts of it didn't fit with things she had told me earlier. Suddenly I felt very cold and very alone seated across the table from her. For the umpteenth time I asked myself if this was all just a waste of time.

I insisted she let me buy her another can of pop from the vending machine. I bought us each a candy bar and was half way back to the interview room when I decided we each needed two, so I fed more change into the machine. I longed for the sedation of the sugar. Maybe I shouldn't have cancelled my doctor's appointment. Something was wrong with me. My legs felt heavy and my brain was having difficulty following Laura's ramblings.

Walking across the empty visit room gave me time to think about what to ask next. When I got back with the cold beverage and candy she changed topics. Did she realize her stories weren't fitting together very well?

"I think ya' should write Dave a letter for me. Maybe if he heard how much I love him he would think again about breakin' up with me."

"I got the CD's he sent me. His music is quite beautiful."

"You got 'em? Isn't he great? I love his music. So you'll write?"

"I need to be a little careful about that, Laura. I could write and let him know that I like his music, but I'm not comfortable telling him to shuck his wife and stick with you. That would be meddling."

Laura thought about this. "Yeah, I guess it would be." Her shoulders hunched back over and she blew her nose in a Kleenex. I suspected the nose blowing was mostly for dramatic purposes. When she was done there was a large, white piece of slime on the end of her nose.

I tried not to laugh. "Um, Laura?" There's never a really polite way to say this to someone. "There's a booger on the end of your nose."

We both started laughing. The tension was released. For a brief moment I was able to see her as human.

While waiting for the bus to take me back to the dock, I was tired and discouraged. Hopefully it didn't show.

Nonetheless I had a chance to talk to one of the staff, a man I respected. He divulged that one of the residents I knew from the prison was scheduled for release from the SCC. He'd been incarcerated in one place or another since the age of nine. Now he was going to his grandmother's home to build a life.

"Is he ready? I mean, what kind of preparation has he had?" In this case the resident was leaving on a technicality and had not had an opportunity to progressively move through treatment and the housing system that would have given him gradual freedom and time to learn basic life skills.

The employee shrugged and looked intently at his shoes. "Nothing, really. He probably won't be gone long. He's not going to succeed."

What would it be like? He'd never driven a car, used public transportation, balanced a checking account or walked into a store and bought something with his own money. He'd never been on a date or taken a vacation. He didn't grow up with loving parents who taught him the things we all need to know, like separating the laundry by color and always having extra toilet paper available.

But he knew all about manipulation and how to avoid consequences for his actions. He had a Ph.D. and twenty years experience in "Games Convicts Play". He knew how to lie, cheat, and steal just to survive in the insane environments of the Department of Corrections and the Special Commitment Center for Sexual Predators. And he knew how to have pleasure, mostly with children and other men.

"He'll be back. It's sad. But that's just how it is," the employee opined.

I didn't know what to say. For the resident, yes it was sad that he was leaving with no life skills and nothing but his unrealistic hope that there was a world waiting for him beyond the concertina wire.

But that was only half of the story. Before he came back there would be at least one more victim. *That person was also waiting somewhere on the other side of the short ferry ride.*

At home I made a cup of strong coffee. I was still mentally struggling to figure out if Laura was telling me the truth. I pulled out her autobiography. She skipped around and the lack of chronology was sometimes confusing.

When I went to live with Gladys and Damon Purvis they had two teenage daughters, (deleted) who was seventeen and (deleted) who was twelve. I started school at this time and had many difficulties with learning and getting along with the other children. I was not sleeping at night. Sometimes I would be spanked at school and placed in the corner for stealing the other kid's lunches because I would be hungry from being sent to bed with no supper the night before.

One of Gladys' favorite punishments for me was to lock me out of the house with no clothes at night. Sometimes it would be cold and I would cry promising to be good, not to make me go out. I would go to the kennel and sleep with Lady our dog. She was my constant only friend. She kept me warm and safe through the nights I was locked out.

I would wet the bed at night sometimes and I learned to hide my wet stuff because if I did not Gladys would make me wear the same clothes to school the next morning with no bath. In class the other children would not play with me because I smelled from having wet my pants or in my bed the night before.

There were times when my friends would come to play. She would wash my face with my wet underpants in front of them. I was ashamed that I wet the bed and that my friends knew it. I seemed to have a real problem with anger and then there were bouts of sadness. These problematic behaviors at home ranged from breaking my toys to tearing my dolls' heads, arms and legs off. It seemed like I was always in trouble.

I began to cut on my wrists and legs with Damon's razor to watch myself bleed. The cutting helped with the intense fear, pain and confusion I was living with. I actually found it soothing. That was the only time I felt anything other than afraid.

When I was about eight years old I began playing with myself almost constantly. The teachers caught me numerous times in the cloak room and bathroom. I was tested and diagnosed with a perceptual learning disability. They put me in the special education program. I had lots of difficulties in schools. I had problems with wetting myself at school which caused other problems for me. I would get sent home and then I would get a beating for messing up my clothes.

This was the first time I realized Laura's abuse might have been considerably worse than my own. Sex was only a small piece of it. There was also neglect, humiliation, intimidation, starvation, deliberate gender confusion and the list went on.

John interrupted my reading with an offer to eat out. As a treat we drove downtown for Thai food.

"Be very careful," he warned after I told him about DD Guy. Laura and the events at the SCC had dominated our dinner conversation, especially my concern that some of the residents' rights were being violated.

I knew my husband's warning was sincere and justified. We both knew I wouldn't heed it.

"Listen, I can't just let this go, John. That kid is just a hunk of meat at the SCC. You know that."

John continued. "You can't take action on hearsay. You don't really know if he was convicted or not. And maybe he really was committed to be there. You have no proof. You've already discovered that Laura's concept of truth is unreliable."

"True. In fact, I have no personal proof that lots of crimes have been committed: Hitler exterminating the Jews, Idi Amin ordering the murder of hundreds of thousands Ugandans, and don't even get me started on contemporary local crimes." My analogy was absurd and we both knew it.

John audibly sighed with frustration. He knew not to push me once I'd dug myself so deep I was bordering insane. We were silent on the drive home. My mood had changed since I started seeing Laura. Everything seemed to take more energy than I had. And I worried about things over which I had no control. For instance, I wanted to know how a young man could end up in the SCC, attractive to over a hundred starving pedophiles and completely defenseless. I didn't believe escorts would keep him safe. So where did the system let him down? I'd recently met someone in the Department of Developmental Disabilities and I was about to make a second inquiry. Maybe there were good reasons for DD Guy to be locked up. Maybe he wasn't forgotten by the agencies that were supposed to protect him. Maybe it was all just a story, but what if it wasn't?

When we arrived home I called the pay phone located in Laura's living unit. I had not given her my phone number, but I had hers. I'd never dialed it before, but I'd need to know the exact spelling of DD Guy's name. I would have to be careful. The administration at the SCC was unlikely to appreciate my snooping around. I tried to remember if I had signed a "Non-Disclosure" contract when I was approved to visit Laura as a volunteer rather than a visitor. I didn't remember one.

I was beginning to develop a "feel" for the unique culture at the Special Commitment Center and it wasn't good. The SCC originally followed the mental health model, having its roots at the Western State Hospital, a publicly funded mental facility.

When the sex offenders were moved into the prison complex at The Monroe Reformatory, the staff was still treatment-driven and compassionately implemented programs to help the men "get well." There was belief in a difference between sick and evil. The goal was healing and re-entry into society. Sex offenders were diagnosed as mentally ill. Only a psychosis could drive someone to sexually abuse another. Right?

When the sex offenders were moved to a section of the McNeil Island Correctional Center, things began to change. The employees of the Department of Corrections resented having the sex offenders locked up in the middle of their compound. The general public often confused the two, which DOC employees felt somehow demeaned their employment. After all, they worked with inmates, not perverts. The civil committment and prison units were separate entities living together in an uneasy alliance. They were symbiotically joined in providing some services like meals and transportation. They were independent in others.

John and I had watched the cultural evolution of McNeil Island. In the beginning the correctional officers treated the SCC staff like lower class citizens. They were openly hostile. Groups of officers would quit talking when an employee of the SCC walked by. In silence they scowled, waiting to resume their conversations when the "rape-o sitters" were out of hearing range. Likewise, on the passenger only ferry, the two groups didn't intermingle or talk to one another. They were clumped by uniform, the correctional officers in their medium blue and the SCC staff in teal and black. Empty seats separated them whenever possible.

Department of Corrections paid the prison workers. The Department of Social and Health Services paid the SCC staff. And to make it worse, the SCC staff was paid better for doing essentially the same—or an easier job than the prison staff.

One of the big issues was the ferry. Both groups rode the twenty-minute ferry from Steilacoom to the island and back every day. But the prison didn't start paying staff until they reached the island. DSHS began running the payroll clock when their employees got on the boat. Those forty minutes of pay each day became a bitter divider.

Shortly after the SCC moved into its new facility, the inevitable happened. DOC employees began to quit their jobs with McNeil Island Correctional Center and go to work for the Special Commitment Center. The crimes committed by those they guarded were of much less importance than staff salaries.

Soon the SCC culture felt the impact. Somewhere along the line, while working in the prison system, the correctional officers had internalized the inmates' culture. Sex crimes were the worst thing a convict could have on his rap sheet; the lowest rung of a very low ladder. Anything negative they got while locked up, well, they had it coming. Those employees who transferred to the SCC didn't see themselves as guardians of the mentally ill and advocates of treatment. They saw themselves as guards of the "worst of the worst."

John and I watched. The hospital model was replaced with high security policies and procedures. The residents (which was their new title to differentiate them from inmates,) were being held virtually forever, and if abuse was their daily experience, so what? They deserved whatever they got. That's just the way it is when you're doing time.

I was experiencing the SCC as a secretive and evil place where the truth was often covered up and rules were made to empower the union and protect the administration and staff from lawsuits. Oh, and as an aside, to protect the public from sexual deviants. They did a lousy job of healing mental illness, if in fact their residents were mentally ill and curable.

There must be some agency or person higher up the Department of Social and Health Services food chain that could help me rescue a nineteen-year-old man with an IQ less than fifty who was being molested in their new state of the art facility. Someone in state government must care about such things, but I was also realistic. There was a possibility that government workers, as representatives of the attitudes of the people of the State of Washington, didn't care what happened to people after they were involuntarily committed as sex offenders. Finding someone with high moral integrity and the courage to do the right thing could be difficult. And I didn't want to get a "snitch jacket." John was right. I would need to be very careful.

Although I thought Laura understood I would not launder her birthday money, she'd thought of a way to circumvent the system and she intended to see if it worked. A few days later I received a letter and check from someone at SCC named Brandon.

Hi my name is Brandon
I live at SCC
I'm sending you $40.00 when you receive
this money please send this amount
to Laura McCollum at SCC
Thank you very much
May you be blessed every day
through our Jesus Christ

I wondered about a couple things. First, it is common manipulation to attach religious references and blessings to requests for favors. Somehow the volunteer being manipulated is justified in breaking the rules to help a kind, good and clearly misunderstood person who was either erroneously convicted and labeled, or at least converted along the way to a new and moral life. I hoped God didn't think me skeptical if I didn't take this very seriously.

In fifteen years of volunteer work in the prison system I had learned only one thing to be certain. I cannot tell who is sincere in their faith and who isn't. I don't have the capacity to determine another's salvation. Some inmates who vocalized Christian beliefs and morals have shocked and disappointed me when they were released. And others that I didn't believe at all have left the island, joined churches, married nice girls and seem to be living happily ever after. Time and experience has taught me I am a very poor evaluator of a criminal's relationship with God.

The second thing Brandon's letter made me wonder about was what Laura was doing or had already done or promised to do for $40.00. That is a lot of money to someone who is incarcerated. I hoped I was wrong.

If I processed the money and forwarded it to Laura I was helping her break the rules. Who was Brandon? Had I met him when I attended church services with John? If so, he didn't seem significant at the time.

Since I wasn't sure what to do with the money order I tucked it away with Laura's autobiography. The Chaplain would tell me how to handle the matter.

Chapter Six

WILL YOU LOVE ME?

For as the heavens are higher than the earth, So are My ways higher than your ways. And My thoughts than your thoughts. (Isa 55:9)

E ach visit, I invested a little time and effort toward developing a friendship with George. John and I were only required to sign in at the visit desk when George was there. Other staff denied knowing there was a sign-in book. Despite the animosity between John and George, I was determined to build a rapport with him. It was hard. Being nice felt like a betrayal of my husband.

On one visit there was a fifteen-minute interval from my arrival and Laura's. George was marching around with a strange contraption that looked like a suctionless vacuum cleaner. On the foot was a large mirror facing up. He was intently rolling it through the visit room looking under the tables.

"George, what are you doing? Practicing for pretty girls in skirts?" The suggestiveness was inappropriate, but given what I'd seen in George's behavior it seemed like the kind of comment he would find flattering.

He looked up in alarm, and then his face relaxed. He knew the jab was meant in fun. "No, not today. Besides, I have a smaller, less obvious mirror for that. It mounts directly on my shoe." He chuckled, amused by his clever humor.

"So what are you really doing?"

"Checking for contraband. You'd be surprised what we find here. Lots of drugs. Family members come in with them all the time. Then they tape them under the table. We have to check nearly every day."

In my mind I pictured the family members I'd met. They didn't strike me as drug smugglers, but I gave him the benefit of the doubt.

"Mind if I ask you something?" I reminded myself that building a rapport was an investment.

He eyed me suspiciously. "Like what?"

"What are you doing here?" I watched him flinch and the muscles in his face tightened. He was instantly defensive. I wanted to diffuse him before continuing. "George, what I mean by that is, what are *you* doing working in a sex offender unit?" I decided a slight lie might further my cause. "You are obviously very bright. You handle authority and responsibility well, and you know how to interact with people. So what brought you here for employment?"

He smiled and continued to look under the tables. I walked with him.

"Oh, this isn't the ultimate job for me. But I needed something to get me by. My dad's a Baptist minister in New Mexico. Everyone just assumed I'd take over his position some day. But religion isn't really my thing. Then I came up here and got married and then divorced. I needed a job just until something better comes along, so I took this one. I suppose I could still go home and join my dad leading the church, but I'm just not sure that's what I want to do."

I swallowed the critical scoff that was forming in my throat. George may have been "churched" in his youth, but I didn't think he understood that pastors are called by God, not by their financial needs. There's quite a bit more to it than just making a career choice. Nothing about him so far had convinced me that he even believed in a Supreme Being, an entity bigger than him. I thought he'd make a poor minister to the sick, the unsaved, and the desperate. Nothing in George suggested to me that he was fundamentally loving or compassionate.

"So what would your perfect job look like?" I asked.

George thought for a moment. "Oh, I don't know. I'd probably have to go back to college first, and I'm not in a position to do that right now. So I guess it doesn't really matter."

I watched him in silence while he stopped to examine the underside of a table. How many years would he stay where he was, always unhappy yet continuing his lame excuses for not doing anything else? He could easily retire from the SCC after thirty years of misery and live comfortably off social security and a state pension. Some would consider it a suitable ending to a life of service.

As the Visiting Room Coordinator he was positioned to abuse the families by adding to their stress and distress. George's misery would become part of their misery. As long as his coworkers and supervisor liked working with him, he could continue indefinitely.

"If you aren't sure what you want to do, then it's probably wise of you to wait. A church is a big responsibility. If you want a ministry, you have extraordinary opportunities right here by reaching out to the families with compassion and understanding."

Then I experienced a moment of profound conviction. My chest constricted. My eyes teared up. I felt physically ill.

Were my visits to Laura fundamentally loving and compassionate? What was I doing here? If this was really all about me, was I any better than George? When people asked me why I was seeing her, was I honest? Or did I word my answer to make myself look righteous and cover up my own hypocrisy, inadvertently illuminated by George?

When he went outside for a cigarette I left the visiting room and headed for the chapel. As soon as I was safely inside, the tears of confession began to roll. My time with Laura was a lie. My motive was cheap and self-serving. If our conversations were to continue, I needed to ask for forgiveness and also some direction. I really didn't know what to do.

All my visits with Laura were predicated on what she had done and how she was labeled. It's easy to hate someone if that's all we allow ourselves to see. I hadn't considered the possibility that she was an actual person, loved by God.

When I looked back at the sins of my lifetime, some of them were quite devastating to others. I wouldn't want to carry the stigma and label of any of them for the rest of my life. I didn't

109

want to be defined by my mistakes. But that's what our culture does to sex offenders. It's what I had done to Laura.

I sat in the chapel and cried until deep in my spirit I heard just four words. *Will you love her?*

The staff interrupted to say Laura was waiting for me. I nodded and returned to prayer.

"Love her, Lord? Most days I don't even want to know her. Is that what this is about?"

Silence.

"OK. I'll try; just don't ask me to go to Nineveh."

By the time Laura appeared from her living unit George had returned to his investigation of the underside of the visit tables. Maybe it was my imagination, but I thought he looked a little disappointed each time he didn't find anything.

"So how's your week been, Laura?"

She had on makeup and clean clothes. I thought I caught a whiff of perfume, but it could have been from her freshly washed hair. Apparently she wasn't smoking this week; she smelled considerably better. After having read about her history of bed wetting and poor hygiene, I realized that her progress was quite remarkable.

She closed our door behind her and slid into the plastic chair. "OK I guess."

"Are you and Dave still broken up?"

She smiled sheepishly, her face infused with guilty joy. "Oh yes, it's over. If he wants to go back to his wife, I'm not goin' to stand in his way."

The ridiculousness of her statement struck me. "Going back" to his wife? They'd never been together. However, Laura infused her words with great emotion. It sounded like a line from a Harlequin romance or a daytime reality show. Jerry Springer, here we come.

"You don't look all that tore up. What else is going on?"

Laura smiled. It was the first time I'd ever noticed that her mouth lacked symmetry when she smiled. The right side of her lips was higher than the left side, as if facial nerves had been damaged sometime in her life, or at least the ones that caused her to smile. Even her dimples were located in different places in her cheeks. Then I realized she wasn't wearing her top denture.

110

"I have a new sweetie. I hope ya' aren't disappointed in me. It's L.L.Cool."

"Mr. Underpants?"

She laughed. "Oh, he hasn't asked me for anymore stuff like that. It's probably hard for ya' to understand, but a lot of these guys just want to smell a woman." Laura chuckled, "They get pretty desperate. But now L.L. has the real deal."

"So, do you like this man?"

She thought about it a moment. "I kinda' do."

"He's very handsome."

If she wondered how I knew that, she didn't ask. "Oh, I know." She giggled like a teenager. "I guess I like him alright. We're still gettin' to know each other.

"So why is L.L. here?"

"Rape. He's been down eighteen years. But it wasn't really rape. They was datin' and got carried away. He got the conviction anyway."

Either he was lying or she was. No one gets eighteen years and a trip to the SCC for one case of date rape. Generally the offender needed three or more victims or an element of extreme violence to be eligible for commitment to "long-term inpatient treatment."

"Does he have a family? A wife?" I didn't divulge that he had told John and me that he was happily married and his wife visited from Alaska.

"They're divorced. He doesn't hear from her. He has twin daughters who are grown and grandchildren. They stay in touch. I wanna go to Alaska with him when we're released. I've never been to Alaska."

I noticed a similarity between Laura's fantasies with Dave and L.L. In both cases the dream was to be released and live happily ever after as a couple. As long as the dream remained alive, so did the romance. Like Dave, I was sure Mr. Underpants wasn't telling her the truth about his crimes, his family, or his life. Maybe that was the unspoken rule that made romances initially successful at the SCC. You never told the truth about your previous life, hence you could be anything you chose to be. All you had to do was speak it into reality. And with the strict confidentiality laws, none of the residents would ever hear the truth about each other. Instead, they were whatever they decided to create.

"Laura, I've been wondering about a few things." I waited for her to nod, signaling me to continue. "When you were molesting the children, did that turn you on?" I didn't want to discuss this, but I had to know. It was part of my research.

If she was shocked by the directness of my question, she didn't show it.

Laura's laugh was rigid and uncomfortable. "Oh, yes. It was a huge turn-on. That's the problem. If it weren't, there'd be no reason to keep on it. That's what makes me a sexual deviant." She said this with ease similar to announcing she preferred butter on her morning toast or most people liked Dr. Pepper; she preferred Sprite.

"Do you still fantasize about children?"

"Not as much as I used to. And I try not to. But sometimes it's hard. What about you? Do you have fantasies?"

"Laura, not all fantasies are bad. Most people imagine being with a person they love and are attracted to, especially when they're going through puberty. It's a safe way to prepare us for the intimacy of a blessed marriage."

I chose not to go deeper than that.

Laura slowly shook her head. "Yeah, but yours aren't deviant. Deviant is when ya' have to visualize somethin' where there's a victim."

I took a big breath of air and deliberately blinked a few times. "That's hard for me to understand."

"Because you aren't a deviant. Once that's arousin', it's hard to stop. I tried. I really did."

"So now you're in an adult intimate relationship. Wouldn't that indicate that you're getting healthier?"

"Not to these people. They would say that havin' sex with a consenting, male adult is deviant behavior because of who we are and where we are. It's not expected. And they tell me that havin' fantasies about little kids is deviant, but it's normal for me. It is expected."

"That is absurd. Shouldn't the treatment goal be for you to quit being aroused by children and learn to be intimate with a consenting man?"

"You'd think so."

I wanted to think about this for a moment. I took some change out of my coat pocket and excused myself. The walk to the vending machines wasn't long, but I felt exposed and vulnerable. We continued when I returned with soft drinks and a Reece's candy bar which was still her favorite.

"Although I don't condone your sexual relationship with L.L., I think it is substantially healthier than molesting children. It seems to me that you get lots of therapy and psychoanalysis here, but no experience in healthy, adult relationships. How can you be expected to ever leave and have a normal life, Laura?"

"You're missin' the point. No one here expects any of us to leave and have normal, healthy lives. They're not workin' towards that. The goal is for us to leave and not re-offend. That's different."

"But wouldn't you be less likely to re-offend if you had a healthy, intimate relationship with someone who loves and is committed to you?"

Laura shrugged and answered with sarcasm. "You'd think so, wouldn't ya'?"

I very slowly opened the chocolate for her. It gave me time to think. What would treatment look like if the goal was healing instead of crime prevention? The state was spending $200,000 a year to house and treat each predator committed there. With that kind of money, I thought they ought to be able to create a virtual world where sex offenders had an opportunity to work toward real relationships with real people. Or maybe with robots. Or computer-generated people. Something. And if that wasn't possible, why couldn't L.L. and Laura go to their therapists, be honest and work on having a real relationship, one that didn't demand they have intercourse on the floor of an empty restroom, staring up at the toilets and smelling the disinfectant?

There was no opportunity for human beings to be appropriately intimate in the SCC program. It seemed like a big oversight to me. Treatment focused on forcing the perpetrators to become asexual.

Laura abruptly changed the topic. While she talked about one of the staff who had insulted her in the gym the week before, my mind wandered to a recent email exchange with my friend, Lynn.

Lynn was extremely intuitive, psychologically savvy, and appropriately concerned when I started seeing Laura. I sent her a copy of my journal entry from the first few visits. I needed a reality check. Lynn emailed back almost immediately.

Sylvia, my first reaction: "What is she doing? She doesn't need to do that. Why is she doing this? Surely there are others who could minister to Laura. Sylvia needs to stay safe. Is she crazy?" I read the journal as soon as I had opportunity. How could I not? Here are my random thoughts:

I love you so much Sylvia. My little girl wanted you to run, run, run away. She says don't go back anymore. Please don't go back. Please Sylvia. OK, so I thought I was OK reading it, but it has me in tears now. Actually, that child in me is in tears as I wrote the above paragraph, urging you to run away and never go back! Thought I could handle it. I can, but not without emotion. I really thought you were being over-protective when you warned in your letter to be safe when reading that. After the fact, I see why you warned me. If I had the small reaction to your writing that I did, and the fear, I can only imagine the depth of the despair, fear and anger that is stirred up in you.

Sylvia, there is a reason God has delivered Laura to you. You know that. Your God is big enough...you know that too. That you are willing to feel those feelings again- well that says a lot to me about your willingness: Is it willingness to serve God, to heal yourself further, to heal another? I don't know.

If your job is to go into McNeil and be her friend, then my job may be to be your friend and help you to stay in an emotional place where you are safe enough to continue? What can I do? What do you need?

Still, I feel heavy hearted and concerned for you. We aren't scheduled for lunch again for over three weeks. Thank you for sharing, and please, please keep current with this, OK? Sometimes you report after the fact, you know. This may be one of those times when it would be best to report in real time.... This is heavy, heavy stuff. If you are indeed fighting evil (and you are), it makes sense for you to use all of the weapons given to you by God.

This would include your friends, who have strength also. I believe with all of my heart that you are not supposed to be doing this by yourself.

I so love you, Lynn

Three weeks later we met for lunch. I was uncharacteristically late. When Lynn asked how things were going at the SCC my answer was flippant and defensive.

"We're both getting what we want while we use each other in a game of mutual mental manipulation." I managed to extract God from the entire experience.

Lynn pointed out that my voice was filled with sarcasm. "Why are you so angry at Laura?"

After unloading twenty minutes of frustrations, most of which revolved around the slow pace with which Laura was willing to divulge information about her life, Lynn made several astute observations.

First, Laura was a sociopath. She'd never said anything to me that suggested she felt bad about the harm she had done. So my expectation that she would make some radical emotional revelation was probably unrealistic.

Second, I was trying too hard to control our dialogues. I poked around trying to find what made Laura tick, but as soon as we got into the rough stuff, I wanted to run. Lynn suggested that I relax and let the sessions flow at their own pace. "Release control," she said over and over.

Third, Lynn suggested that I re-commit to being a detached observer. This would allow me to listen without being devastated by the abuse details when they came up. We agreed that one of my challenges would be to listen without dissociating. Deliberate emotional detachment would help.

Fourth, she advised I remain curious, but also guarded.

And Lynn's final reminder to me, the one that was now surfacing from my memory was that I should not expect to have a normal relationship with Laura. She wasn't capable and if that was my expectation, I would be disappointed over and over again.

Laura would continue to test me with great consistency. I needed to expect the behaviors and not be surprised.

Sitting in the small interview room, listening to her discuss the staff and their various dealings with her, I wondered how much of our conversation was a test. Did I love Laura enough to take her side against the staff? Did I love her enough to buy her a Sony PlayStation? Did I love her enough to pick out just the right games? And even more important, did I love her enough to keep coming back, even though most of the time I didn't want to, and I was pretty sure she knew it?

Laura desperately wanted someone to love her. I didn't want to be that person. The best I could do for now was to ask God to soften my heart.

I waited until she finished telling her story. "Laura, what do you believe about God?" This was the first time she'd appeared startled by my question.

"I'm not sure what you mean."

"Do you believe God exists? What is He like? How do you feel about Him?"

Laura looked uncomfortable and began fidgeting like a small child who'd been caught doing something wrong. Regardless of her verbalized answer, her truth was communicated through a face filled with fear, guilt, and some other quality I momentarily had trouble identifying. I thought it might be yearning. If I was right, the very God whose love she desperately wanted was inaccessible to her because she was terrified she didn't deserve it.

How could I explain to Laura her experience was universal? We all feel like that

There was no further opportunity to talk about God. She abruptly changed topics.

"Hey, you'd be happy to know that the DD guy is gettin' out. They're sayin' he came here straight from juvenile. There's a law against that, so he's goin' home to his mother's house."

"What's the mom like? Does she come for visits?" I was thrilled to hear this news and hoped Laura's information was accurate.

"Nobody knows for sure. I heard she's not mentally all there either. But, hey. It's his mom and it's sure better than bein' locked up in here. And they're payin' more attention to where he is and who he's with. Hopefully he'll be out in a few days."

Any resident released was big news. It brought a flash of hope to the remaining two hundred residents. Unfortunately that flash was quickly followed by increased depression. In each man's heart, and in Laura's, was the never-ending question. "Will it ever be me?"

Laura seemed genuinely pleased that "DD Guy" was leaving. In spite of all she had done that was horrible, she frequently expressed a generous heart. She rejoiced when residents were released and felt sad when she heard of men who weren't doing well. I couldn't tell if her caring for others was the result of healing that had taken place somewhere along the way. Or could it all be just part of the show so that I would like her and keep coming back, part of the game we were playing? Or maybe I was seeing glimpses of who Laura could have been with a real family who loved her.

I didn't see or hear from Laura for almost two weeks. My full-time job had expanded and I was working longer and more hectic hours. I felt unusually tired and I was pretty sure I'd gained weight; I didn't want to stand on the scale and know for sure. There was lethargy about me that I didn't like, but couldn't quite get over. I was taking long naps on weekends and then I couldn't sleep at night. Everything seemed to take too much mental, emotional, and physical energy. I still hadn't made an appointment with my physician.

Since starting to see Laura I had stopped taking care of myself in every area of my life. It was beginning to show. Maybe before I could love Laura I needed to start loving myself.

John and I went out to the Special Commitment Center the evening of Thanksgiving. He was insistent that the residents needed a Thanksgiving service and communion. I didn't want to go. There was a biting cold wind blowing steadily, with gusts up to thirty miles an hour. I didn't feel especially spiritual, and I didn't want to spend my holiday with sex offenders. I knew John would be gracious if I announced I wanted to stay home, but I felt unrealistically afraid that he wasn't safe out there without me. At the very least he needed to be covered in direct prayer, so I went anyway.

We left on the five o'clock boat. The water was black except when the moon occasionally broke through the clouds. There were seven people on the ferry, and four of those were the family of staff who lived on the island because they were essential in case of an emergency. The smell of holiday leftovers followed them to their seats.

We were the only two people going out to the north side of the island and had to wait in the blowing cold for a van to pick us up. The sky was menacing. I didn't feel good about the visit, more unsafe than usual.

When we got to the SCC the staff's welcome was somewhat wary. It was obvious they wondered what kind of people would visit their "throw away" population on a family holiday. The employees were having a party in the visiting room, which was adjacent to the chapel. Their laughter and noisy banter was hard to ignore. They didn't seem to care.

Seven men joined us for church. Then to my delight Laura arrived. I was genuinely glad to see her. We sat together at the end of a row and whispered back and forth every chance we got, without being rude or disruptive. She said the holiday was hard for her. She was depressed. And bored. I told her I'd shop for her Sony PlayStation and she could have it early, before her birthday and Christmas. That seemed to brighten her up.

While the piano player— who obviously needed more lessons— and the guitar player consulted between songs, I leaned over and whispered. "Is DD guy out yet?"

Laura shook her head. "Not yet. Did ya' hear about the letter?"

I hadn't. The music started back up and we obediently listened and mouthed the words. Between the next two songs she continued.

"He got a letter. Nine residents were plannin' to... well, I think ya' can figure it out. Fortunately he had enough brights to take the letter to his counselor. Now he has two guards with him everywhere... even the bathroom and shower."

I felt relieved he had protection. Listening to snippets of conversation on the boat, I'd already heard that the SCC didn't "have time" to release him. They were very busy, too busy to correct a critical error that had gone on much too long.

"What about the other guy that got out? Has anyone heard from him?"

Laura nodded sadly. "He doesn't call me, but he calls some of the guys. He's been drinkin' a lot. Calls here drunk. That's not a good sign."

"Drinking is a good way to get into trouble. It impairs judgment. If he's drinking, he's going to re-offend. That means there is at least one more victim out there, Laura."

She nodded in agreement. "Maybe he'll get picked up on a DUI or somethin' instead. I don't want him to hurt any more children." Laura's voice became soft and childlike. She looked away from me as John started his sermon.

We both listened to him preach an exceptional Thanksgiving message, but neither of us was thinking about the spiritual implications of George Washington's proclamation.

I looked around the room and inventoried the men who had shown up for the service. It is easy to have preconceived ideas about what child molesters look like, and the SCC residents were a constant visual surprise to me. They look like most people. They were all ages, body types, nationalities, and temperaments. It could have been a cross-section of society taken from a church or a grocery store line or a sporting event. Not even one looked like a violent sexual predator. Yet collectively, they felt creepy to me. I felt the heaviness of their crimes and their diseases.

Sitting in the relative safety of the chapel I began to have intrusive thoughts, sexual and violent Polaroid snapshots in my mind. I forced myself to look at the bland faces of the men. I didn't believe the holiness they were portraying. All I saw was what they had done to get locked up. Instead of focusing on the sex offenders, I forced myself to concentrate on the prayer John was leading.

Laura and I visited for a few minutes after the service before the staff gestured for her to leave. I promised to visit in eight more days.

John and I had a forty-minute wait for the van to pick us up for the ride to the dock. We walked slowly outside. The night was dark and fiercely cold. The wind caused a rhythmic clang as the ropes from the flag pole whipped back and forth. The almost-full moon was eerie. The grounds were quiet. When the clouds passed by, I could see a lone deer standing in the field across from the front entrance.

The worst part of the wait was the blackness of the cold, more brutal and biting than either the temperature or the wind. It felt like a steel knife on the back of my neck. The dark cold of evil was whispered into the night from two hundred cells tucked behind concrete and concertina wire.

Happy Thanksgiving.

When we arrived home I was chilled to the bone. A long, hot bath would have warmed me the quickest, but I couldn't take one. I didn't even want to stand in my own bathroom with my clothes off. John thought I was losing my mind when I crawled into bed for the night. I was still fully clothed.

As soon as I could carve out a couple hours of uninterrupted time, I returned to the story of Laura's life. Finally I felt like I was getting into the revelations that explained how she became the person I was getting to know.

I always worried that Mrs. Purvis would kill me. I would tell my caseworkers, but they never saw any bruises so I was left there. Gladys began to physically abuse me when I first arrived. Sometimes she would not feed me if I was bad or got an F on my report card. She did not approve of bad grades.

When I was about eight years old CPS brought another child to live with us. The boy's name was (deleted). We called him (deleted) for short. He was four years old. I loved him a lot and used to play with him. We shared a room together and even slept in the same bed. I began to fondle him a lot. He would always cry, so I had to stop. I was afraid he would tell Gladys and Damon.

I began having more problems controlling my behavior. I began sexually acting out with the younger neighborhood children. I was caught by the neighbors peeping in their kitchen window with a flashlight. I did not understand being beaten by Gladys for this behavior. I was not doing anything that Damon had not done to me.

There were times when I would touch myself multiple times in a day every day and this went on for years. I would get a beating when Gladys would catch me and told that I was going to hell and that my hands would fall off and that I was a bad, dirty kid. Her favorite was that I was the devil's spawn. There were times when she would have the neighborhood preacher come and pray for me to remove the evil within me.

My social skills with others were non-existent. I took whatever I wanted and beat up and sexually hurt younger children. The intense rage I was exhibiting was out of control.

There were many times I would go into Gladys and Damon's room at night and cry and beg her to forgive me, that I would be good just don't hurt me anymore. I was never able to keep this promise. I was always in trouble for something.

Damon's sexual contact with me was a nightly happening. There seemed to be no escape or safe haven for me. After some time they became more sporadic. It almost seemed like that was a punishment too. I would lie awake for hours scared to move, to breathe. I feared he was waiting there in the dark.

That year they put me on birth control pills.

When I was nine years old I tried to kill myself for the first time. I overdosed on the pills I was given to control my seizures. I was found by Gladys. I was rushed to the hospital where my stomach was pumped and I remained for awhile.

I believe what I was doing was screaming for help for someone to notice that I was being hurt. I think all children do this when they are being abused maybe in different ways. I was begging for someone to rescue me from this nightmare of crazy people that were slowly destroying me.

When I was ten years old, in one last attempt to get away from the Purvis family I told my case worker all the things Damon and Gladys had been doing to me over the years. I told her how on a regular basis he would touch me and how Gladys would beat me for the least thing and that if she left me there after we were done talking that I would be hurt again.

She confronted them with my allegations. They denied any knowledge of such actions against me. Even though she investigated my story nothing was done I was left in this home.

After she left we had dinner. I was doing the dishes while Damon was skinning a rabbit. He told me if I ever told on him or Gladys again he would do the same to me. I believed him and I never told again for many years.

After that my one focus was not to anger Gladys or Damon. I found it safer to be out of sight. I continued to hide under the house or go to Lady's kennel to sleep with her. I always thought that if my own family did not want me why would anyone else?

When I was ten or eleven years old I tried to stab Damon with a steak knife because he wanted his brother to have sex with me. I grabbed a knife and every fiber of my being wanted to kill him.

I met Gladys brother Marion who came to visit. Even when I first met him I did not care for him. I was scared of him. He smelled bad and looked like a big hairy ape. His hands were huge and he had a large scar on his face. His eyes were like ice, a cold steel color. He tried to rape me in the bathroom one evening when everyone was sleeping.

I began to notice things were weird with my body. I was getting hair and my chest had lumps that had not been there before. I started my periods at this age and my body was changing rapidly. I remember I told Gladys I was growing hair. She told everyone

**that evening at dinner. I was so embarrassed I cried
running from the table and out the house.**

I quietly set the autobiography on the table next to me. Her
writing was as random, repetitive and confusing to me as her conversations. This wasn't the first time I had actually caught her in a
lie. Laura insisted that she didn't start molesting children until she
was in her thirties. According to her autobiography she started in
grade school. *Then it struck me. She had more victims out there.
Many more.*

I now recognized Laura's abuse was considerably worse than
mine because it had the added elements of psychological, verbal,
and emotional battering. Her actual needs had been severely
neglected. Even more, she had been punished for having them.

However, I was plagued with the notion that I could be reading
a fictionalized account of her childhood. Or maybe I just didn't
want to think it all really happened the way she said it did. It didn't
matter either way; I couldn't quit reading. I also couldn't quit
having mini-conversations with her in my head as I responded to
her writing.

I kept reading.

**When I turned thirteen I met my friend (deleted)
and spent more time at her home. She was my best
friend. One day she and I were playing with her
father's gun. We didn't know it was loaded. It went
off shooting her in the chest. She died later at the
hospital. She was only fourteen. I cried for days it
seemed and was not the same for a long time.**

I was immediately angry. Didn't (deleted) rate more than
eight sentences in the story of Laura's life? There would have
been policemen, an investigation, distraught parents, and media.
Instead it was eight short sentences. Laura killed her best friend
and she reported it with less emotion than Damon skinning the
rabbit in the kitchen after dinner. Eight lousy sentences.

Then I realized with definitive acuity, it was a lie. It never happened. I read on.

This was the same year I told Ms. Spain my teacher what Damon and Gladys were doing to me and had done for years.

Really, Laura? I thought you just reported that at age eleven, you never "told again" for many years. I was becoming increasingly agitated.

I told my teacher what was going on at home. She asked me why I came to school with bruises on my face and arms so often. I told her and shortly after this I went to juvenile. I stayed there for three weeks till there was an opening in Lebonur's Children's Hospital on the psychiatric ward. I stayed there for about a month. My medication was changed. I was placed on Thorazine and many others.
Gladys and Damon used to visit me. This I did not understand.

I didn't understand it either. In fact, I didn't understand very much at all. Who was this woman? I felt like I was trying to identify Laura from a piece of jiggling Jell-O. Whenever I moved close enough to see the edge of her, she moved and changed.

When I started seeing Laura I hadn't really stopped to consider what was in it for her. Certainly she had groomed me in a sense, requesting gifts that I had purchased for her. Cotton knit sheets. A comforter. The makeup. And of course the Sony PlayStation II and games. But I rationalized it in my mind. It was a fair trade. There were things Laura needed from me and there were things I needed from her. My cost was too high if that's all it was about.

The other issue I kept buried just out of mental reach was my marriage. During the months I'd been traveling back and forth to see Laura my true feelings were hidden from the people around me. John knew I was always tired when I got home. He didn't realize the depth of my exhaustion. I wasn't sure I did either. My appointment with the doctor was in a few more days. My fear was that I was now mentally ill. Since I didn't really want to know, I decided to cancel the appointment.

My sweet husband has always championed my causes and supported my passions. We were pretty good by ourselves; together we were great. We held each other in mutual esteem, and I wasn't willing to risk losing even an ounce of his respect. What if he knew everything I was really feeling and remembering? Would he think less of me? Reliving my abuse through conversations with Laura made me feel dirty and shameful. I'd do anything to keep John from seeing my filth so I learned to smile, and to pretend, and to lie. I let all the coping mechanisms of my childhood resurface. In addition, because my motives were wrong, I closed more and more of myself away from him. Gradually my marital integrity would erode and I knew it.

Sometimes sitting alone in the night I still felt the unmistakable tickle of spiders' feet crawling up my arm. Then it disappeared and I prayed myself to sleep.

Chapter Seven

FREEDOM ISN'T FREE

But where sin abounded, grace abounded much more...
(Rom 5:20)

My next letter from Laura was fairly short. She thanked me for sending her the Sony PlayStation, although the SCC staff confiscated all the games. Apparently I hadn't screened them closely enough. Or there was another possibility; the holidays were coming. I wondered how much of what was taken away from the residents ended up under employee Christmas trees. It might be a lucrative gig this time of year.

Included in the letter, Laura sent me the report her attorney had entered with the Pierce County Superior Court, requesting that she be considered for a less restrictive living alternative (LRA) in the community. The document interested me. I knew before reading it that I could not support a lessening of her restrictions. I hoped this report would give me a professional's perspective.

I didn't want to read it from an emotional position of compassionate friendship, so I tried to put myself in Laura's place. If I could get out of the SCC and all I had to do was follow the enclosed conditions set by the court, would I? Could I? When I first scanned the document I found it to be a little tedious. When I imagined myself as the offender it wasn't tedious at all.

On 11/29/04, the Superior Court of the State of Washington, in and for the County of Pierce, ordered the Department of

Corrections (DOC) to investigate a proposed Less Restrictive Alternative (herein referred to as an LRA) for Laura F. McCollum. The investigation began with a review of DOC electronic records, all chronological entries entered into the Offender Based Tracking System (OBS), police reports regarding the instant offense, monthly status reports generated by the SCC, and an extensive interview with Ms. McCollum that occurred 11-16-04. This report will reflect any concerns and recommendations for the Court to review that are subsequent to completion of the LRA investigation.

Next there were details of the place in Spokane they recommended because of its strategically placed video cameras, managerial staff, and the fact it was essentially an apartment building for sex offenders only. I suppose her attorney thought she'd be more at home with "her own kind," and the NIMBYs would be easier to appease.

Reading just these barest of details of the New Washington Apartments I felt immediately skeptical. They sounded sleazy and secretive. Although Laura would at least have other women around, that didn't necessarily mean it would be an environmental improvement.

The next section addressed the issue of "Approved Monitoring Adult(s)". Laura was supposed to find an adult who would escort her into the community. I assumed this would not be a highly coveted or high-paying job. She indicated in her interview that she didn't know anyone in the Spokane area who could do this for her and didn't have information about the process or her resources. If this step was an expectation, had anyone told Laura?

Another condition of her release from the SCC was ongoing community-based treatment.

Ms. McCollum has reported no contact with a local Sex Offender Treatment Provider other than through her attorney. Ms. McCollum has reported her attorney has provided very little information regarding community based Sex Offender Treatment and has provided no insight regarding programming with a community based Sex Offender Treatment Provider.

The attorney had contacted an appropriate provider on Laura's behalf, who had received 5 compact discs' worth of information regarding assessments and crimes. However, the attorney admitted she hadn't spoken directly to Laura regarding her ability to live in the community. As of the date of the paperwork, no known treatment contract had been signed.

I made a note that if her attorney hadn't "had an opportunity" to even meet with Laura, how could she be represented fairly?

Apparently Laura was also required to secure employment. She was given a black mark because she hadn't made any employment contacts in the Spokane area.

When interviewed regarding any educational advancements she had made, Laura admitted to the interviewer that she "had taken several courses, but drops out or quits." Her treatment team stated she was resistant to completing classes that were offered to her. I had already identified Laura's belief that she was stupid and therefore incapable of learning. Of course she dropped out; it was better than failing.

Laura was asked a series of probably standard questions regarding her preparation for release. Her answers sounded unenthusiastic.

- She had made no effort to contact the prospective treatment provider.
- She wasn't sure how to pay for treatment. "I would like to find some employment perhaps working graveyard shift as a custodian, but I have no plans at the present time."
- When asked why she was moving to Spokane, Laura didn't know. She admitted feeling "scared of being released to Spokane, not knowing anyone, and not having a support network." She had received absolutely no information about the apartments and asked the interviewer if she would be the only sex offender in residence.
- Laura had no plan for how to pay rent.
- When asked how she proposed to pay for routine polygraph tests, a requirement of ongoing monitoring, *"Ms. McCollum was unable to provide any additional information regarding this question, as she wasn't aware she would likely be required to participate in polygraph testing."*

- Laura also didn't know she would be subject to wearing a Global Positioning System and had no plan for how to pay for that.
- She had made no attempt to re-apply for Social Security benefits, as "DSHS isn't supportive of her release at the present time and this matter has not been addressed."
- She was interviewed regarding her "offense cycle." She said she hadn't worked on that yet in treatment. The same for her "relapse prevention plan," although I distinctly heard her use its existence to pressure George.

I began to wonder why Laura was even going through these motions. I guess the interviewer wondered also. "Why do you feel an LRA is appropriate at this time?"

"I don't," she responded. "I have a lot of concerns about being released. Sometimes I get tired of having two staff with me at all times, and would like to be released, but I've made a commitment to this program and would really like to finish or complete the program prior to being released."

The next portion of the report addressed her Clinical Team Review. It began with her current diagnoses: pedophilia, paraphilia, sexual sadism, poly-substance dependency, and borderline personality disorder with anti-social traits.

The report went on to state that Laura "continues to have sexual urges and fantasies directed at children and also at adults as evidenced by self-reports. She also continues to demonstrate episodes of sexual coping with anger and aggression, resulting in inappropriate behavior. She has also had periods of sexualized preoccupation as evidenced by the touching of other residents or residents' clothing. It was also reported that she has poor cognitive problem- solving skills and gets easily frustrated when environmental changes, directives, and lack of control become overwhelming."

A trickle of fear slid up my spine. Had Laura fantasized about me? Was that why they watched us so closely?

"Some of the residential/problems that were reported are that Ms. McCollum still has periods when she engages in verbally aggressive behavior on the unit and yard, resulting in negative behavior observation reports. She has also demonstrated problematic behavior in her interaction with other residents, resorting to biting, touching, and the exchange of personal items."

Like underpants?

I was glad to see the report also outlined Laura's strengths.

"She continues to acknowledge her need for treatment and acknowledges that she still has the potential of sexually acting out when not in a structured environment. She verbalizes that her past behaviors were destructive and she needs to focus in on addressing these behaviors. Ms. McCollum also demonstrates and verbalizes transparency in her sex offender issues and her own childhood abuse issues and is able to recognize when she needs guidance by asking for treatment assistance from the clinical and residential staff. She is also presenting issues in group sessions and has emerged as a strong group member.

"Ms. McCollum was able to identify her targeted risk factors and high-risk situations that would be of high importance for her to be cognizant of. However, Ms. McCollum was unable to identify or provide with certainty that she would be able to avoid these situations. Ms. McCollum presented information as though she is knowledgeable about what she needs to do to remain crime free in the community, but stated on several occasions that she 'could tell us what she knew we wanted to hear, but couldn't say for sure what she would do given a specific situation."

The remainder of the document summarized the findings, recommended against release, and then stated what conditions would have to be satisfied should the court release her anyway. There were so many of them and I could not imagine anyone successfully meeting them all. Laura would be required to do the following:

1) Change her residence only by court order.

2) Register as a sex offender within 24 hours of release.

3) Not be at large alone in the community, nor leave her residence except for activities pre-approved by her Transition Team and prepare, in advance, a two-week schedule of her requested outings for approval by her CCO (Community Corrections Officer.)

4) She could not leave her residence unless accompanied by an approved monitoring adult who was always in close

proximity, sight and sound. I was relieved that the state intended to maintain a tight grip on Laura when and if she was released to the community, but the farther I read, the more impossible the conditions looked.

5) Continue sex offender treatment, fully comply with the provider's plan, and pay for it out of her pocket.

6) Although earlier she had 24 hours to report to her CCO, now it was a much shorter time-frame. She had six hours. I couldn't figure out why it had changed.

7) Carry a cell phone at all times (and pay for it,) log all calls and keep it charged.

8) Laura could have no intentional direct contact with minor children (age 17 and under,) could not enter onto the premises of any schools, day-care facilities, parks, recreation areas, malls, theatres, or other public or private facilities normally frequented by minors without the explicit approval of the Transition Team and in the presence of an approved monitoring adult.

9) She could not enter any public washroom or other rest facility until it had been checked for the presence of minors.

10) There was to be no intentional direct or indirect contact with any prior victims or their families, and she was prohibited from forming/engaging in relationships with persons who have minor children.

11) She also could not purchase, possess, or view any pornographic materials, have access to the Internet, use or possess alcohol or illicit drugs, enter bars, taverns, or casinos. Laura could not own, possess, receive, ship, transport, or have access to any firearms, ammunition, incendiary devices, explosives "or any parts thereof."

12) She was court-ordered to make regular payments toward any financial obligation.

13) She had to submit and pay for random urinalysis testing and could be searched at any time without a warrant. Of course, there were also periodic polygraph assessments.

14) And finally, Laura could not leave the State of Washington.

I had to set this document down after reading all the conditions. Most caused me relief for the safety of our communities. The state was certainly working hard to protect its children from Laura's eventual release, and I was grateful for that.

On the other hand, there were logistical items that I questioned. I have driven from Seattle to Spokane. It is a five-hour drive if you don't stop to eat, stretch, or use a restroom. In the winter the mountain pass is unpredictable; it's easily a seven-hour trip on snow-packed roads sprinkled with wrecked cars. Then there was routine avalanche management that closed the pass without warning. Unless she was released in July or August there was no assurance she could drive there in six hours. Right out of the box I thought it looked like a set-up to fail.

I made a list of the things Laura was expected to pay for out of her own pocket: rent, living expenses, therapy, random urinalyses, a cell phone, lie detector testing, and a paid escort. The cost was adding up in my head. Cha-ching. Cha-ching. Cha-ching. Oh yes, and the Global Positioning System. That had to be pricey. Would she be expected to pay for all this working for minimum wage as a night custodian? Or would my tax dollars be tapped to keep the community safe from a woman who, at least for now, wasn't safe to release? Was the State of Washington really willing to spend twice the amount it cost to keep her at the SCC and take on the legal risks of releasing her into the community? Why did the document list Laura's financial responsibilities when they knew she was indigent?

Laura desired to escape constant monitoring. Her discharge plan didn't move her any closer to that goal. It eliminated the razor wire, but re-created its intent with pages of restrictions.

Also, her release plan did not address the issue of church. This bothered me. In the church where John and I attended, the issue of sex offenders has been openly addressed. Everyone is welcome to worship God with us. However, registered sex offenders must meet with the pastor. Some firm restrictions are established and a contract signed to keep the children and vulnerable adults safe, as well as the offender.

In one case, an offender who worships there regularly began to spend his time before and after services talking to a specific nine-year old boy. Our pastor met with him and re-formalized his boundaries with a more detailed contract. The offender was defensive and angry, and eventually left the church. "I'm not going to worship where people don't trust me."

My response was "Prove trust is warranted, and there won't be a problem."

John and I are vocal advocates for developing church infrastructure. It is unfortunate, but at this time faith-based groups need to adopt policies and procedures if they hope to keep everyone safe. No parent should have to worry when their child goes to the bathroom unsupervised at church.

It didn't sound to me like the State of Washington intended to permit Laura to attend any kind of religious service when she was released. Maybe she needed to ask them. Or maybe the state assumed that anyone who had molested over a dozen young children had sinned themselves out of a spot on the pews. I knew an extremely long list of Christians who believed that to be true; many of them were pastors.

Laura's interviewer made her sound unmotivated and unfocused. She may want to be free of her (nearly) continuous escorts, but she hadn't displayed a willingness to take any action steps towards her goal, if she even knew what they should be.

I was also more than just a little unnerved by the stark references to her crimes and fantasies. I felt ashamed for her and of her. It took a conscious act of will for me to wiggle my way out from under Laura's shame, or where I would have had shame. Her crimes were hers, not mine. I pictured her in my mind, stuck in a quicksand-like quagmire of perversions and sexual triggers. I could reach out my hand to her, but I would need to be careful of my own footing. I couldn't afford to be emotionally sucked into her bog. That would be of no benefit to either of us.

I cancelled our next visit. The holidays were fast approaching and I needed to create enough space so she wouldn't intrude on my time with friends and family. Laura wasn't going anywhere, at least not in the near future.

John and I did agree to attend the Christmas banquet at the SCC. Friends and families of the offenders, and the offenders themselves had a holiday party in the visit room. John went over early to help the chaplain set up. I stayed home until catching the last possible boat to McNeil. I knew Laura was counting on me, but I really didn't want to go.

The room had been decorated for the holidays. A little Christmas tree hid in the corner, tinsel sagging and lights flashing in obnoxious intermittent cheer. Tables were set up banquet-style. The residents had laboriously made little candy favors and placed them at each seat. The entire room felt like it had been created by people who were trying too hard to appear merry.

Laura was waiting for me with make-up and clean clothes. She looked good.

There were about twenty families, a few with children, so she'd arranged for us to sit in one of the private rooms we used on my visits. Because of the full wall of glass, we could see and hear everything. "I can't be around the kids. It's in my relapse prevention plan," she announced as casually as if she was telling me it was raining outside. I didn't point out that I knew she didn't have one.

"Okay, Laura. I'll greet the other families and meet you there." I was beginning to know the names of several of the male offenders and they greeted me warmly by name. L.L. Cool was there and flirtatiously winked at me. I worked the room as quickly as I could and met Laura in our private room.

It struck me as odd that she wanted to be apart from the rest of the party. I didn't believe that the SCC required us to separate from the others. Most of Laura's peers were pedophiles and they were allowed to socialize around children at the banquet. I suspected that the real reason for us being sequestered had to do with ownership. Laura was letting everyone know that I was hers.

The banquet began with prayer and singing. One of the residents invited his family to entertain, and I was pleasingly surprised. There were eight of them, mostly children. They sang professionally and the music was outstanding!

While I was focused on the performance, Laura bounced in and out of our room. I gave it very little concern. L.L. Cool joined us for awhile, and then he left also. If they were still "dating," it wasn't obvious. I wanted to ask him if he still had her underwear, just to see by his reaction if that story was really true, but I needed to let it go.

When the music ended John and I left, although most of the families were taking a later boat. It was Sunday night and we both had things to prepare for our workweeks. I decided my trepidation about the evening was completely unfounded. Maybe I was just over imaginative.

Or maybe I was still naïve.

I didn't see Laura again until January. The weather was cold and the rain knifed through the gray in stinging pellets. By the time I arrived I was dripping wet and cold to the bone. I walked over to the snack machines and bought her a Coke and a Reece's while considering a new diet. Then I bought a bag of licorice. It would flush down the toilet quicker than candy or cookies.

Before she arrived I had time to silently pray. "Lord, you want me to love Laura and I don't know how. In fact, most of the time I feel afraid of her. Protect us both and soften my heart so I can experience compassion. You created her. You sent me here. I thought this was all about me, but it isn't. Over the next two hours I choose to set that aside and let you teach me about love. Amen."

The snacks were waiting for Laura when she arrived from her living unit. She gave me a quick against-the-rules hug and sat down across the table from me. I could tell from her face that she was in a dark mood and I immediately felt guilty. I should have kept up our visits over Christmas and the New Year's holidays. But Laura didn't even mention the lapse. She had other things on her mind.

"Well, I told the staff about me and L.L."

"Why? What did they say?"

She leaned back in her plastic chair with a heavy, dramatic sigh. "I just don't think it's right, what we're doin'. I don't wanna have sex with him no more. So I told my therapist. But guess what? Nobody believes me. They think I'm just makin' it all up."

I considered this predicament for a few moments before answering. "They have a problem here, don't they? If you are supposed to be guarded by staff everywhere you go, then how is it you found a way to be alone with Mr. Underpants? What does that say about the system keeping you safe from the men? It is easier for them to decide you are lying."

"Yeah, I thought of that, too."

I watched her rip into the candy, finishing it in four quick bites. "So how does he feel about you telling on him?"

She let out a long whistle. "He's pretty mad. He denies it, of course. But then he calls me on the phone from his unit. Yells at me one minute. Then wants us to meet and have sex the next. I told him to quit callin'. I don't know what ticked him off the most- that I told, or that I quit meetin' him."

She had a good point.

"My counselor's gonna arrange for me to take a polygraph. Then he'll have to take one. Then let 'em say I'm makin' it up!"

Laura stood up and I followed her to the snack machine. This was going to be a multiple-candy bar day. When we returned to our room, she made a point of making sure the door was securely closed before continuing.

"I gotta tell you somethin' else. I don't want you to think bad of me, but I gotta get it off my chest."

Under my breath I prayed. "Please, Lord, protect me. I want to be obedient, so I choose to love her regardless of the information she shares with me on this visit. Don't let my heart become hardened. Keep me soft." I braced myself and nodded for her to continue.

"It's about the Christmas banquet. You remember those kids that performed?"

"Yes. They were outstanding."

"Yeah, well this isn't about their music. You remember that littlest girl?"

I did. She looked like she was about five or six. She wore a deep-red velvet dress, and her blond hair hung almost to her waist. She sang a solo that brought down the house. "I remember her." I heard the immediate, protective concern in my own voice. I didn't know for sure what Laura was going to divulge, but I knew I didn't want to hear it.

"Yeah, well, I thought she was real cute. Remember when I kept getting' up and goin' to the bathroom?" Laura looked at me, and my face must have registered my panic. "Oh, don't worry. I didn't touch her or nothin' like that. But I had fantasies. That's why I got up and left you here a couple times. I needed to, um… relieve myself." She waited for me to react. When I didn't, she continued. "I just thought you oughta' know."

The room was silent. Nothing I wanted to say would have come out in a softened-heart, compassionate tone of voice.

Instead I thought about the LRA paperwork. If Laura couldn't handle even being in a large room at a Christmas party, celebrating the birth of Jesus with a live child in proximity, how could she ever think of being released back into the community? Disgust surged through me in a toxic wash of revulsion. I shook it off.

"OK. So now I know," I stated very matter-of-factly. "Did you self-report to your therapist?"

"Nah. He's pretty busy tryin' to figure out what to do about me and L.L. I will though, when I'm ready to talk about it."

Suddenly, being in a separate room at the banquet seemed like a good idea. In fact, maybe Laura needed a separate room for life. I was angry and I felt dirty, like I had somehow been an unknowing participant in her sick secret bathroom life. I gagged on the licorice and covered it with a cough.

"Sometimes I just can't help it, Sylvia. I know it's wrong and God don't like it, but I don't know what to do."

I didn't want to talk about little girls anymore. I usually tried to soften my voice when I asked her the hard questions. After hearing about what really happened at the banquet, I rather hoped she'd be a little offended by my tone of voice.

"Laura, what would keep your future victims safe from you?"

Laura appeared to think about this for a moment. If she was offended it didn't show. "Well, I know a few things that could, but I'm pretty good at keeping' my actions secret. For instance, there was this one time; it was right at the end before I was arrested. I used to go to the park and watch the kids a lot, so I knew the regulars. One day, I went into the public restroom and waited to see who'd come in. These two little girls came in there together. One was young and the other- probably her sister- was bigger. Maybe around six or seven. That was the only time I used a weapon. I had a knife and I … "

My brain switched off. I didn't hear anything else she told me. I began to shake; my throat constricted in horror.

Maybe it was all a lie. Truth or fiction, I had heard enough. God may have sent me to love her, but that didn't mean I had to stay the allotted two hours.

"Laura, I'm not feeling well. I'm going to leave an hour earlier than usual."

Somehow I managed to get off the island and into my car. But once I was inside, I just stared at the keys until I finally remembered how to drive.

The Diagnostic and Statistical Manual of Mental Disorders (DSM-III-R, 1987), defines dissociation as "a disturbance or alteration in the normally integrative functions of identity, memory or consciousness".[8] It is an innovative defense mechanism used by many survivors of childhood sexual abuse. It minimizes the victim's perception of the trauma and effectively blocks cognitive, sensory, motor and affective memory. It causes amnesia, but dissociation also interferes with the victim's ability to cope effectively with reality. Somewhere inside me, the horror of her confessions juxtaposed against my own abuse was too big for me to process. I had spontaneously and completely dissociated.

I got home and couldn't remember if we talked about anything after the little girls in the park. My head was pounding and I went to bed. When my husband asked me what was for dinner, it seemed like such an inane and insignificant question that my response was not kind. I don't know if he ate, and I didn't care.

Sometime in the night, I got up and moved from the bed to the downstairs sofa. I couldn't stand the idea that John might inadvertently touch me in the night. I didn't want to ever be touched again. I began to cry deep, wracking sobs for two little girls I would never know...and for myself. In the end my prayer was only two words, over and over again. *Why, God? Why?*

Laura's next letter arrived a few days later. I was trying to forget our session together. She wasn't trying to forget me. I had become her lifeline to the world, a conduit to everything material she wanted, and her list of "I-wanna-do-fer-me's" was nearly endless. Before I settled down to read, I scanned to see if she acknowledged having upset me. An apology was more than I dare hope for. Of course, there was neither.

Dear Sylvia,

Hi, it was sure good to see you today. I have had such a hard time since I spoke to Ed about sexual contact between L.L. and I. I don't know if our working relationship will ever be the same again. Unfortunately I know now to trust that I can be candid with him is a big mistake. Being candid is what got this whole situation snow balling down hill. For nine years the SCC staff have said how I am not ready for an LRA. But now that this sexual contact took place they want to shove me off on someone else instead of helping me address the issues that led me to needing to act out this behavior with JR. I feel the SCC has no reason to be angry with me. I am not the first person to make a poor choice here.

Sylvia, will you contact my lawyer and explain who you are and express your concern about me going to Spokane with no friends or support system and how that will make my success harder? I will miss you and your visits. Will you still write and call me periodically? Maybe once a year for my birthday and Christmas you will be able to come visit me. I would like that very much. I must say I am scared to death about going to Spokane. I don't know the town and anyone there to be my friend or support persons. I have no job or money to start out with nor any of the things I will need like bedding, towels, dishes, ETC.

I want to thank you and John for taking the time to love me and give me a chance to be more than a statistic or diagnosis. Your love and friendship means a lot to me. I thank you for the gifts and things you have purchased for me and for the visits and words of encouragement you have given me. I love my gown, socks and yarn. I will make you a boa scarf out of the brown and gold. I will also make you some hair scrunches. I have started the next blanket project; it is denim and assorted pinks. It is very pretty, I think.

Sylvia, I love you and you are my one and true friend. Thank you for loving me. I am going to send you some money periodically to purchase a couple things for me. I hope you won't mind doing this for me. Are you a member of SAM's club by chance? They sell 1,200-minute ATT calling cards for $50.00. I will be sending you a $100.00 the 25th of this month to purchase me two large backpacks, hopefully purple or black for packing my property when I leave. I also need a footlocker and a combination lock. These things I want to pay for. I don't want you to have to do it. It is good practice for me to also do these things for myself because it will teach me to budget and buy things I need. It is important to me that I also do things for myself. I don't want to be dependent on you. Here is (deleted) phone number she is my lawyer. She is in Tacoma, Washington. I don't know my other lawyer's phone number. I want you to call her so she knows I have someone to care about me.

I am feeling a little better today. I must say though that it hurts that L.L. is being a horse's behind. I gave him more credit than to behave so childishly. You know that my heart is and has always been with Dave. I love him. I have never felt this way about anyone before I met him. I know that he is doing the right thing and sticking by his wife and trying to make their marriage work out. I respect him as a man for this because it is not easy for him. I would have liked a life with him but I wish him and his wife the best of everything.

Hey, did you ever get the Christmas pictures I sent to you of our party here? If you did, would you make copies on your computer if you can and send to me please? I wish things could be better and more positive and therapeutic for us all here so that we could get real treatment and life skills so we can return to public and be successful. However this is nothing more than a maximum security prison to warehouse us.

It is really scary to think about leaving here after being programmed by therapists here for nine years and that I will fail because I am not ready for a LRA. I will give it my best. That is all I can do. I am worried about how I will get to the first few places I have to attend as soon as I get there. I have to report to my CCO. (Community Corrections Officer) Go to the social security office and DMV for identification. I also have to get the address so I can send for my birth certificate. I can have a pet there so I want to find a newspaper with a free pet section and a kitten. I will name her Mouse. Anyway, I should close this to get it in the mail. I love you and will see you soon. Take care. God bless you both.

Love you always, Laura

She wrote as if there was nothing out of the ordinary in her life. Perhaps there wasn't. I determined to move past the Christmas party. There were very legitimate reasons for Laura to be at the SCC. Dwelling on her pathology wouldn't help either of us.

Despite her apparent belief that the State of Washington was eager to move her to Spokane, I didn't think she was realistic. She wasn't working towards the goals that would precede her release. I believed she was diverting most of her attention from treatment to sexual/romantic liaisons with the other residents.

I wasn't sure if it was yet another self-absorbed letter, or an accumulation of issues and manipulations. I'd reached my limit.

Even talking about her had become a trigger for me. I felt tense and weepy when her name came up in casual conversation.

"Hey, Sylvia, are you still seeing that sex offender lady?"

"Hey, Sylvia, what's going on with the sick woman you go see all the time?"

"Hey, Sylvia, how much longer do you have to go to sex offender prison?"

Why did people keep asking me these things? I was sick of talking to her; I couldn't even talk about her anymore, except with my husband and Laura's chaplain. John gave me tender and protective support; the chaplain was teaching me about healthy boundaries. Other than that, what was I doing?

Chapter Eight

CIRCUMVENTING
THE SYSTEM

Cast your burden on the Lord, and He will sustain you...
(Ps 55:22)

S omething changed inside me after the Christmas Banquet. Up until then, compassion was the foundation on which I hoped to stand while God taught me how to love Laura. Now, compassion was at an all-time low. Regardless, I wanted to be able to articulate my thoughts in a way that wasn't hurtful or in anger. I had no experience loving someone from a place of biblical commitment, but not liking them at all. I hadn't forgotten Grandpa Ed; he was now secondary. God told me what He expected of me and that was my focus, even though I wasn't sure how to proceed.

The list of items Laura wanted me to purchase and errands she wanted me to run were growing with each contact. I knew she didn't stay on any one topic for long, so I had quit responding to requests that only came up once or twice. If she locked onto a genuine need, then I considered it. I was still a little burned financially from the Sony PlayStation. After the staff confiscated her games, I felt compelled to go out and buy more. What good is the unit without games? By the time I was done, I realized that I had spent as much on Laura for Christmas as I spent on my husband.

Granted, her needs were greater, but I couldn't reconcile that in my financial plan.

I called the chaplain at home.

He explained to me the systems whereby Laura can purchase anything she honestly needs. Maybe the bathrobe wouldn't be her favorite color, purple, but it would do everything a bathrobe was supposed to do.

I also shared with him my concern that Laura was setting the stage for me to be part of her release plan. She made me nervous when she wrote, "I don't know the town (Spokane) and any one there to be my friend or support persons. I have no job or money to start out with nor any of the things I will need like bedding, towels, dishes, etc."

His reply was gentle, but firm. "All you have to do is tell her no."

The chaplain allowed me to vent, process, and speculate. When I tried to picture Laura outside the rigid confines of the SCC, panic set in. I didn't want her sitting on my sofa, riding around in my car, or meeting my neighbors. I now believed there was a violent, dangerous side of her that I had yet to experience first-hand. When I imagined incorporating Laura into my "real life," I felt actual fear. The victim that I had been was terrified by the perpetrator she still was. Those thoughts were flat up against my commitment to love her. Could these opposites coexist in a reasonable brain? The chaplain assured me they could if I gave it more time.

I also talked with him about Laura reporting to me her relationship with L.L., Mr. Underpants. I couldn't tell if he believed me, and it would have been inappropriate for him to divulge whether there was a complaint/confession/investigation. I did point out it would be difficult for the SCC to accept that the two of them had opportunities to be intimate together.

Also, it could come down to which of them was more believable. L.L. was active in the little church at SCC, attending a variety of denominational services. Laura was on the periphery. L.L. presented himself as respectable and moral by SCC standards. Laura didn't. In short, when it came to "He said/she said," he was the more believable of the two.

I knew the chaplain would receive my information as a man committed to providing spiritual support to the residents at SCC, not as a sex cop. I completely trusted his judgment, and I wanted him to know that if she was lying, she had sure done a great job planning it out over several months and building a whopper of a story while meeting with me. It would have required more focus than either the chaplain or I had previously seen from her.

When we hung up the phone, I thought about him and the many things he did for residents without funding or anyone noticing. The chaplain drove forty miles to pick up animal hides for the Native Americans, and returned again to deliver the beautiful drums the residents made. It was the chaplain's job to personally supervise the Wiccans during their "weekly worship" and casting of spells. He ordered and transported fresh donuts on the mornings when religious volunteers or A.A. met with the offenders. Because they had no money, he also bought tobacco and rolling papers for the indigent residents, which explained how Laura could afford to smoke. The SCC was extremely fortunate to have a chaplain with that degree of commitment to the residents' spiritual lives, regardless of what they chose to believe. Most of the time no one even bothered to thank him.

This is what I had wanted to explain to George while he looked under the tables for contraband. Either it's a ministry or it isn't what God intended.

Later that night, I settled in with a cup of tea and a few more pages of Laura's autobiography. I had deliberately avoided it during the holidays.

When I started to read I discovered that she was returned to Gladys and Damon. She didn't document when, why, or how that felt. I assumed there was a price to pay, but true to her conversational style, Laura moved quickly from one thing to the next.

During this time (deleted) and I began to become very close. She was thirteen at this time. She and I became very close and began to explore with a lot of touching, hugging and holding each other tightly at night when we went to bed. She began to spend more time with me. When Gladys would finish beating me or giving me an embarrassing gift such as a doll with its panties pulled down, (deleted) would feed me and take me to bed where she would hold me and talk to me. We would steal money from Gladys' purse and go to the store and buy candy. One time Gladys took my walking doll and drew a spot on her head that said "spot to hit to kill.

I was still getting into lots of fights at school. I had no real friends. The kids called me "Dirty Sally" because I smelled of urine when I would go to school because I had not had a shower. I only got to shower when Damon or Gladys gave me one.

We ran around naked a lot and would shower together. I didn't understand why my family was so different from my other friends. I used to think about this and wonder why I was treated so differently from my friends I played with and went to school with. I would cry because I was ashamed my dad and mom had to bathe me. I was not allowed shower time alone. I was afraid of bath time. I learned showers equaled touch that was painful yet pleasurable. I would become angry and frustrated with these feelings of pain and pleasure. Sometimes when I was with my Damon the pain and confusion was more than I was able to comprehend.

I was eventually sent back to live with Damon and Gladys. I was a liar. When I returned things were different. (Deleted) had married a man named Gary and they lived in their own house. (Deleted) was engaged to a man in the Navy. His name was (deleted.) They were married not long after I came back from the nut house.

The Purvis family had taken in a new daughter. Her name was (deleted.) She was fourteen. They gave her my room. I now resided in the family room. I had no space or privacy to do my homework.

Things were really no better as far as the beatings and Gladys' fits of rage. Damon stopped touching me for awhile and for that I was grateful. I hated being back in this family's care. I believed they had had their chance to be good parents and they blew it.

In some ways things were worse now that I was back. I felt like I was living in a dream waiting to wake up. At least when Damon would hurt me I felt I mattered. I served a purpose. When Gladys beat me I knew I existed and was good for something. I still continued to strive for her approval, love and affection. There was no hope of this however I tried.

The hope that she would love me seemed to be what kept me alive. The possibility one day she may accept me to be a daughter of hers. This was not the case. I seemed to be able to bring out the worst in her.

I turned fourteen and was enrolled in Fairview Junior High. My teacher's name was Mr. Bagwell. I was able to find refuge in school. I actually began to make some lead way in my grades and my behavior seemed to be much better.

I did not have many friends. I did meet a boy; his name was (deleted.) He was a senior and the captain of the football team. He was tall and slender with beautiful eyes and a smile that could melt the coldest of hearts. I met him while at a pep rally at school. I thought he was the most wonderful thing I ever saw. I began to write him notes and send them through one of his friends. Little did I know he had a mean streak. I learned he thought this was funny.

One day after school I had agreed to meet him by the smoking tree where all the older popular kids hung out. When I arrived I found the joke was on me. He and some of his friends grabbed me and tried to hurt me like Damon. I believed he liked me. I was so embarrassed.

I still felt scared and very alone. I missed my foster sisters. I used to peep on my foster sisters dressing and in the shower. I found this exciting and arousing.

Once I caught my Gladys and Damon having sex. I did not know this was the sex that married people did. I only related it to what he was doing to me at night or when Gladys and the girls were gone. I was curious why she was not crying and wiggling to get away from him. I was told not to ask such questions or I would be whipped, and to go to my room and play. I was hurt and jealous and confused why he broke this special time we spent together. I felt he had ruined our time together.

I looked forward to his nightly visits at the same time I dreaded them. I would lie awake waiting for the bed to move, my heart racing and tears in my eyes wondering when it would begin again. At least someone touched me.

I'd noticed a slight change in Laura's reporting. She had developed a sense of relationship with Damon. She felt jealous when he was intimate with his wife. She was now calling him "my" Damon as though he belonged to her in some strange way.

It's not unusual for children to become attached to their abuser. Somehow it lessens the trauma if there is a degree of relationship. Laura desperately wanted to be loved. She wanted to belong to a family and have parents who protected and provided for her. Unfortunately, she was forced to create that love and sense of "belonging to someone." The same two people whose job it was to protect and nurture Laura, were the same two people who abused her and used her up. Gladys and Damon had indeed "blown it."

I was still disturbed by our last visit and her report on the two little girls in the park restroom. I didn't want her to know my memory hadn't recorded the remainder of the conversation, or if it had, I wasn't able to access the memory at will. Appearing vulnerable was always a risk. Earlier in the visit we'd talked about Laura's tips for keeping children safe from people like Laura. Now I was curious what she'd recommend to concerned parents and care providers, so I picked up the phone and called her.

She answered the pay phone in her unit and was thrilled I had initiated a conversation.

"Remember last time I was out to see you, and we were talking about your advice to keep children safe?"

"Yeah, you asked me how I'd keep kids safe from people like me."

Laura had apparently missed the part of my question that asked about her "future victims." I let it go.

"I can't take notepaper and a pen when I see you, and sometimes I can't remember everything when I get home." That statement was truer than she would ever know. "Now that I'm sitting at my computer, I wondered if you'd re-tell me your ideas on this. I think it's important and I want to keep the information."

Laura was flattered. "I'd love to help ya' with this. When I did a interview with one of the local television stations, they asked me the same thing. I'll try to remember everythin' I told 'em."

John was gone for the evening. The house was quiet and dark. I took a couple slow, deep breaths and determined to remain present through the entire conversation.

Laura continued, speaking extemporaneously, but with passion. "The most important thing is that adults need to believe kids. No little kid is goin' to make up a story about being molested just to get an adult in trouble. I know how awful it is to report and not be believed. You know it, too. Kids need to be given permission to say 'no' to adults. And when they don't want to go visit a particular adult's home, their parents- or whoever is responsible for them- need to find out why.

"I think when kids have been overnight somewhere, someone needs to notice if they have bruises or cuts. It's not really hard for a mom to check the kid's underwear when she does the laundry. If there's blood, she better find out why. If a kid has rectal bleeding, or a little girl has a vaginal infection, they're being molested. One of my victims, a little boy, had anal bleedin' and I don't think anyone even noticed."

My stomach began to churn as it fought to keep my dinner down. I imagined my insides discussing the French Onion Soup. *Should we let this go through, or send it back in the direction it came from?*

Laura had warmed up to her topic and she kept going with more and more volume and speed. Was it igniting her deviant fantasies?

"I also think parents who hire live-in housekeepers oughta' come home sometimes in the middle of the day to check and see what's really goin' on. The same for kids in daycare. The parents need to show up at odd times and see how the staff and children react.

"Sometimes parents need to play with their kids and their kids' toys. That's how I got busted. Annie was playin' with her dolls one day at her dad's house. She undressed them. Her dad wanted to know what they were doin' and Annie told him, 'What Laura does to me.' If kids are actin' out sexually in their play, they are sendin' a signal to their folks. Parents need to pay attention."

I'd heard this part of her story before, but I listened intently to her re-runs. I was always watching for discrepancies.

"Also, I don't think little kids should ever be sent into public bathrooms without an adult."

"Until what age?"

Laura thought for a minute. "They should be at least thirteen or so. And even then, they aren't completely safe."

There was a lull in the conversation. I was thinking about the two little girls in the park. I wondered if Laura was also. "Anything else?"

"Yeah, go to the 'America's Most Wanted' website. They have some really great ideas. I'm real glad John Walsh never came after me!"

I tried to join her laughter, but it sounded metallic and forced. Part of me wished that someone had "gone after her" a lot sooner than they did. How many children did she molest after the mental health system knew she was dangerous?

"I'll write ya' a letter and include all my ideas," Laura said. "I need to think on it some more. Hey, Sylvia? One more thing. I'm really ticked off at one of the female staff here. She's new and she's suppose' to be escortin' me. Well, yesterday she said to me, 'Laura, are you still a lesbian?' Like it's any of her business! I told her I never was one. I'm proud of that fact. When I was locked up with the women I did have this one girlfriend, but we didn't fool around or nothin'. We was just good friends. I loved her, but not like I love Doug. Well, I jus' think it wasn't right for her to ask me that, so I've filed a complaint. I doubt they'll do anything. But I want the staff to know the... stuff I have to put up with here. What do ya' think?"

"It sounds like she asked you an unprofessional question. I think you did the right thing by reporting the conversation."

"Yeah, me too. I'm not a lesbian. I've always been proud of that. I think homosexuality is the worst sin you can do to God. I would never do that."

After we said our good-byes I sat for a long while and thought about her last statement. The full irony of it hit me. Did Laura believe sins were rated according to some nebulous measuring stick that placed homosexuality farther up the scale than pedophilia? Or was that statement an attempt to make her look better in my eyes?

Until I started seeing Laura, I wanted to believe God had a measuring stick. It comforted me to know her sins were greater than mine. I looked pretty righteous in comparison. But is one really more heinous than another in the eyes of God? Imagining myself better than Laura might make me feel good in the short run, but it accomplishes absolutely nothing eternal.

Every time I looked deeper into the pathology of Laura McCollum, I tripped over the basic doctrines of my faith.

The next week I received two interesting and completely unrelated pieces of mail. I opened the thick one first. Apparently there had been an escalation of Laura's issues at the SCC. She finally sat down and wrote a letter to her two counselors and sent a copy to me. No one wanted to believe that she and L.L. had figured out a time and place to meet privately. Laura had decided that her living environment was the source of her poor choices. I read the letter twice. The first time I noted the letter's content. The second time I focused on her experienced attempt to manipulate her therapists.

How can I be tested for aids without having to reveal I have had sex here? Also, so you know I cannot get pregnant. I have had a hysterectomy. I don't believe he had aids, but better safe than stupid.

151

I don't trust the RRC (Residential Rehabilitation Counselor) staff to keep the fact that I have had sex in the gym restroom with a male resident between themselves and my treatment team. I have been witness to many RRC staff discussing residents' problem behaviors ETC. with other residents, which I believe to be harmful and unprofessional.

I don't trust RRC staff to be aware of this matter. You are the only two people I can turn to with this. I realize you are unaware of a few things that have been on going with me because I have not told you, which has created great stress and more problems for me. From the day I arrived here my stay thus far, which is partially my fault, has been difficult. Because I have not come to you sooner with these difficulties and problems with RRC staff that work with me, you may now not want to help me because I made some poor choices. I did not tell you I was having sex in the gym bathroom.

I did not express the truth of why I wanted out from under the strict escort procedures. The reason I want to be off the escort strictness is for several reasons. They are all listed here. Most have to do with RRC staff. I am sick to my stomach because I have to ask and depend on RRC staff to take me to groups, class, yard, etc., especially when I hear the comments they make when they don't know I hear them. They do not express this to you or ask you to change it. Instead they verbalize it passively and aggressively around me. Which in turn I feel like I don't have the right to ask them. I am asking for something unreasonable from them. Like it's my fault they have to follow me around. They have no idea how much I despise the fact I have to depend on them to take me everywhere. I try not to ask to go many places until I get so anxious I feel I will explode.

I also have been stressed and in knots due to the bickering and arguing between the swing shift and day shift staff. The negativity and backbiting is awful. It is not something I need to hear. How am I to respect staff that doesn't respect each other? You ought to hear them on the phone. They use profanity I don't even say. A lot of the bickering is about staff stealing from other staff or not cleaning up their messes. It's worse than when I lived at home. It is so bad at times I put on my headphones and blast my stereo so I don't hear it.

This is why I want my freedom to get away from the craziness of having to hear the RRC staff back stab each other. Then when they are face to face, they smile at each other like everything is hunky dory. The RRC staff really doesn't care for waiting outside of the class and group room when there are two staff present. When I walk in the yard I like to walk for at least an hour, sometimes two. The RRC staff doesn't like to walk in the yard, especially for this amount of time or go to the gym. I hate having to depend on the RRC staff, especially when I know I can do these things for myself. My experience has been when people are doing something they don't want to do they are miserable which makes everyone miserable. I never told you this, but after the biting incident with Bill, I had to deal with the RRC staff's negative comments among themselves and to other RRC staff. Comments like why didn't SCC send me back to Purdy? Why was I brought here to begin with? Why were RRC staff burdened with the responsibility of supervising me day and night. That I act like a dog in heat around the male residents. They said that I don't watch or keep boundaries with the men and that I should be kept separate from male residents at all times. That it places RRC staff at risk by them having to watch me.

Please don't discuss this with RRC staff or REC staff. The bathroom is off limits for sex now because it remains locked at all times when not in use. When the bathroom is being cleaned it is unlocked then locked as soon as the janitor is done. I don't want this all over the campus. I personally don't see the benefit of telling the RRC staff now it is done and over with. I really don't want them questioning or talking to me or other residents or staff about this. I don't ask you to keep secrets, but I am asking you not to share this. What would be the therapeutic value of the RRC staff knowing? Believe what I say here. RRC staff is not as calm as they appear when you are present.

I just think you need to know what has really been going on in my life here. I am tired of stuffing what I am really feeling and going through, what it is I really want and need to get better. It is making me ill. I am more depressed. I over eat as well as over sleep. I don't shower or clean my room or do my job very often or take my meds like they are prescribed because I am uncertain how to get myself out of this funk other than by telling you what has and is still going on with me. I need your help exploring how to cope with my resentment toward authority figures i.e. RRC staff.

I understand that L.L. was most likely not the best choice I could make. I care very much for this person and wanted him to feel/care for me. I truly believed that he did care for me and that he was different. He called me on the phone and spent lots of time with me and even told me he loved me and wrote me letters which I cherish. He always had a smile and words of encouragement for me when I needed them most. When I looked in his eyes I always felt warm, safe and secure around him. I was truly happy with him. It was like eating fresh warm chocolate straight from the oven or running through fresh grass on a warm spring day. I have never felt this way before.

After we were done having sex he told me to get out of the bathroom to go back to my unit. I immediately felt a great sadness enter my breaking heart.

I have never felt such an utter emptiness. I felt my heart literally shatter. It felt like glass breaking into tiny shards. When I see this person now it causes great conflict within me. This man made me feel special. Then he stole that back. Why? He was just one more person that does not want me. Will I ever have someone who loves and wants me? I believe the reason this is becoming more difficult for me as time goes by is because he doesn't even speak to me or look at me anymore. It is though I don't exist and that is an awful feeling. I feel invisible.

I give you my word. I will never have sex again while I am here. I hope you will consider all I have said and disclosed here and still consider lessening my restrictions so I am not dependent on RRC staff that don't want to do things with me in the first place, but will not be honest and tell you this. I really believe the gym and kitchen are the two places I need one to one supervision because there's a large group of males at one time in a closed space at one time and there is no security in there at times. Sometimes my staff is the only staff present. I should be able to walk to class and groups, clinic, in the yard alone with my peers with line of sight supervision from staff. I would like RRC staff to stop sitting at the table with me also when I eat my meals. And allow me to walk through the food line alone.

When I go to court eventually for an LRA to Spokane I will be living with sixty other male sex offenders without one to one supervision. I need to learn here how to do this appropriately and safely. I would like the opportunity to learn this while I am here.

I am making a commitment to you and myself. I will start tomorrow to shower and clean my room and do my job morning and evening and take my meds as prescribed every day. I will also commit to attend all my classes and groups with punctuality and I will complete my assignments. I will follow staff directives and even work on setting and keeping my personal boundaries with all the male residents. Just don't ask me to give up the desire and hope to have the restrictions lifted.

I know it must be costly to keep two staff with me all the time. This is money that could be spent on a second nurse for swing shift or training for staff etc.

I happen to know that the SCC issues body alarms to the residents here with medical problems so staff can quickly respond. Why can't one be issued to me so I can have my restrictions lessened? I could use it in case of emergency. I hope you understand I don't want to come across pushy or demanding. I just want to have more freedom and be treated equal to the male residents. If I can be housed here then I deserve the same privileges and opportunities the men do. I know that this freedom will be good for me. It will give me a light at the end of the tunnel that seems bleak and never ending at this time to me.

Will you just let me try this for a month so I can show you I can handle this request? I will come to you the first sign of any problem. I promise. Good night.
Laura Faye McCollum

After my second reading, I set the letter down in disbelief. Her justification for meeting L.L. in the bathroom was the intolerable condition of having one-to-one staff assigned to keep her safe from people like L.L. And she had taken it a step further. Now that she had broken the rules and broken trust and violated the conditions of her treatment plan, she believed it was an opportunity for the SCC to lessen her restrictions. Her complete lack of insight amazed me.

While I did think Laura had the right to question her treatment by the staff, blaming her sexual inappropriateness onto their internal bickering was absurd. Although I'd never met them, I was certain her therapists weren't going to take Laura's requests seriously.

I moved onto my second piece of mail. The return address identified the sender as "Ron". I was pretty sure it was the same Ron I had seen Laura talk to at the Christmas party. I assumed she had given him my Post Office Box to circumvent the system. I was about to learn why the SCC had rules about such things.

The letter was written on a piece of common, yellow legal paper. His handwriting was large and printed. It may have been done with a color crayon which would explain its childlike appearance. There was nothing childlike in its content.

DEAR LARUA.
HOW ARE YOU DOING? I'M DOING JUST FINE
FOR NOW. IT REALLY MAKES ME HAPPY TO
HEAR YOUR VOCIE. I HOPE YOU LOVE THE
BEARS. THANK'S FOR PUTTING ME ON THE
BACK OF YOUR BOOK OF LIFE AND I FIND IT
REALY FUN AT TIMES SWEETY. I LOVED TO
SPINE MORE TIME WITH YOU BUT AS YOU NOW
THERE IS TO MUCH HET RIGHT NOW AND I'M
WORKING ON GOING HOME BACK TO MY KID'S.

The remainder of Ron's letter was gross, raw, and passionate pornography. He told Laura exactly what he wanted to do to her, and what he wanted her to do to him. His ideas exceeded anything I could even imagine.

He abruptly ended it,

SORRY SO SHORT OF A LETTER FOR NOW
SWEETY. LOVE ALWAYS. BABY BOY
P.S. WRITE BACK ASP.

I grabbed the edge of the kitchen sink, leaned over and threw up. The stark repulsion of the images that had invaded my home, made me ill. Then angry. I didn't hold Laura responsible for what Ron had written, but I did hold her responsible for giving out my address without my permission. Once again I was struck full in the face by the abusive and sexually inappropriate treatment she endured from the men at the SCC. Now it was spilling over into my house also.

Whoever Ron was, he was sick. I didn't want anything about him to ever again intrude uninvited into my life. I wasn't sure what to do with the letter. I had no intention of forwarding such filth to Laura. I couldn't protect her from her environment, but I didn't have to be another conduit of sexual malignancy for her.

I decided to tuck the letter away and not mention it for the time being. I didn't even show it to my husband. As angry as I felt, I couldn't begin to imagine what his reaction would be.

Then I heard His voice in my spirit. *Sylvia, they are just like you...and I love them.* That's all. The words fell on me with a thud. What did that mean?

"I quit group." Laura plopped down in the chair across from me and immediately ripped open the candy bars I'd purchased while waiting for staff to escort her from the living unit to the visiting room.

"Why'd you do that?"

She shrugged as though it wasn't really very important. "I'm not gettin' that much out of it right now. And besides, L.L.'s best friend's in my group. I can't even talk openly about what's going on between me and L.L. I took a polygraph, but the interviewer says the results were inconclusive."

"What about L.L.? Did he take one?"

"Nah! He refuses. That ought'a tell them somethin' right there. But they still don't believe me. I'm sick of this place!"

I watched her break off big chunks of the Reece's and shove them into her mouth. Today she had on jeans and her favorite purple T-shirt. Both were worn, but clean and she'd taken time to shower and apply her makeup before coming to see me. There were little pieces of chocolate on her chest and the table between us. I imagined clouds of Reece's dust punctuating her words of frustration.

"Are you and L.L. on speaking terms at all?"

She scrunched up her face. "Are you kiddin'? He only calls me when he wants me to put out. The rest of the time he still denies it all. I hate him for that. At least I take responsibility for my part of it. And I never really cared that much about L.L. It's nothin' like the way I love Dave."

Just then, one of the other residents walked by our interview room window. Laura jumped up, left, and returned. "Did you see him? His name is Ron. He has issues with me."

She had my renewed attention. His letter to her was still tucked away in my desk at home.

"Meaning what?"

"Oh, he's sometimes inappropriate with me. I think he has a crush on me or somethin'. One time he gave me..." She looked to see if I could figure out what she was talking about without her saying the actual words. I could. She wasn't talking about urine. I nodded. "I guess he thought I could get pregnant. He doesn't know I've had a hysterectomy. And I don't think it woulda' worked anyway. I don't know. What do ya' think?"

"It would not have worked." My voice was deliberately deadpan.

"Yeah, that's what I thought. But he said he wanted to have a baby with me. Ron's sweet, but in a kind of real stupid way."

Sweet? I couldn't imagine standing in the same room with a man who wrote the kind of filth Ron had mailed to my house.

But there were conflicting issues. I briefly thought back to the opinion piece Ken Schram had written about her. Few people would have any concerns that she was being manipulated and victimized by the male residents, and possibly some of the staff at the SCC. They'd insist that she was getting what she deserved. No, they'd insist she was getting better than what she deserved. She had "three hots and a cot," three meals a day and a place to sleep.

I didn't agree. Regardless of her crimes, as unspeakable as they were, the ongoing abuse she experienced was re-victimizing her by virtue of her own childhood history. How could healing and transformation occur when Laura lived daily with grossly inappropriate sexual behavior in her face? If the State of Washington intended to eventually release Laura, they needed to first find a way to fix whatever snapped when she was a child. I'd yet to see any evidence that her current living situation and treatment regime was making actual headway towards that goal. If, however, the goal was permanent incarceration and punishment, maybe Ken Schram was right and none of us should feel sorry for Laura McCollum.

She roused me from my thoughts. "Hey, I wrote ya' a letter to help with your ideas 'bout keeping little kids safe. Did you get it?"

John and I checked our post office box irregularly.

"No. When did you send it?"

"A few days ago. You shoulda' had it by now."

"I'll check the box on the way home." When I came to visit without John I rarely went to the Post Office. I liked him to be with me when I read her letters.

Laura seemed pleased with herself. "I think you oughta' talk to some groups, like the Lions Club or somethin'. You could tell them about me."

Suddenly I saw what she was doing. Her list of ideas wasn't about keeping children safe. It was about her. I could use it to talk about *her*. She was the center of the project, not the children. I felt angry, no longer reluctant to ask penetrating questions that would have been offensive to someone healthier.

"So how did you choose your victims, Laura?"

She considered this a moment and looked uncomfortable. When she answered, her voice was uncharacteristically quiet, almost remorseful.

"I chose really young ones because I knew they didn't have the verbal skills to tell on me."

We were both quiet for several minutes while I pulled at a hangnail on my finger. I didn't know what to say. It was absolutely clear that her molestations were calculated and deliberate. This wasn't the case of a woman whose intimacy with her victims started out as nurturing and somewhere crossed the line. Laura had made a conscious decision to victimize children who were incapable of telling anyone what she had done to him or her.

When I looked back into her face she glared at me with eyes that were cold, malevolent, and not quite human. The woman sitting across from me now wasn't feeling bad for the innocent lives she had destroyed. There wasn't enough makeup in the world to soften that face.

"Can I get you more chocolate?" I needed to get away.

"Sure. And another Coke Classic if ya' have any money left."

I did. How like Laura. For every act of kindness I made towards her, however small, she managed to ask for more. I was beginning to see that in Laura's world everything was all about Laura. Her childhood had left huge wells of unmet needs and now nobody could ever give her enough to fill the holes.

There would never be enough.

When I returned with the Coke I told her about Ron's letter without the sick details. When I finished justifying why I had not forwarded it, Laura seemed somewhat touched, perceiving me as protective.

"I think I'd better talk to the chaplain or my therapist or someone about it. Ron's not suppose' to do that, write me like that. Are ya' mad at me for givin' him your address?"

"No. Just curious why you did."

"He wanted to send me some stuffed bears, so I figured he could send them to you and then you could give them to me. Otherwise the staff wouldn't let me have 'em. But the bears I wanted were out of stock, so that's why you never got 'em. I guess he just took it upon himself to write me the letter."

"It was pretty sick stuff, Laura."

"I'm sorry. Want me to talk to him about it?"

"No, but I do think you need to let someone here know that he found a way to write you an inappropriate letter. I'm sure that's in violation of his treatment plan."

"Yeah, we aren't allowed to write stuff like that. I'll see if anyone wants to see the letter."

"Okay. I'll hold it until I hear from you, but one other thing, Laura. Do not ever again try to use me to circumvent the system. I will never forward things to you from other residents. This time I talked to you about it. Next time I will talk with your staff. Do we understand each other?"

She nodded. I was pretty sure the letter wouldn't come up again, not with me and not with anyone else.

I stopped at the Post Office on the way home and Laura's last letter was waiting. What would she expect me to buy in trade for the information?

Her recommendations were neither new nor insightful. Most were common sense; all were included in everything I'd ever read on the topic. I was disappointed. How much of Laura's own advice would have kept her victims safe from her? I didn't see where she was exactly giving away her "trade secrets."

The months had sped by, and I didn't feel I understood my own abuse any better than when we started. Perhaps I was beginning to see into Laura's disturbed mind. Perhaps I was realizing how hard it is to love someone whose life was the antithesis of love. Perhaps I was serving some sociological purpose. But that isn't what my visits were supposed to be about. Loving Laura did not preclude figuring out what I came for. Then I could gradually back out of her bizarre world.

I sat at the computer and devised a more organized plan to look at the potential causes of pedophilia. I was certain that break-through was imminent.

Chapter Nine

CRAZY OR JUST PLAIN EVIL?

For I am the Lord who heals you. (Ex 15:26)

I made a list of anything that might contribute to pedophilia: chemical imbalance, fetal alcohol syndrome, personality disorder, low intelligence, family genetics, and childhood experiences. I didn't need to dive very deep. The research noted that all of these could be contributing factors. Was it possible that there are no diagnostic explanations for the horrendous actions of sex offenders? Are they all just plain crazy, or worse... are they pathologically evil?

I decided to research the last two. Were there similarities between Laura and Grandpa Ed? When I isolated the characteristics they had in common, I would be well on my way to an answer. I started with mental illness because the alternate possibility felt creepy.

Coincidentally, it was about this same time that I was scheduled to teach a class on mental illness for my employer. I'd taught the same class many times, and— as usual— I waited until an hour before class to pull the materials together. Unlike usual, I couldn't find the training manual. I went through all my office drawers and cupboards; it wasn't there. Rather than cancel the class, I pulled a different author's work that covered the same material and hoped I could teach it coherently. The new curriculum included a slightly different presentation, and I found myself looking at mental illness with new eyes as the day progressed.

The materials explained mental health as an individual's ability to express a wide range of emotions, both give and receive help in times of trouble, and concentrate on a task until its completion. A healthy person is able to express their feelings and fully participate in a life that included physical, emotional, social, and spiritual activities.

When I first started visiting Laura, one of the questions I wanted answered was, "Is she mentally ill?" Based on the class I was teaching, and the material I was presenting, and based on my limited time with her, I would have to say no. Based on the treatment report that was submitted in considering her transfer to an LRA, I didn't believe Laura had a qualified mental illness, although she'd been labeled with quite a few.

Pedophilia is not a disease, just like murder is not a disease. It is an action, albeit not a healthy one. I am personally disinclined to let people off the hook by labeling them. Laura had molested children and that made her a pedophile. But being a pedophile is not a suitable excuse for molesting children, any more than compulsive disorder is an excuse for washing hands all day long. It was, however, her core issue.

Laura was able to exhibit a full range of emotions. Her life was balanced between the mental, emotional, physical and spiritual, even though she was never very functional in any one of the four. This related to her extreme narcissism.

She seemed to be adapting pretty well to a very structured environment, making the most of it while she was there and learning how to get what she wanted in spite of the very sick internal culture. Her cleverness was sometimes impressive.

I saw no evidence of hallucinations or delusional thinking. Laura had no false ideas about herself or her crimes. Lack of reasonable, adequate remorse did not equate to mental illness.

However, if Laura wasn't mentally ill by clinical standards, then what was wrong with her? Somewhere back in one of our earliest conversations she had suggested that her childhood abuse caused an actual chemical or electrical change in her brain function, thus suggesting that she wasn't entirely responsible for her actions against children. Personally, I thought it sounded like hogwash.

I was determined to explore all possibilities. Some online research might help. I also wanted to look at the effects of Fetal Alcohol Syndrome. Based on Laura's autobiography her mother was drunk all the time. I presumed her intoxication included pregnancy. What impact might that have had on Laura's mental and emotional development? I wanted to talk to Laura about whether she saw herself as mentally ill, but our next visit was not the right time.

At the onset, there was a darkness about her that was immediately noticeable when she sat down in our interview room. We were the only people in that area, but Laura still insisted that we meet privately and close the door. Her mannerisms were very masculine, and her words snapped shut at the end of each sentence. She appeared to be barely controlling an inner rage. If she exploded, would I be in danger? Would the staff even care?

After the briefest of greetings she motioned to the Coke Classic and Reece's bars on the table. "These for me?"

I thought it was a stupid question. Who else would they be for?

Laura ripped open the candy, barely chewed, and swallowed it with quick and efficient gulps. I watched her without speaking.

Her haircut had grown out unevenly; she reminded me of an old, worn jacket I had in the back of my closet. The hem was coming out in some places. There were permanent stains on the front and the sleeves. The elbows were worn through. The original colors were fading, but not with the choreographed look recently popular in teen clothing. Laura looked like a human version of that jacket, all used up in a careless and neglectful way.

She'd applied foundation, but with too much on some parts of her face and none at all on others. She wasn't wearing eye makeup or lipstick. I'd never before realized wearing a little make-up could look worse than wearing none at all.

She looked to me like a very tough "dike" in a bad mood. Although she had molested children of both genders, I'd never thought of her as a lesbian. Today I did and I felt afraid of her.

"I thought you'd like to know, I have a new honey."

"Really?" I leaned forward slightly. This isn't what I expected. "Who?"

"His name's Anthony. He's real sweet. We're getting married. Will you be my... what's it called? You know, the lady that stands by me."

"Your Matron of Honor?"

"Yeah, that's it." In spite of the happy announcement, her tone of voice was droll and flat. She didn't sound like Laura in the throes of a new romance. "We're goin' to ask the chaplain to marry us, but I don't know if the state will let him do that. Hey, maybe John would marry us! Yeah, that's a great idea. What do ya' think?"

I knew exactly what my husband would think, and I would never consider being the Matron of Honor for two incarcerated sex offenders. "You'll have to ask John," I said hedging. "I don't speak for my husband."

"Yeah, I'll ask him. We want to get married next summer."

"So how long have you and Anthony been seeing each other?"

"Two weeks. But we've known each other a lot longer. He's a pedophile just like me, so we really understand each other."

Did Laura really think pedophilia was a solid foundation for a lasting, committed, and blessed marriage?

"Are you having sex?" I couldn't resist asking.

"Oh, no. We're goin' to wait until we're married. That's one thing I like about Anthony. He's very old-fashioned."

I tried to hide my sarcasm. How "old-fashioned" could he be? My judgments were bubbling to the surface in the form of extremely harsh criticism. I wasn't there to judge or to hurt Laura, or anyone else for that matter. I forced my voice to soften. "Tell me about Anthony."

Laura leaned back on the legs of her chair, resting against the wall. Her heavy thighs were positioned apart and in the air. I felt uncomfortable and began to perspire.

"He's young. Only twenty-nine. He teases me about that. He's young enough to have been one of my victims." She laughed without humor. "I tried to bring ya' a picture of him, but the staff found it when they frisked me. They'll hold it 'til I go back to my unit. But he's real cute. Maybe I could mail it out and ya' could make me some copies."

"Do the staff know you and Anthony are seeing each other?"
"Oh, yes. We're not keepin' it a secret. In fact, I ordered him a silver ring. Can ya' go by the bookstore and buy me some more lanyards for my ID? I want to give them to Anthony so we have matchin' ones. Also, he'd really like some new sunglasses. Maybe ya' could pick up some little round ones. He wants to look like John Lennon. Hey, that reminds me. I need a new bra. A 40 DD. In here we call 'em 'boulder holders.'" She grabbed her bra strap and yanked a couple times, causing her to bounce back and forth from her shoulders to her lap. "Some of the guys been makin' fun of me. I need more support. But no underwires. I don't wanna set off any metal alarms."

I started to make a mental list. Then I stopped. In less than five minutes the "I-wanna-do-fer-me's" were too numerous to remember. Besides, I wasn't feeling all that generous.

Laura read my mind. "Better yet, maybe I should send ya' a letter with the list. It might be hard to remember everything, 'cause I need some flip-flops too and I'm almost out of makeup."

"Okay, a letter is a good idea. I'll see what I can budget over the next month. Certainly the lanyards; they're pretty inexpensive." I hoped she heard that she wasn't going to get everything on the list. If so, she didn't acknowledge it.

I decided to change the subject. "Laura, we've talked about a lot of the things in your life. But you've never told me about your children. How many did you have? Who were the fathers? Where are they now?"

She crossed her arms and stared me down. Finally she leaned forward. With a *thud*, the front of the chair hit the floor. "You really wanna hear all this?"

Without knowing what "all this" would be, I nodded. Children of her own might have partially filled Laura's deep hole, psychological isolation, and spiritual disconnectedness. Although I was certain she'd be a lousy mother, it was possible that motherhood would comfort her, and protecting her own children would add meaning to her life.

Once again, I was extremely naïve.

"OK. I left my foster parents' home when I was nineteen. I just went to the streets."

I was surprised she had stayed that long. She could have emancipated herself much earlier from what was, by all accounts, a very abusive home. At some time, the older foster sisters left. I wondered what it was like when Gladys and Damon had fewer and fewer witnesses.

But I couldn't afford to wonder for long. When Laura told a story she fired her words like a semi-automatic rifle, with precision and a finger that never left the trigger.

"I moved in with a guy and got pregnant. Then I moved into a shelter. Mostly I lived on the streets. I wasn't real smart. I didn't know about pre-natal care and vitamins and stuff like that. And I was real sick the whole time."

"Where did you have the baby?"

"One day I was just sittin' at the bus stop. My ankles were swelled up and I was big as a barn. This nicely dressed lady came up to me and asked when I was due. Well, I didn't know. Turns out she worked in the neo-natal department of the hospital there. So she told me I better go with her. I told her I didn't have no money or anything, but she insisted. I think she musta' signed me in on her insurance or somethin'. I don't know. When I got there they admitted me right away. It was the first clean bed I'd had in months. And they fed me real good.

"They wanted to do an X-ray, but I said I'd heard that pregnant women shouldn't have X-rays. But the lady— turns out she was a nurse— came up and explained that I was far enough along. It wouldn't hurt the baby. I now know they did an ultrasound to look and see what was goin' on. By then it was evening. I'll never forget it. She woke me up just after midnight and gave me the news. I was having twins. I didn't really know what to say, so I just rolled over and went back to sleep. The next day I had 'em.

"I remember they gave me one pink armband and one blue armband. So as soon as I could, I went to see my babies, but when I got to the nursery there was two girl babies. I argued with them. I said, 'Those aren't my babies. I got a boy and a girl.' But they finally convinced me that I really had two girl babies."

"How did you feel about your daughters?"

"I didn't feel nothin'. I thought they were awful little. They'd come almost two months early. A couple days later it was time for me to leave the hospital. I hadn't even named them. So I told the nurse-lady she could name them. She called them (deleted) and (deleted.) They'd be twenty-nine years old by now."

"So what happened next?"

Laura sighed and leaned back against the wall again. "I jus' walked away. I figured they'd have to be in the hospital for awhile and I sure couldn't take care of 'em. I didn't have a job or a place to live or nothin'. So I just left them."

There was a moment of silence between us. I couldn't imagine a mother just walking off and leaving her two tiny, newborn daughters, assuming someone else would come along and take care of them. I thought of what God said in the Book of Isaiah, "Even if a mother could forget the child from her womb, I will never forget you." I'd always wondered what kind of a mother could forget; now I knew.

"A few years later that nurse who was so nice tracked me down. She hired a private investigator and found me. She and her husband had taken the babies home and raised 'em like their own. They wanted me to sign away my parentin' rights so they could adopt them."

"Did you?"

"Oh, sure. I didn't want 'em. By then I was in the mental hospital. That's probably how they found me. That's where I got pregnant the second time."

I didn't ask how she had ended up back in the mental hospital. It seemed like every story led to more questions. With Laura, nothing was ever as simple as it sounded.

I was relieved she never abused her own children and was anxious to move on. "In the mental hospital?" It didn't sound like a good gene pool to me.

"Yeah. It was kinda funny. I was having sex with this guy and we was in the shrubs. One of the staff must'a heard us, 'cause he yelled, 'Hey, what're you guys doin' over there?' The guy I was with, he yelled back, 'Oh, we're just plantin' roses.' And I guess that's what we must have done. Planted roses... because nine months later I had me another baby girl. This one I named myself. I called her (deleted.)"

"Did you take her home and raise her?"

169

"Well, I tried. I really did. But I didn't know nothin' about raisin' babies. She cried all the time and I used to just shake her and shake her. After a few months I realized I was goin' to kill her if she stayed with me. I jus' couldn't take it anymore. I called CPS and asked them what a mother should do in my situation. I didn't tell 'em it was me; I just made it sound like 'what if.'"

"And what did they tell you to do?"

"They said to take the baby to the hospital, tell the social worker why I was there and jus' leave her. They'd put her in foster care and find her a home. So that's what I did. The last time I looked at (deleted,) I realized I'd got her there just in time. She had little broken blood vessels in her eyes from me shakin' her and bruises from places I hit her, tryin' to get her to shut up."

I excused myself to the restroom. Tears flowed before I was even out of the visiting room. George watched me fly by and I didn't care. He now seemed petty and inconsequential.

The bathroom door locked with a deep, throaty thud and I sank down to the cold, tiled floor. The incongruity of her stories struck me. She didn't want an X-ray when she was pregnant the first time because it might be harmful. But she almost killed her third child. And how could the hospital social worker let her just walk away? She should have been arrested. Child abuse charges should have been filed.

Maybe if Laura had gone to prison earlier there would have been fewer victims.

Those thoughts were all in my head and going nowhere. When I blocked them and tried to feel, the emotions were overwhelming. I saw the tiny baby and all I wanted to do was hold her and love her and protect her from the monster mother who brought her into the world. I was angry with Laura, but I was even more angry with God. Where was He when this innocent child was being shaken and beaten? How could He stand off to the side and watch? Couldn't he have struck Laura dead, right then and there? After all, he struck down Uzzah the priest. The whole world would have been better off if Laura wasn't in it.

I was in the SCC visitor's bathroom for a long time, crying for babies I'd never met. My anguish consumed me. The tears went on and on, dripping down my face and splashing onto the tiled floor.

When I couldn't weep for the children anymore, I wept for myself. Where was God when I needed Him most? *What could I have possibly done to merit His indifference?*

Finally I got up and washed my face in the sink, holding soggy paper towels over my eyes in an attempt to lessen the swelling. It didn't help.

When I returned to Laura she looked surprised. "You OK?"

"No. No, I'm not OK." My words were laced with anger. "Laura, I cannot begin to comprehend how a mother could purposely hurt her baby. I realize no one loved and cherished you as a child and I'm sorry that was your experience, but that is no excuse. Somewhere inside all mothers there is a desire to care for and protect their offspring. Animals have it. Birds have it. Humans have it...

"From what you just told me, you hit and shook your daughter because she was crying and it annoyed you. I don't understand that kind of selfishness and I don't particularly want to."

For just a fleeting moment Laura looked like she would cry, but just as quickly the moment passed. Her eyes returned to cold, steel blue.

"You wanna' hear about my last child or not?"

I didn't know if I could stand to hear more, but maintaining her trust was vital for me to answer my questions about my own abuse. Also, it was impossible for her third pregnancy to lead to anything worse than I'd already heard.

"OK. Yes, I want us to finish the conversation. Do you know whatever happened to (deleted)?"

"No. I never heard nothin'. I signed papers right there at the hospital so they could find her a home and never have to talk to me again. I didn't want another private eye knockin' at my door."

I think she knew there could be legal ramifications.

We took a break and walked outside. The weather was cold and damp one hour, sunny and warm the next. It depended on whatever was floating over us in the ever-changing sky. I watched the clouds form and reform while Laura had a cigarette. It kept me from being forced to look at her face.

Three children, three daughters. The first two were abused through a lack of pre-natal care and abandonment, although they probably ended up in a loving home with kind parents. The third girl was physically abused and then abandoned. So far, Laura hadn't admitted to sexually molesting any of her own children, although she certainly treated all three like "throw-away" kids, less than dolls and much less than pets. She did to them what had been done to her. But she wasn't finished.

As soon as we returned to the small room, she continued.

"A few years later I got pregnant again, just some guy I knew. This time I moved in with my sister so I'd have some help. I named the baby (deleted) because there was this lady in our neighborhood. I watched her and I thought she was a real good mom. Her name was (deleted) so I named the baby after her.

"But I had trouble with her right away. She cried and cried, and I couldn't get her to stop. I tried shakin' her and yellin' at her and hittin' her, but she just wouldn't stop. Except that sometimes when I held her up she'd start shakin' like she was afraid of me and then she'd just make this little whimperin' sound. It made me feel real bad."

I put my hands under the table so Laura couldn't see them tremble with rage.

"I told my sister that I couldn't take it no more. After a few months I wanted to take her to the hospital just like I did (deleted,) but my sister and I had a real big fight. She said 'You've had four kids and it's about time you raised one of 'em!' She didn't understand that I couldn't do it. A few months after I had her, we took her to the pediatrician. She was all messed up. She had bruises and gonorrhea. My sister wanted to know how (deleted) got gonorrhea."

"Did she get it from you?" I was hopeful that perhaps the baby contracted a venereal disease passing through Laura's birth canal.

"Yeah. I explained to my sister how I gave it to her. Do ya' want to know how?"

"No! I do not want to know!"

If Laura realized I was shouting, it didn't faze her.

"She said I was a terrible mother and I better give up the baby. After my sister left to go somewhere, I signed papers and left the baby cryin' on the balcony of our apartment. I called the lady downstairs and she came up and got her. That's the last time I seen her. I moved out.

172

"A few months later, I went back and stayed a couple weeks with my sister. I was off my meds. I was really out of it. I didn't even know how long I'd been there, but I remember one night my sister asked me if the baby's cryin' had kept me awake. I said, 'No. When did you have a baby?' She told me she didn't have a baby. She never said it was (deleted,) and I didn't ask. But I think it was. I think she kept (deleted) and raised her. So I packed up my stuff and left. I didn't wanna see her again. I didn't wanna know if that was my baby, so I never went back or talked to my sister ever again."

I thought I didn't have anything more to say until I opened my mouth. I stood up, placed my hands flat on the table in front of me, and leaned forward, crying, shouting, and trembling with a deep and seething fury. I couldn't take it anymore. Months of filth had backed up in my brain like a clogged toilet.

"Why do you tell me this stuff? Why? You spew these horrible, lurid, fetid stories from your life, and when you are finished, all you can say is, 'Go get me another candy bar, Sylvia. I'd like another Dr. Pepper now, Sylvia.'

"In my whole life I've never heard such filth. And I hope I never ever have to hear it again. Maybe you get your 'jollies' by recanting your crimes, but what about me, Laura? What about *me*? You expect me to keep coming in here week after week and pretend like we are friends just 'shooting the breeze?'

"I'm sorry you had such an extreme, abusive childhood. But why do you keep telling me these things?" I slumped back into my chair and tried to breathe. There was no eye contact between us.

Finally, Laura spoke and I looked up. She didn't appear angry, remorseful, or even terribly upset to be the recipient of my screaming rage. "I tell you this stuff about what I did because... because I want to know if ya' can hear them and still find a way to love me. Nobody else ever has. I've been prayin' and askin' God if maybe you can. Maybe if you can love me, it means God does too."

I didn't know what to say. We were both silent for a very long time. I spoke first.

" Laura. I apologize for my outburst. It wasn't the kindest way I could have said what I did. As for love, it is a decision. We make up our minds to love someone, and then we ask God to make the decision real. That's kind of what God does. His mind was already made up about you before you were even born. He made a decision to love you, and God never changes His mind. There's nothing you have done or ever could do—we could do—that is so terrible He would ever stop loving us. What you also want to know is whether or not I can love you, even after knowing the horrible things you have done."

Laura's voice was so quiet I could barely hear her speak. "Yeah. That's what I want. Someone who knows the truth about me and still loves me."

I reached out and held her hand. Let the staff write us up for lesbian contact. Suddenly I was flooded with compassion, grace, and love for her, even though I despised the things she had done. God had supernaturally made my decision real.

"Laura, I do love you. I don't like the things you have done to children, but somewhere along the way I made a commitment to love you. And I do."

"Thank you. That's all I want. I'm goin' back to my unit now. Is that OK?"

There wasn't anything left for either of us to say. I went home early also.

Later, John found me asleep. Apparently I had set out some hamburger for dinner before I crawled in bed. He reported it was dripping onto the kitchen floor.

I cancelled our next visit. My "compassion pipes" were unplugged, but emotions had flooded my basement.

Sexual abuse isn't just a physical violation that is over when the perpetrator stops. It returns in waves of memories, both mental and physical. It slips and slithers through the subconscious mind, then bursts through to the conscious mind when the victim least expects it. My conversations with Laura had kept mine "local" for months.

I deliberately developed small patterns of behavior to increase my sense of safety: park in the same area of the parking lot, keep the car keys in the same pocket, pray on the boat ride over, take breaks in the restroom, pray and take a nap when I got home, etc. The best visits were the ones when John went over with me and helped the chaplain for two hours while I talked with Laura. I always felt safest when John was nearby.

No place felt safe now. I was trapped by my survivor symptoms: an exaggerated startle reflex, extreme anger bubbling just under the surface, and an agitated anxiety that made it impossible for me to focus and complete any task. I felt the spiders day and night, on my arms, legs, and face. I saw them everywhere. Not only that, I became instantly afraid whenever I saw a shadow, convinced it was something evil I could not fully see.

I stayed home from the Commitment Center for a few weeks, choosing instead to send her funny cards and notes that affirmed God's love. She continued to write. I let Laura's unopened letters pile up on my desk.

Before my next scheduled visit I read a stack of them and her latest mandatory annual review. It said basically the same things about her. Not surprisingly, each legal document included details she either hadn't shared with me, or that contradicted stories she had already told me.

I got Laura's list of requests out of the way first. In the current manila envelope, she had enclosed pages from a catalog in case I felt compelled to replace her Sony PlayStation; it was already broken. Her television set had also "died," so there were pages of options to replace it. Early on, John gently reminded me that a commitment to love isn't a commitment to buy.

Laura was always struggling financially, although she could easily make about sixty dollars a month by cleaning her living unit. She had lots of unscheduled time she could use to pick up even more work hours and increase her income. Not only did she choose not to do that, she didn't consistently work the hours to which she already agreed.

If Laura wanted a new television and PlayStation, she had the means to make, save, and spend the money. I made a conscious decision to only acquire those things for her that she truly could not purchase through the established SCC systems. And I was not interested in replacing big-ticket items just because she didn't adequately protect them from breakage.

My husband was right. The most loving thing I could do is encourage her to find ways to meet her own needs.

When I fingered through the packet Laura sent me, I pulled out a report done by the SCC. As part of Laura's annual review, the Acting Forensic Services Manager submitted a twenty-one page document to the courts. I found nothing new until near the end. One very significant item stuck out from the others, a detail that conflicted with previous information and could not have been "forgotten" in both her autobiography and our conversations.

I made a mental note to talk with her about the discrepancy and actually looked forward to presenting my discovery. A part of me wanted to confront Laura until she verbalized some feeling of remorse for the people she had hurt. At the very least I wanted her to feel embarrassment for withholding information of significance.

I wasn't sure how Laura would respond to my little bombshell, but I was tired of playing games if I intended to ever wrap this up. I trusted that God would give me gentle words that expressed who He is, and not what I thought Laura deserved. Riding the ferry to my next visit, I tried to find words that would do that.

While I waited for her in the main visiting room, I purchased our first round of beverages and treats. The vending machine was out of Reece's so I had to make a substitute decision. Even this small deviation from normal would irritate Laura.

I was never sure what time she would join me. George always searched her thoroughly before he'd allow her into the visit area. After she tried to give John the CD's that Dave made, those searches were even more invasive.

Finally, Laura came striding in. She had permed her medium brown hair and cut it shorter. It looked good, softening her features. She had on the expensive jeans I'd sent her, then put on an ugly, polyester, brown-flowered blouse with stains and cigarette burns down the front. I thought Laura might be working to look like me in some ways; I hoped the blouse wasn't part of that. She gave me a quick hug under the watchful eyes of the staff before we headed to our same small visit room.

Neither of us wanted to discuss our previous visit.

"So tell me, what's the latest news at the SCC?"

Laura's eyebrows narrowed and her face scrunched up. "Well, ya' know DD guy is still here." It was a statement rather than a question.

"I figured as much. I assumed you would tell me if he got out. That would be big news."

Laura nodded. "Yeah, well now listen to this. The SCC had one staff assigned to him, but 'they' got to him anyway. Ya' know who I mean. Someone wasn't payin' much attention, I guess."

My head was spinning with questions. How could that happen? Does the staff person who allowed this still work here? In my perfect world, that would be cause for termination. "Do you know who did it?"

She shook her head with genuine sadness. "Yeah, and here's the deal. That person who was suppose' to keep the little guy safe, still works here, just not with him. I don't know for sure who did it. But now he has two escorts instead of one."

"Laura, you had two escorts and you still managed to meet L.L. off the radar scope."

"Yeah, but that was different. I'm smart enough to figure out how to do it. He's not. This kind of thing happens all the time out here. You have no idea how evil the gym is and what the guys do in there. I went in last night, and I was walkin' in front of my two escorts. Well, just as I walked in I saw Ron. You know, Ron that sent ya' my letter? You know, that nasty one." She waited for me to nod, before she continued. "Well, he and one of the guys- . . ."

"Laura, stop! I do not need to know this. It's not my business and frankly, it isn't yours either." Her stories had lost most of their shock value. "Is anything else going on? How are you and Anthony?"

Laura immediately sagged in her chair. Everything about her— facial expression, posture, and gestures— screamed, "I'm a victim."

"Anthony and me met with the Chaplain to discuss our marriage and I don't think we're goin' to get married. Chaplain asked us what kind of life two pedophiles could have together. He thinks we wouldn't be safe because we would trigger each other's fantasies. If Anthony ever brought a kid home, what would I do? I mean, I wouldn't touch 'em or nothin'. But would I call the cops on my own husband? That would be real hard to do. So, I think we'll just stay really good friends. Besides, I still love Dave. What do ya' think?"

177

I was relieved that Chaplain had addressed the issues boldly. I knew he would also have been kind, encouraging them both to do the right thing. My admiration for him kept growing and growing.

For a moment, I pictured Laura and Anthony living outside the SCC in happily wedded bliss. Then one of them brought a child home. They wouldn't have to necessarily abduct one; offer free babysitting to almost any harried, working single mom, and who would turn them down?

But here's the kicker: was I really supposed to believe that Laura would be able to keep her hands off the child? Laura's attestation that she "wouldn't touch 'em or nothin'" didn't fly for me. Also, what if the child started to cry? What would she do then?

"Laura, I think you and Anthony have done the right thing. You want a marriage where you and your husband always bring out the best in each other, not share the worst."

"Oh, it's OK. I'd rather be with Dave, unless I have a chance to take John away."

I looked into her eyes and realized she was serious. Laura didn't want just my husband; she wanted to be me. She tried to dress like me, look like me, and now she wanted John. Her complete transference felt cloying, sexual, and just plain creepy. It also met the definition of "covet." When people truly covet, they don't just want something *like* someone else has; they want *what* that person has. I'd never had an actual life example until now.

It was time to talk about her annual review.

"I got your review in the mail. Are you up to a couple of questions?"

"Sure, but I wanna smoke first." Laura stood up and led me outside. She sat down and straddled the concrete bench. Then she blushed and sat down with her legs together. "Better not get us in trouble for not sittin' like ladies," she said sarcastically.

Then she switched topics. I was pretty sure she was deliberately leading me away from prying into her annual review, but I motioned her to continue.

"The grandfather who hurt ya', did he get to your younger brother and sister too?"

Her question was abrupt and intrusive. It hit me hard. For a moment I felt ill, but then it passed. I let the question hang in the air while Laura tried to light her hand-rolled cigarette. There was enough of a breeze to blow out the paper match her first four attempts. Each time her audible comments became more profane, but she politely apologized one match at a time.

When she finally inhaled deeply from her cigarette, I decided what to say. "I have only a few memories from that time in my life, so I don't know."

"Have ya' ever asked 'em about it?"

I felt myself becoming defensive. I should have protected them better. I should have told someone what was happening. My shame was permanently indented with "should haves," like little BB holes in the old fruit tree we used for target practice at the farm. I didn't want to talk about it anymore. I wanted to go home. Instead I took several deep breaths.

"My brother and sister don't believe me. They insist I'm making this all up. When I told them it could have happened to them too, they quit speaking to me. Neither one socializes with John and me; they deliberately avoid being at our parents' home whenever I am there. They are both angry because I said Grandpa Ed did things to me. They think I'm a fruitcake. No. Worse than that, they think I'm a liar."

Laura looked at me with concern. "Why would anybody make up a story like that? It's the most horrible thing that can ever happen to a child! Nobody would invent a story like that. How can they call ya' a liar?" She was immediately defensive and protective.

We were silent. In some odd way, her words were comforting. My eyes welled up with tears. I wanted to reach out and touch her hand, but her staff were standing nearby and watching us more closely than usual. I blinked the tears down and nodded.

"Do they have any signs of abuse?"

I didn't know how much detail I wanted to share. Part of me felt protective of my siblings. But another part was angry and hurt. They had both been persecutory, punishing me for putting words to the unspeakable. Who could trust the ramblings of a liar?

While Laura sucked in the tobacco from one cigarette, she was already searching her pockets for another. It gave me too much time to remember the past. Her annual review was all but forgotten.

My grandparents' farm was several miles outside Myrtle Point, Oregon. It was a convoluted drive over rural dirt roads. Then there was a long driveway up to the old, white farmhouse on the right and the barn on the left. I loved the country. We caught tadpoles and watched them grow tails until they hopped away. There was a tractor to ride. One time we stayed up all night and saw a calf born. There were always litters of kittens and fresh canned fruits and vegetables. No food ever tastes as good as home-cooked after doing the evening chores on a small farm.

I'm not sure when Grandpa Ed married Grandma Gertrude. He wasn't my father's biological father. It must have been Ed's farm, because she lived in the adjacent city before they were married, if you can call a population of four thousand a "city."

When we were there with our parents, the farm was fun, a treat for children who lived in town. Then things changed.

I'm not sure when it first started. I do remember the weekend my brother and I were there when Mom was giving birth to our sister. Maybe that was the first time. If so, I would have been seven or eight. My brother must have been three or four. The memories are sketchy.

Grandma Gertrude was a tall, buxom woman with big hips and big breasts and no-nonsense mannerisms. She was strong and well-suited to farm life. I remember watching her throw bales of hay. Where did she get such big muscles? Although she wasn't affectionate, I thought she cared about me in her own gruff way.

Grandpa Ed stood about six inches shorter than Grandma. They looked quite odd together. One of his legs had been amputated above the knee after a hunting accident. He wore a fake, plastic leg that fit onto his stump and strapped around his waist with a worn leather belt. He walked with a limp because the plastic leg didn't bend. Another feature I remember was his ears wiggled up and down. He tried to entertain us by making funny faces with his edentulous mouth and wiggly ears. When I looked back, he rarely spoke.

Grandpa Ed's only other feature was a musty smell that made me gag.

I may be unclear on the date, but I am very clear remembering the first time he touched me. Grandma Gertrude had already tucked me into bed. My brother was in the other bedroom on the second floor of the farmhouse. Grandpa Ed came hopping into my darkened room. He'd taken off the plastic leg. Then he took out his false teeth and carefully removed his wire-rimmed glasses. There was a hole in the end of the sock on his real foot. His big toe was peeking out and I could see his jagged, unkempt toenail.

What I remember the most vividly was that I felt dirty when he was done. He had filled me with shame and disgust, made me bad in a place very deep inside. I would have screamed, but he covered my mouth with his hand. I will never forget that hand. It was hard and callused. His nails were long and ripped in places. There was black dirt permanently imbedded in both the crevices and cuticles. I had to look at that hand until he was finished. It was the hand of the man who murdered my ability to believe in my own goodness. Where his shame should have been, my shame now was.

I never ever shared the details with anyone in my family, but it didn't matter to my brother and sister. It was enough that I said something sexual had happened. That was enough to ostracize me. Part of me felt like I deserved their punishment because I didn't protect them, if it had ever been their turn at all. On some deep subconscious level I was afraid their anger was justified. The whole complex, fetid mess was somehow my fault.

Over the years I tried to heal the breach. I wrote letters to my sister. I sent flowers when my brother got married. I asked to be let back into the family. Neither my brother nor sister ever answered me.

My mother and I had an agreement. When there were family reunions, John and I would not be invited. She didn't want the fun times ruined by the tension and anger that would have been leveled against me. I got used to celebrating Christmas on the twenty-sixth. I arranged for gifts and dinners the day before or the day after birthdays, anniversaries and holidays. As the years went by, there were times I resented always being the one who had to create alternate celebrations. Paradoxically, the best way— the only way— I could communicate that I loved my brother and sister was to never be present.

Laura was looking at me as I sat there watching her smoke her cigarette down to the last little bit. She repeated the question. "So are there signs of abuse? Is there anything about them that makes you think Grandpa Ed got to them?"

My mind had wandered far, far away. "I suppose there could be, but I don't really want to talk about my brother and sister." I still wanted to protect them in whatever small way I could.

I was the liar to everyone, except maybe my mother. She and I had grown into a relationship that I cherished. She was the only member of my family who saw good in me. She and my husband were the only two people who had ever really loved me.

"All three of us have some of the behavioral characteristics of survivors, but there are lots of things that could cause that. I'm the only one who remembers, and the only one talking about it."

"Do ya' think they really don't remember?"

"I've read several books on repressed memories and I don't think they remember. That's what makes this so hard. They are being true to what is consciously stored in their memories and I'm being true to mine. Children often forget their abuse because it's so traumatic they don't record the event anywhere in their brain where they could easily trip over it later. And retrieving lost memories is very controversial work. How do you know the child isn't just making it up?"

We moved silently back into the visit room. I glanced at the clock and was relieved the bus would be coming soon.

As soon as we sat down, Laura ripped into the third candy bar of the visit. They weren't Reece's, but she was taking the loss in stride. "You're not talkin' about little kids reportin' abuse. You're talkin' about adults rememberin' what happened to them when they was little kids. Like I said before, nobody's goin' to make up a story like that. Nobody."

"I agree, but if my brother and sister can't remember anything like that happening to them, I can't convince them it did. Their lack of remembering could be just part of their mind keeping them safe, if indeed anything happened. The problem is I can't convince them that it happened to *me*. What proof do I have now?

"And, Laura, here's the thing that I've finally realized. I'm not even sure I can articulate it to you. If they really think I'm a liar and I'm making this up, then why don't they just accept that I'm weird and go on loving me anyway? For them to be this angry and put all this negative energy into cutting me out of the family, they are really shouting that they are terrified it might be true. Otherwise, there wouldn't be any reason for them to continue to be mean to me. Does that make sense?"

Laura thought about it for a few minutes. "Yeah, it does. They are goin' so far overboard to say it isn't true, they are being mean. If they really thought you was makin' it all up it makes more sense for 'em to just shrug it off and love you anyway. After all, you are their big sister. You're a nice person. You're funny and generous and there's nothing for 'em to be afraid of, whether it's all a lie or not."

"Yes. That's what I'm saying. We each have to live our own reality in life. The thing that hurts me is that we haven't found a way to live our lives and still love each other. I miss them more than they will ever know."

We were silent for several minutes. I hadn't wanted to talk about this. Every holiday I cried, missing them and not knowing how to fix what was broken between us.

I waited while Laura went to examine the vending machines and returned.

"How hard is it for 'em to stock Reece's? I gotta smoke."

Laura excused herself to the restroom first and I closed my eyes. "Lord, what is this all about? Why am I here? All I wanted was to understand Grandpa Ed enough to be able to forgive him and move on, healed. When does that part begin?"

Laura didn't bother to sit down when she returned. She knew what I wanted to talk about. She was avoiding the topic and we both knew it. I talked to her in my head as we walked. *OK, Laura. Smoke all you want, but when we go back inside our room I will not drop this matter. You can't run from me forever.*

Chapter Ten

PREPARING TO FORGIVE

When you pass through the waters, I will be with you.
(Is 43:2)

"OK, I figured you'd notice a couple things don't match up. Where do ya' want to begin?" Laura fidgeted a little. I thought she might feel guilty for her past or for lying by omission. I didn't know which and felt no need to conversationally ease into the discrepancy.

"How about with the son you had at age sixteen, conceived with your Damon. The review says you lit his crib on fire and killed him. You've never mentioned having a son, much less killing him. It doesn't seem like a detail that would be easy to ignore, but I don't see it in your autobiography."

I didn't disguise the accusing tone that was spitting the words out of my mouth as quickly as I could breathe in more air. In all our conversations she never talked about being a murderer.

"I think I need another cigarette first." Laura stood up, brushed candy crumbs onto the carpeted floor, and walked out of the visit room, leaving me completely alone and unable to read her face.

With relief I watched her march outside. Talking and remembering my own childhood had sent me to the shame place deep inside. I was grateful for a few minutes alone.

I couldn't remember a single time when I hadn't followed Laura outside while she smoked. This time I wasn't budging. I hoped my refusal would be like an exclamation point behind my question. What kind of a monster mother could watch her own son burn to death? Although absurd, I didn't want to be anywhere around Laura and a pack of matches.

One of the many things that didn't make sense was Laura getting pregnant. She said that Gladys and Damon put her on birth control at age eight. They seemed to be going to the extreme, preventing pregnancy even before she was old enough to conceive. So how did Laura manage to get pregnant? Wouldn't someone at school have noticed and initiated an inquiry?

Regarding the fire, I didn't have much difficulty believing that Laura was capable of arson and violence. I'd read a little more of her autobiography, where she finally retaliated against Gladys Purvis:

> About this same time (deleted) was not home a lot during this time. She met a man and was engaged to be married to (deleted.) It was (deleted,) Damon, Gladys, and myself living at home. I would become angry and outraged with my foster mom because she would beat me. When I was thirteen I tried to stab her with a paring knife because she was not listening to me. I told her what Damon was doing to me. She did not care; she left me every chance she got with him.

> I began making some neighborhood friends but was often fighting and touching them. We had a lot of fun together. The kids would tell their parents and their parents would tell Gladys. I would get a beating and was not allowed to play with them.

> I was eleven when I began to hit puberty. This was weird I did not understand why I was changing in my body.

Had Gladys and Damon slipped up when they were administering Laura's birth control? I considered that to be unlikely, although possible.

Laura returned from smoking, looked me straight in the eye and said, "I lied."

This wasn't exactly what I expected.

"I made it all up. I was just makin' my life sound even worse than it was so I could get some attention. I guess it backfired on me."

"Backfired?"

"Yeah, I'm here aren't I?"

"Are you saying you are here because of things you made up or because of things you actually did?"

"Some of both. But the story about havin' a son is definitely a lie. I only had the four girls."

Listening to Laura, I thought this made sense. I did think she probably made some things up to get attention. It was a life pattern for her, something she used to compensate for an early childhood where no one paid attention to her needs.

"One of the things they do here is check up on what we tell them. They tracked down Gladys and Damon. They're both deceased now. No little boy child ever died in their house in a fire. But a little girl did die in a house fire next door to us. The therapists think I was just transferrin', you know, thinkin' like it was my child when it wasn't."

While I was thinking about how desperately she had wanted to belong to someone who would love her, Laura adroitly changed topics.

"I think we need to both write letters. Have ya' ever written a letter to your grandfather?"

The question startled me. "No. He's been dead for many, many years."

"Not that kind of a letter. I've been thinkin' about this a lot. A few months ago ya' said somethin' about us both needin' to find a way to heal and move on. Maybe we should both write letters— you write to Grandpa Ed and I'll write to Damon. You said we have a right to be mad when people hurt us. I want them both to know how messed up our lives got."

Her suggestion irritated me. I wasn't the pedophile; Laura was. This wasn't *my* therapy time. But at the same time, I sensed God urging us to do more than rant and blame.

"Laura, we can tell them everything you are suggesting, but there is one more thing... we need to forgive them. Damon and Grandpa Ed aren't keeping us stuck. We are. Our unforgiveness is chaining us to the past."

She appeared to think about this for several minutes. When she spoke again, her voice was small and childlike.

"Sylvia, I don't know how to forgive. No one's ever talked to me 'bout how to do it, just that I gotta do it."

"Would you like me to send you some materials I wrote last year on forgiveness? Maybe it would help if you understood what it is and what it isn't. For instance, it isn't letting the bad guy off the hook and it doesn't mean we didn't hurt. And it doesn't mean we have to like the person and be friends again."

"It doesn't?" Her eyes were open wide. This was new information.

"I'll stick them in the mail for you to read while we are writing our letters. If you can get yours done by our next visit, I will finish mine too."

When John and I got on the bus to the dock, he reached over and held my hand. "How'd it go today?"

I smiled wanly and I looked out the window, but gave his hand a squeeze so he'd know I was OK. Talking about my family and remembering the details of my first sexual encounter with Grandpa Ed had opened up the old wounds and I wanted to cry it away again. How many times had I done this already? How many more would it take before it was all cried out?

Could Laura be right? Would a letter help?

A miracle happened between that visit and the next. I didn't think it would happen in my lifetime.

My mother and I had danced all around the Grandpa Ed issue. We never really talked about it. She knew I said it happened, but most of her information was secondhand through my brother and sister, so I was never sure what my mother thought she knew.

Age had softened us both. We discovered we were able to give and receive the gift of each other with deep gratitude and without competing. The few things I didn't much care for about her were the same traits that I detested in myself, and we had learned to laugh about it together. My mother had a way of meeting me in the deep water of my soul and swimming alongside me when no one else in my life saw an ocean. Sometimes she surprised me with her courage.

I was at work when she called. "Sylvia, are you still seeing that lady, you know, the sex offender?"

One thing my mother and Laura had in common is that they are never given to small talk or easing into conversation.

"Yes. I get in to see her a couple times a month." It seemed an odd question. I felt certain she knew I was still meeting with Laura. An agenda was coming. "Why do you ask?"

She was quiet for a moment too long. My mother and I read each other's silences with precision. I could feel her measuring words. I inherited my verbal skills from her side of the family. The longer the silence, the more important the word selection. I braced myself.

"Do you ever talk about what happened to you?"

There it was. The little girl inside me had waited forty-five years, since the day my sister was born. Now the door was open just a crack.

"Yes. We have talked about what Grandpa Ed did to me. He sexually abused me." I waited. I had said it out loud to the person whose belief I wanted the most. I could scream it in the night and beat the sofa until my knuckles were raw, but nothing mattered at all unless my mother knew and she believed me.

The silence was too long again. I wasn't breathing and I thought, *I might pass out before she says anything. Wouldn't it be sad if she said she knew it was true, but I was dead because I held my breath too long waiting for her to speak?*

I heard her voice about the same time I decided to inhale.

"I would have killed him if I had known. You know that, don't you?"

This was harder than I had imagined. I was sitting at my office desk with a line of people waiting to see me. I had to make a decision. I didn't have a long time to talk, but I couldn't lose this moment with my mother. It had taken great courage for her to initiate this conversation.

Before I spoke, I had to quickly make a decision. I could continue to believe Grandpa Ed, the monster who convinced me to keep the secret. Or I could believe my mother, who loved me with all her heart. It was my choice.

Sometimes we have to choose the good people just because they love us.

"I know."

I could hear the relief in her voice, but she wasn't finished. "I've been remembering a conversation I had once with your Grandma Gertrude."

I motioned to the staff at my door, giving them a hand signal that they recognized to mean I would be tied up for a few more minutes. They left.

"Gertrude told me once that she was worried about Grandpa Ed. When the neighboring farms would slaughter the cows each year, he would go and help, but instead of coming home at night, he would sleep over. Sometimes he slept on neighbors' sofas, even though the farms weren't that far away. She thought he did that so he could molest the children."

I felt my mouth go dry. Grandma Gertrude knew. And to some degree my parents should have known also. It was all true. My mind hadn't made it up. I wasn't a liar. Even more important, my mother *knew* I wasn't a liar.

I didn't know what to say. Suddenly I felt very tired. Mom instinctively rescued me.

"Well, what I really called to say is that Dad and I are looking forward to getting together with you and John for Dad's birthday. I've taken enough of your time at work."

We signed off with our usual "I love you" and smoochy kissing noises. We were locked into the rituals of conversation as though nothing significant had just passed between us.

I sat and looked out the window for a very long time. Whatever the staff had needed, they must have figured it out. No one returned to my office door.

My conversations with Laura had set me on the course of healing in two ways. They prepared me to receive my mother's ultimate gift. It was, perhaps, the most sacred thing she would ever bestow on me other than life itself. Something precious that Grandpa Ed took away had been returned to me in a conversation that took less than five minutes. My mother had given me back my self-respect.

Second, I now believed in my ability to forgive Grandpa Ed, with or without fully understanding.

On our next visit I asserted control at the onset. "Laura, I want to ask you about something." She looked good. Her eyes were bright and she had on the latest round of makeup I had sent her. Around her neck was a lanyard with her ID and a man's ring, which I knew meant she was back in love again. There would be time to get into that later.

"Sure. What's on your mind?"

"You've had many years of experience in the mental health system, both as a child and as an adult. But when I look at your paperwork, it doesn't look to me like you have a significant mental health diagnosis. So, let me just say it outright. Are you mentally ill?" I always expected Laura to be hurt by the bluntness of my questions, but she never was. In fact, coming from her history, she felt cared about that I would ask and take the time to listen to her response.

"I know what you mean. All that 'Axis I, Axis II ' junk can be a little confusin'. I'll explain it the best I can." Then she looked around.

I realized she noticed I had Dr. Pepper, but no candy bars. "The machine is out of Reece's again. I thought we'd go pick out something together." I felt like I needed to apologize.

Laura stood up. She wasn't about to discuss her mental health status without chocolate. As we walked to the vending machines, I had time to see who we were sharing the adjacent visitation area with today. There was a very attractive African-American couple in their thirties holding hands and flirting on the bench in the smoking area. The girl I'd seen on the boat was visiting her significant other and they were deep in conversation. Another resident was meeting in a private room with several people who appeared to be professionals, attorneys I guessed. There were briefcases and lots of note taking. A usual day at the SCC.

George wasn't there, but the other regular staff was. When he was gone things were more relaxed and friendly. We were able to exchange comments and smiles, which felt good. It had taken a long time to develop relationships with these people.

When we returned from the vending machines, I closed the door— our private signal that we would talk about things we didn't want the staff to overhear.

"I'm not crazy, Sylvia, if that's what ya' mean. We have a couple guys out here who are schizophrenic in addition to being pedophiles. They are real sick and they need to be locked up somewhere, though probably not here.

"They aren't able to take care of themselves. They don't eat right. They don't keep themselves clean." She looked at me a moment. "OK, I have issues with showers, but at least I take 'em. These guys don't. One of 'em, Joe, is *real* sick. Doesn't matter if it's summer or not; he wears as many layers of clothes as he can get on. One day I was there when the staff made him take off his shirts 'cause he was walkin' around like some freakin' Frankenstein. He couldn't even bend his arms. Ya' aren't going to believe this! He had on thirty-six T-shirts, and he was real upset to take any off."

I nodded. "So how safe is he here? He sounds vulnerable to me."

"He's safer than some of the guys. At least Joe has the sense to put on a bunch of pants. And then there's Bart. He's schizophrenic too. He can't even tell anyone what he wants because the words don't come out straight."

I thought about the two men. "How could they self-report if they were abused here?"

"Couldn't. This is no place for people who are really mentally ill. One day, Joe wanted to come to group with us, and the therapist wouldn't let him. He said Joe is too sick for treatment. Well, if he's too sick for treatment, why is he here? Shouldn't he be at Western State Hospital instead of locked up with a bunch of men who want him for a sex toy?"

I thought Laura had a point, but we were off topic. "How do you know you aren't mentally ill? What you did to those children sounds insane to me." I said it gently and could tell by her expression that she took it as genuine curiosity, not a judgment.

"Yeah, it's hard to understand for someone like you. Let me tell ya' why I know sex offenders aren't mentally ill, except for a few like Bart and Joe. We are cunnin' and manipulative. And we are cowards. Most of us preyed on children because we was afraid to have real relationships with adults. We're also insightful and very intelligent. You'd be surprised if you heard the degree some of these guys went to in plannin' their crimes. They didn't intend to ever be caught. And me? I picked kids who were too young to rat. A lot of us have 'mental disorder' written in our files. You know why?"

I didn't.

"What society doesn't understand, they stamp 'mental disorder.' And they sure don't understand me. That's why they don't know how to fix what's wrong. Also, they are desperate to label me. They will work and work just to make us fit in their diagnosis categories. They don't seem to understand it just makes us sicker."

"You're on a roll today, sister."

Laura laughed. "Yeah, and I ain't done yet. But I need a cigarette first."

When we came back in she didn't miss a beat. "The other problem is that nobody is goin' to get well out here. The therapists don't know what they're doin'. I was talking to one of the guys, and he had to go for his... his... just a minute. I don't know what it's called, and I sure don't know how to spell it. You'll need to know how to spell it 'cause someday ya' might wanna write a book about us. You know, you and me and our conversations."

I watched Laura bounce around the visit room and return with a resident who was emptying trash. He appeared to be in his forties, clean-cut and articulate. If he was embarrassed, it didn't show. His tone of voice was respectful when he spoke to me. "The word is plethysmograph. You want me to spell it?"

I did and then thanked him. He left without introducing himself. If he had intruded in our conversation in any way the staff would have infracted him, and Laura would have received a verbal warning. There was no room for social amenities at the SCC.

"So what is a plethysmograph?" I said the word several times in my head so I wouldn't forget it. I also made a mental note to find a way to bring in a pen and paper.

"It's a thing where they hook a guy up to electrodes, ya' know, down there." Laura pointed toward her lap. "Then they show him porn to see if he's reactin'. If he does, he's still sick. But here's the thing I'm mad about. The guy who was tellin' me about his test said that they made him sit through movies of little kids. He says that wasn't even his crime. He raped adult women, and the videos made him sick."

It made me sick, too. Was this how the State of Washington was using my tax dollars? Were they purchasing "kiddy porn" and showing it to sex offenders. I was livid.

"Laura, how is this supposed to be therapeutic?"

"It's supposed to be a way to measure progress in treatment."

The scientific model had been applied to the SCC. They had to find objective data to legally and indefinitely incarcerate the men and Laura. Although I saw logic in the goal, the methodology infuriated me. Without being an expert on sexual reconditioning, it made no sense to me that the cure for deviancy is to stuff more deviant material into the person's conscious mind. That is absurd.

This led me into a further restatement of my fears. "Laura, as a taxpayer in this state I am outraged that my money is being spent on this kind of junk! What is this place? The more time I spend at the SCC, the sicker it looks to me. What really goes on here beyond this room?"

Laura seemed comforted by my anger. Maybe there had been too few times in her life when anyone had stood up for her in righteous indignation.

"Sylvia, I don't tell ya' most of it. I don't want you to have a stroke or nothin'.

"These people are nuts. And I'm not talkin' just about the residents. We both know they're nuts. I'm talkin' about the staff!"

"Look, I can't stand this anymore, Laura. I can't stand keeping my mouth closed. I'm sick and tired of worrying about you and DD guy, and now there's Bart and Joe. How many other vulnerable adults are here? How many of you are being tortured instead of treated?"

Laura was obviously pleased at my tirade. She finished off her candy. I knew the routine and stood up so we could go outside while she smoked. I needed a few minutes to cool off.

When we came back in I checked the clock. We had plenty of time left. "So you don't believe you are mentally ill." It was a statement.

Laura leaned back and emitted a very unladylike belch that smelled like Dr. Pepper and chocolate. "Oh! Sorry. But that sure did feel good." She giggled. "No. Here's why I don't think we're mentally ill. We can take care of ourselves. We can dress and take showers and stuff like that. We can make plans and follow them. We have relationships with people who are healthy. Ya' know what really bugs me? It's when the therapists here say stupid stuff." Her voice changed and was nasal with sarcasm. "'You need to address your childhood victim issues which are why you are mentally ill.' Sylvia, that's a lie! I molested little kids because it was fun and I could get away with it."

The clarity of her statement caught me off guard. "So, there is a difference between being mentally ill and being sexually deviant."

"Yep. That's what I think. I admit I'm impulsive. If somethin' sets me off, I get really mad. You haven't seen me do that yet. And, I'm compulsive in some other things too."

"Laura, *I* am compulsive. I have certain odd things I do because they help me to feel safe. Compulsive behaviors only become a problem if we don't know why we're doing them and we can't control them and they are keeping us from doing other things we want or need to do."

I was sure Laura McCollum was not crazy. Neither was Grandpa Ed. And now I knew my mother didn't think I was crazy either.

True to form, Laura abruptly changed topics. "Anthony and I are back together. He's pretty screwed up."

"Laura, you don't have to marry everyone you have a relationship with. What if God brought Anthony into your life so you could have someone to care about who cares about you, and someone to practice having a relationship with while you are here and it's safe?"

"I like that idea. Well, kinda. I want a husband."

"Based on what I know of your childhood, I think there's a really big hole in your heart, Laura. You need someone to love you and fill it up. You may not be ready for a husband, but that doesn't mean you can't love Anthony and let him know you and love you too. You deserve to be loved. By God. By Anthony. By me. By lots of people. We deserve to be loved, not because we've done anything to earn it, but because we're human. We were created to love and be loved."

I watched her face, and I thought she was going to cry. The pit of loneliness and unworthiness was deep and dark inside her. The thing I was beginning to see was a warped thread leading from that emptiness to her crimes. It was as if she had thrown the lives of fifteen or more children into her pit of despair, in a hopeless attempt to meet her need to belong to someone. It was all about Laura, because that's all it could be for now. Her entire being was wrapped up in layers of narcissism that blinded her to any degree of empathy, sympathy, or the ability to consider the feelings of her victims. Hence, she had no remorse for her crimes.

Inside Laura, relationship and orgasm and affection had been twisted together those nights she lay in bed with Damon while he used her for his own purposes. For the first time, I could see how nurturing became confused with molesting.

"Sylvia, I don't think I know that much about love. What the state teaches here is Care-Safety-Control-Treatment. Those are their four goals. They do a pretty good job of controllin' us. But they don't know how to treat us. We aren't safe. Nobody cares what really happens here. Well, I know you and John do. And so does the chaplain. But across the water, they want us to be locked up here forever."

"Laura, they are afraid of you."

"Yeah, I know. But how can I get better living in here? I wanna get well and not hurt no more kids. And I want to have a real life, with a home and a dog."

On the boat ride back to Steilacoom, I was haunted by Laura's simple goals. A home. A dog. A husband. Things that most of us take for granted in life. To Laura, they were monumental. If the NIMBYs, forensic psychologists and sex therapists had their way, she'd never have any of them.

I was driving home before I remembered—we didn't read our letters.

Later, I put John's dinner in the oven and pulled out Laura's autobiography. Ron's letter and Brandon's money order both floated to the floor. Sex and money. Our society was completely fixated on both. Was there a cure? The techniques Laura reported weren't going to fix anyone.

I settled down to read more of her autobiography.

When I started my menstrual cycle I was eleven years old. I was at school. I thought I was injured or dying. I was very scared and did not say anything till I got home. I ruined my dress and I got a whipping from Gladys. She told me to let her know when it was over. I was so ashamed that I wet myself when she scolded and whipped me for ruining my dress. Puberty was an especially difficult time for me.

That summer when school let out it was nice and we went on a family vacation. We went to Shelby Forest for a picnic and then drove to Sardis, Mississippi, which is a tourist sight. We spent two wonderful weeks there. We fished. I caught a crawdad. I did not know what it was. It scared me. We cooked on an open fire and swam. We roasted hot dogs and marshmallows. I burned my fingers and have not since cared for roasted marshmallows. We were a real family and did things that families do. I was happy. There was no abuse. It was great. I was not locked out of the house naked with only my dog to confront me. When we had to leave I cried because I was sad to leave this part of heaven I had found.

When I was about thirteen I attempted to stab Gladys again because she did not listen to me about what her husband was doing to me and she did not protect me.

We bought a shanty that was partly burned down for fifty dollars and tore it down and used the part that was salvageable to build a house in Byhalia, Mississippi. We would go down every weekend and work on it, straightening the nails and building the

196

foundation. We were building it from the ground up. We all were very tired at the end of the day and would wash in a fifty gallon drum warmed by the sun then we went to bed to start again the next day. I remember there was an Indian mound in the back forty and I dug on it for days looking for signs of buried treasures. I was disappointed when I found nothing.

Laura's autobiography, though interesting, wasn't helping me to understand pedophilia.

I agreed with Laura that, with only a few exceptions, most of the residents at the Special Commitment Center were not mentally ill if their deviancy was all the psychologists could legitimately find. She had confirmed my earlier feelings. I thought it was insightful for her to verbalize, "What society doesn't understand they stamp 'Mental Disorder.' Society certainly does not understand pedophilia."

I did on-line research into every possible cause. Nothing fit. Chemicals and hormones and neurotransmitters and genetics — none of them were diagnostic markers for sexual abusers.

If my grandfather wasn't crazy, that only left one possibility.

It seemed less offensive to ask her if she was mentally ill than to ask Laura if she was evil. Before my next visit I reviewed some books John and I have accumulated over the years. I also stuffed my Grandpa Ed letter into my shoe in case we had time to read to each other. There was no other way to take it inside.

John didn't go with me on the visit, which left me feeling more vulnerable. To make matters worse, the vending machine was out of Reece's again. That was never good.

Laura arrived unsmiling, her motions rough and masculine. I could tell she was irritable.

"What's going on?" I asked. "You don't look very happy today?"

She sat down and ripped open the candy. "Out of Reece's again?"

I nodded.

"This stupid place. How hard is it to fill a candy machine?"

The sugar and I usually had a sedating effect, so I waited for Laura to unwind. "The therapist who's in charge of my treatment team died. Went home and dropped dead of a heart attack."

"That's horrible! When?"

"Couple days ago."

"Is that why you look so down?"

She looked up, surprised. "How'd you know I was down? Nobody around here ever notices my moods."

My answer was soft, deliberately gentle and a complete surprise to me. "Maybe nobody around here genuinely loves you, Laura."

She started to cry, then the moment of vulnerability passed. "No. That's not why I'm down. It's just that I really hate this place. They denied my request for a court review to go to less restrictive housin'. I gotta get outa here, Sylvia. I'm goin' nuts."

I tried to ask with tenderness, but I was getting better at boldly addressing the issues. "Laura, why did you become a pedophile? You weren't born this way. I know we've talked about it before, but I don't feel like I've found the answer yet."

She thought for a moment. "I think the fact that nobody ever really loved me is a big part of it. Even as a tiny baby, nobody took care of Laura. I could just cry and cry..."

I wasn't sure how she could know this, but I let her continue because I believed she was probably telling me the truth.

"I was neglected in every way a child can be. Food. Clothin'. Shelter. Love. Kindness. Encouragement."

"There was no safe lap you could ever crawl into, was there, Laura?"

Her voice was barely audible in our soundproof room. "No."

I watched her do what I predicted she'd do next. She fished around in the pocket of her jacket until she came up with a crumpled, hand-rolled cigarette. "I gotta smoke. You mind?"

I followed Laura out to the smoking patio. The sun was bright and we found a bench where it wasn't bearing down on us. As soon as we sat down she pulled up her pants leg. "I got bit by a spider. Wanna see?"

I didn't, but it was too late. Her leg was indurated and red. It looked sore. "How do you know it was a spider?" I felt myself shudder involuntarily.

"Saw it. A big old black and white one. I had to go to the clinic and get some antibiotics."

"Where were you when it bit you?"

"In my unit. Just mindin' my own business."

This immediately distressed me. My husband is well aware of my spider phobia. As a result— and because this man truly loves me— he hires a professional exterminator to crawl under our house and kill the spiders each year so that they don't even *think* of coming inside. And if I see so much as a tiny one, my husband instantly turns into "Bwana, The Great Spider Hunter."

Looking at Laura's swollen leg I couldn't imagine living in an environment where I had so little control that I had to live with spiders biting me and no one showing up with bug killer.

"Laura, are they going to do anything? I mean, you shouldn't have to worry about being bitten in your living unit. I can understand if you'd been outside, maybe."

"Oh, yeah. They said they'd spray. But that doesn't mean much. You know what *does* mean somethin'?" She looked at me and her eyes softened. "It means somethin' that you care I got bit. Thank you."

I felt a lump rise in my throat. Something had changed. I hated everything Laura had shared with me about her treatment of children. I hated the things that were done to her. Yet, more and more I saw her as separate from her actions. She had been in prison as punishment for what she did. She was at the SCC because of who people thought she was.

Despite my firm attestations that I would never like her, we had reached a place where humanity had bridged the gap between us. On our first visit I had perceived her as a perpetrator and me as a victim, frightened, but determined to see her anyway. Now, I was able to put all of that aside and love Laura Faye McCollum just as she was, sitting there beside me frowning at her sore leg.

Once inside the security of the small, soundproof visitation room, I told Laura about the conversation with my mother.

"Good for her! She sounds like a good lady. I'm glad she told you that. Now ya' know you aren't crazy. As for your brother and sister, I think they're the crazy ones, but it's jus' my opinion."

"Let me ask you something," I said. "You are pretty smart about the people here. Do you think any of the residents held at the SCC are evil?"

Laura thought about the question and didn't answer for several minutes. "What do you mean, evil?"

"This is the darkest place I have ever been. I think some of the people here are flat-out evil. Certainly not all of them." I gave her time to think before I continued. "There's a distinction between doing evil and being evil. Just like there is a distinction between doing bad things and being a bad person."

Laura wrinkled her forehead. "I'm tryin' to follow. I think I get it. Like it was bad for me to do what I did with L.L., but that doesn't make me a bad person."

"Exactly."

"Well then, yea, I think some of these guys are evil. But I don't know which ones. I'm not good at figurin' out stuff like that. I'm goin' to get matches."

This spoke to my continued concern for Laura. She didn't know how to assess people and set appropriate boundaries with the ones who were even just plain bad, much less evil.

In my own limited reading experience no one had explored human evil from the psychological perspective as articulately as M. Scott Peck in "People of The Lie."[9] His work resonated with me when I read it. In fact, I made a checklist to evaluate people as I moved through life. Now, I could see my reaction as a little extreme.

I had looked at Peck's material before ever coming in to meet with Laura. He did an excellent job of articulating an ambiguous topic and making evil definable.

Peck deduced that maybe it is time for psychiatry to recognize evil as a distinct diagnosis, which he suggested would come under the umbrella of personality disorders. He named four characteristics of those who deserve the label "evil." In extremely basic terms, the person would exhibit:

- Destructive, scapegoating behavior.

- Excessive intolerance to criticism.
- A narcissistic concern with public image, and
- Intellectual deviousness, with greed.

I had never heard Laura deny her sins or offenses. In fact, by her own admission she had made up additional ones to make herself look worse than she actually was. This was dishonest, but not evil.

On the other hand, her destructiveness had been fairly consistent in that she had so many tiny victims. This again was by her own admission.

In her conversations with me, Laura consistently bore the trials of being displeasing to herself and was willing to risk being displeasing to me. The fact that I had been consistent in my visits, except for a couple brief breaks, and had not judged her, had built a level of trust between us. And because of that trust, Laura told me things that were candid and especially unflattering about herself, her crimes, and her intentions. Were they all true? Of course not.

As far as evaluating her greediness, I could not honestly say I perceived her as such. Yes, she did manipulate me to purchase all kinds of things for her. But she also knit blankets for the homeless and for me. She made hats for the elderly in the nursing homes in Tacoma. And she had a generous spirit when it came to caring about some of the other residents at the SCC. Often she was reprimanded for giving them gifts. The one area where I did experience her as greedy was in our relationship. When other people were around, Laura did not want to share me. Given her history of abuse, neglect, and abandonment, I understood why she wanted exclusive rights to my attention.

At times I could see how she attempted to control others, but given the unnatural environment in which she lived, I didn't think she had any choice. It was manipulate or be manipulated.

Laura did not have a self-image of perfection. She saw herself, albeit realistically, as damaged goods. She certainly didn't sacrifice others to maintain an image that she was perfect. I thought about her relationship with L.L. If anything, he was closer to fitting the model of evil than she was in their situation. She was willing to face her moral failures. He wouldn't even submit to a polygraph.

I think she worried that the things she had done emanated from an evil nature. The evil don't ponder this question. It's interestingly the opposite of what I had heard in 12-step meetings: "If you are sitting around wondering if you are an alcoholic, you probably are. People who aren't alcoholics don't stop to ask themselves if they are drinking too much." With the evil, they don't wonder if they are evil. The rest of us do.

Laura wasn't always the first one in line when it was time for therapy, but she wasn't trying to hide from herself. She knew she was messed up. She wanted to find her motives and exorcise her personal demons. Laura's greatest fear seemed to be that the system didn't know how to fix her. As each year went slowly by, a little more hope drained out of her.

There was nothing in Peck's material that suggested to me that Laura was evil. In fact, in reviewing it and looking at the significant people in my life, it startled me to realize there were a few "normal" folks that did fit the model. Furthermore, all of us display those characteristics at various times. The thing about true evil is that it is incredibly subtle, consistent, and very difficult to pinpoint.

I was fairly certain that some of the men at the Special Commitment Center were evil in addition to having committed horrific crimes. But committing sexual crimes doesn't mean that people are either mentally ill or categorically evil.

While she was gone, Laura apparently decided she was still hungry. We walked back to the vending machines. A family with children was using the visiting room next to them. Laura started to fidget, then turned her back so she wouldn't see them. "I'd like a Dr. Pepper and a Banana Nut Muffin if ya' have enough money left. I don't think I should stand out here this close to the kids. I'm goin' back to our room."

I nodded. While I fed dollar bills into the vending machines, I peeked out of the corner of my eye into the room with children. It looked like any normal family. Dad and Mom were holding hands. Two children of preschool age were playing with toys. There were cartoons on the television in the corner, but no one was paying attention.

I assumed the dad's crime wasn't against children, or they wouldn't have been allowed to visit. That meant he was an adult rapist. I looked into his wife's face. She was listening to him and they were laughing at some private joke. I couldn't help wondering if he was just a normal old rapist or if Peck would categorize him as evil.

When I got back to Laura she was obviously agitated. "You OK?"

"Oh, yeah. I just don't like being around kids. That's all."

"Laura, how are you going to make plans to get out of here if you can't be around children, even briefly? The world is full of them, and people keep making more every year."

She chuckled at my attempt to lighten her mood. "I don't know. I can't go to Spokane. I think it's just a set-up to fail. There are drugs sold out of that house. And I don't know anyone in Spokane. Sylvia, you're the only friend I have. Why can't I stay here and be close to you and John?"

I didn't know how to answer. On the one hand I wanted to keep her from being hurt anymore. On the other hand, I didn't want her in my neighborhood, my church, or my place of business. How could I keep my neighbor children safe if Laura was there? Maybe it didn't really matter.

I was about to find out my neighborhood wasn't safe even without Laura.

Chapter Eleven

CREATING PEDOPHILES

No one has seen God at any time. If we love one another,
God abides in us, and His love has been perfected in us.
(1 John 3:12)

Laura's next letter came rapidly. John and I picked it up on our way home from visiting the prison side of the island where we taught a class. I read it aloud while he drove.

> Sylvia,
>   I want to thank you for believing in me, for getting to know me, for not judging me, but instead getting to know me. You are a true friend and sister. I thank God I have you and John in my life. I want and need you to know how special you are to me. You have blessed my life. You bring fresh air and sunshine in to my dark, lonely world here. Your visits are a renewing of my hope and belief in mankind.
>   Sylvia, you have no idea how very much I need and value our friendship and the love you give. You and John are my family now. Is that OK with you guys? I know you can't be, but I wish you had been my parents. I would have known much love. Know that you and John are in my prayers and in my heart. Sylvia, if you could, if you ever write a book about

us and you talk about SCC remember we are not all
monsters. We are children of God also. We did bad
things, but we are not bad people. We only need a
chance to prove ourselves. It is growing late so I will
close for now. I hope to see you soon.
    Love you, Laura

She wanted me to tell the world that she and the men weren't
all monsters; they were children of God, just like the rest of us.

I kept thinking about Annie and the other children. God's love
was difficult for me to grasp. How could a loving God let things
like that happen and then come back to redeem the perpetrator?
Who was this God who loved both victim and perpetrator equally?
Was that the kind of love He was asking me to develop for Laura?

I was certain God was able to look deep inside each of us
and see the person He created us to be. Perhaps the life experiences that distort our character are considered mitigating circumstances, although they will never be adequate explanations for our
atrocities.

When Adam and Eve sinned in the Garden of Eden, God was
very angry. There were severe consequences to be paid by this "first
family." He gave them the ability to experience shame. He made
childbearing painful. He made them toil for what had been freely
given prior to their disobedience. And finally, He banished them
from the Garden. But He never banished them from His heart. One
of the first things God did next was fashion clothing for Adam and
Eve so they could cover their naked shame. No matter how grievous
our actions, God never gives up providing for us and loving us.

Sometimes when I was with Laura I wanted to cry in frustration. I didn't want her to be released. I didn't believe, given the
chance, she'd resist molesting children again. I fully sympathized
with the NIMBYs. My gradually developed, compassionate love
for her didn't mean I wanted her released. But I didn't want to
consider that Laura Faye McCollum could live the remainder of
her life at the SCC.

I was ready to accept a level playing field at the foot of the
cross. I could kneel there next to Laura. But with my grandfather?
Regardless of my willingness to forgive, there was still a place

inside me that was held hostage by the memories of Grandpa Ed. In that that place I hoped all pedophiles would rot in eternity. Well, maybe everyone except Laura.

When I began our visits, I saw her as a short-term project. I didn't visualize ours being an extended relationship. Each visit deepened the roots that were Laura and me, together an entity entirely different than what we were separately. Regardless of the crimes she had committed in her lifetime, I couldn't be just one more person who abandoned her.

At home later that night I pulled out Laura's autobiography. I was almost finished with what she sent me. Everything predated her adult crimes.

When I was nine years old I tried to commit suicide on an overdose of medication I was on for my behavior problems called Thorazine. I was hospitalized for three weeks and then placed in on-going mental health counseling. I was on medications at a very early age for my behavioral problems... and sleeping problems. I was on Melaril, Prolixon, Haldol, Navane, Dilantin, and Phenobarbital. Once every two weeks I had to visit with a team of neurophysiologists at the child development center. I am not sure why this was. I had to be photographed and measured and weighed and have blood and urine work-ups each time.

School still held its problems. I was suspended for peeping on the other girls using the facility. When I was thirteen the team of doctors wanted to hospitalize me for a tubal ligation so I could never mother children. The concern was great that I would become pregnant.

We had ducks, pigs, chickens, a cow named Candy, and a three-quarter horse named Daisy. She was a beautiful horse and I loved her very much. I used to go to the field and if I was eating she would come to me for a bite. Once I was eating some cherry yogurt and gave her some off my spoon. She did not like it. She made the funniest face.

We had a lot of fun working on the house. Our nearest neighbor lived five miles away. There was an African American family and they had lots of children that I played with. The little boy I liked the most was named (deleted) and I used to carry him around everywhere.

One day we were at the farm and I was washing dishes and a news announcement came on the radio that there was a fire on Ogden Street and I ran out of the house and told my foster parents. We rushed home. It was not our house, but our next-door neighbors' house and their little girl (deleted) was killed from smoke inhalation. She was only eighteen-months old when she died. I was very sad for her parents. They loved her very much. They moved away shortly after her death.

I began Fairview Jr. High school that fall. I had teachers named Ms. Spain and Ms. Cappage. I loved them very much. They were the ones that turned in my foster parents for physically and sexually abusing me. I was then sent to juvenile and placed in protective custody. I then went to a mental hospital in Bolivar, Tennessee. I stayed there for six months and was returned to the same foster home.

By this time they had a new foster child. Her name was (deleted). She was twelve with long dark hair. She took over my bedroom and I was upset to find this out. I felt pushed out and angry at her that I was so easily replaced with a stranger. When I arrived back home things were very strange and I began school again and things calmed down. My foster dad changed and would have very little to do with me. My foster mother was cold and indifferent to me.

I adjusted to the family again and (deleted) and I became fairly close. We spent a lot of time talking about her twin sister, (deleted) that she was separated from and how much she seemed lost without her.

There was no more abuse when I returned to Gladys and Damon. I thought this to be too good to be real. It was hard returning to the Purvis family. I felt alone and misplaced in the family, like an old pair of shoes that had been tossed aside from too much wear. I resented (deleted) and felt she hated me. She and I later spoke of this and I explained my hurt and resentment of her moving in my home and for receiving the love that I felt should have been mine. We held each other and cried for a long time.

(Deleted) and I began school again in the fall. We both went to Fairview my second year at this same school. On our walk to school was when I first experienced smoking cigarettes. I felt very grown up and proud that I had a friend and a sister now. See, (deleted) and I were not as close as before I went to the mental hospital. She had met (deleted) at this time and began dating. He soon became the man she married. We had the wedding at a friend's house. They lived with us.

I was about fifteen at the time and was interested in boys, however I had not begun dating yet. During this time I was going through the Goodwill Program for job elevation and readiness. I stopped going because I did not like being tested just to gain another label. I spent most of my early years in and out of hospitals and mental health and I felt I had already been tested and labeled enough. I had been diagnosed with P.T.S.D. (Posttraumatic Stress Disorder,) mental retardation and a perceptual learning disability. I had EEG tests and CAT scans and they all showed some abnormalities, but I am not sure why or what they were. I did not care to know in my opinion. I was just a guinea pig they could experiment with. This was not important to me. They had no idea what was wrong or how to help me. I was just a scared, mixed up child with many emotional difficulties in controlling my impulsive behaviors and angry outbursts.

That following summer we all went back to Sardis Dam and spent a month there. It was great. I had lots of fun. I met a boy there named (deleted). He was sixteen and was black. My foster parents had a fit when I introduced him. They said whites and blacks don't date and I got the surprise of my life when they told me that niggers were not welcome in the family.

I was doing well in school as far as math, reading and English, but was acting out more sexually than before in elementary school. I was suspended four times that year for this behavior and fighting with my classmates because they made fun of me because I was fat and unpopular due to the fact that I was a bully who messed with my female classmates.

When I was out of school and when (deleted) would come home we would steal money out of Gladys' purse and go buy cigarettes and candy. Gladys would beat us both and ground us to our room. We became good at lying and stealing. I once stole gum and got caught, but only had to return it and apologize. Nothing more was needed. I was quite embarrassed. I continued the same behaviors of running away and sexually acting out, just begging for someone to notice me and love me. I did not love myself or even like myself.

At age sixteen I was allowed to go to the county fair alone with just (deleted). She had a boyfriend and did not want to be with me. I was very scared I would get lost and not be able to find my way to where Gladys and Damon were to pick us up, but my fear was unfounded. I made it back fine. There were many other trips out to the movies and arcades since I did well going to the fair.

Christmas Day when I was about fifteen I gave a set of end tables I made at school in wood shop for Gladys to her. She seemed quite pleased and impressed at the quality of what I made and placed them proudly in the living room.

Sometime shortly after this Damon's brother, Robert passed away with cancer. We all went to his funeral. I cried because I loved him very much. He and his wife, Margaret owned a ranch and I went there with Damon quite often to cut the grass and ride the horses. That was a lot of fun for me.

(Deleted) left and went to live with her twin sister during this time. I missed her a lot when she left. I began running away again and staying with my friend, (deleted). She was my best friend through Junior High School.

I finished the eleventh grade at Treadwell High. I then was about eighteen and went to live with my boyfriend in Dallas, Texas. I stayed with him for about a year. While we were there we lived and supported ourselves through food banks and working out of labor pools and manpower, doing day jobs like roofing, landscaping and digging water lines for sprinkler systems in front of office buildings.

I was not offending or acting out during this time.

That was the end. I went back to the original envelope, but there was no more autobiography. I'd have to piece together the remainder of Laura's story from our conversations.

That's what was on my mind when I was back at Albertson's a few days later. I was in the condiment aisle reading the labels on sweet pickles when I got stuck behind a mother and her four children. I might have been annoyed except they were a vision worth a moment of watching.

The mother was obviously tired. In the main basket of the cart sat a little girl about four who was partially buried under groceries, but adorable and quite content. The youngest child was facing the mom, his pudgy little legs sticking through the shopping cart seat. He was a full-time job. His ability to lean and grab from the shelves was quite a sight! Walking behind them was the third child, another girl, who was supervised by the oldest, a boy who looked like he might be about eight-years old.

I thought of all this mother had gone through just to get four children dressed, in the car, and moving in the same direction. The analogy of a farm wife herding chickens came to mind. Sometimes life's real miracles are the everyday things we all take for granted, like four young children each wearing two socks and two shoes that match.

Eventually, I was able to steer around the family. I barely noticed the older man at the end of the aisle. It wasn't until later, re-creating the scene in slow motion, that I realized he was watching them shop for their groceries.

Two rows later I passed them all again. We were shopping in the same general direction, but as they went up an aisle, I went down it. Again, I paused to enjoy them. The mother appeared eager to finish and get to the checkout line. She was focused on the list in her hand and the tiny hands of her two-year-old, still grabbing with intent if the cart steered near enough for him to reach a shelf. Child number three had started to whine and was holding her mother's coattail with one hand while she wiped her drippy nose on it with the other.

For the umpteenth time, I wondered why women choose to give birth to multiple children. If they could see into the future to these moments of exhaustion and frustration, would they still? Or was it choice at all? Maybe I was watching the result of failed birth control and a really sexy marriage. Four children in the span of six years seemed to me to be beyond the scope of cognitive choice.

Yet, there was a part of me that deeply admired and envied this woman, and I was unashamedly enjoying the mini-drama of her young family. I knew she could not see how beautiful they all were at this exact moment. *Norman Rockwell would have loved to paint you*, I said to her in my head.

I didn't even notice that the oldest child was shyly engaged in conversation with the man who had been watching them two aisles earlier.

By the time I was ready to check out, so was the family. So was the man. We were all in line together. He was first. They were second. I brought up the rear. I guess that's when I realized that something was wrong. At first, he seemed to be there with them. Then I realized he wasn't.

The man paid for his beer with cash. He looked like he was in his early fifties. The first feature I noticed about him was that he had very hairy legs. It was a cool day, and he had on shorts and flip-flops. His face was worn out and blotchy, as if something stale was leaking out through his pores. His oily gray hair was beginning to thin. His eyes were unreadable because he was looking down, completely focused on the mother's oldest boy.

As she watched her groceries pass by the sensor and the charges appear, Mom balanced the youngest child on her hip with one arm and looked in her purse for money with the other. The little girl still sat in the shopping cart, contentedly sucking her thumb and holding a box of saltine crackers. The other daughter was talking and gently, rhythmically bumping into her mother as if reminding her, *"Don't forget me. I'm the one who is high maintenance. I need more attention than the others. Don't forget me."*

The eight-year-old was on his own, not even visible in his mother's peripheral vision. I suspected he was the one she could always count on. He was the oldest, the responsible child. She didn't need to keep him as close anymore. *"What a relief,"* she must think in her head every day. *"One child is old enough that I don't have to watch him every minute."*

I could hear bits of the conversation between the little boy and the man, his beer now resting on the farthermost end of the counter and nearly forgotten.

"I bet you'd love the farm. I have cows and horses. Have you ever ridden a horse?"

"No." He looked at the man with less shyness than he had in the grocery aisles. They had apparently been talking now for some distance throughout the store. Most boys that age would be pleased an adult was paying this much attention to him. The younger children probably received most of the parental attention.

"What color is your horse?" he asked.

"Well, I'm glad you asked me that." The beer man had sized up his victim with psychological precision. "I have several of them. The one I think you'd like best is named Max. He's brown and white. Why, he's so tame I could sit you on him right now and he'd carry you around the whole field."

"He would?"

"Sure. Have you ever seen a real farm?"

Laura's letters came back in a flash, listing the methods pedophiles use to lure children. Was that what I was watching right in front of me at the grocery store? Every cell of my body screamed that a little boy I'd never seen before was in danger. Simultaneously, his potential perpetrator knew that I knew.

If for no other reason than the sheer concentration of my rage, the beer man looked up. When our eyes met, I am absolutely certain he read my mind. We locked thoughts for what may have only been an instant, but a significant amount of information can pass between total strangers in a short amount of time without a single word being said. Neither of us blinked. No one else noticed. I stared him down with deliberate and precise intensity. To call it a glare would be an understated injustice.

The man immediately turned and disappeared into the crowd of shoppers, leaving the boy, the store, and me in an instant. He was already out the door when the clerk realized his beer was sitting on the end of the check stand, paid for and abandoned.

He didn't need to abduct the little boy that day. Now they had a rapport. All Beer Man had to do was follow them to the neighborhood where they lived, wait a few days and "run into him" playing in the yard or another trip shopping. By then, no one would remember the kind man who entertained one little boy while his mother paid for her groceries. The idea of Max the horse was all the bait he needed.

By the time the family left and I had paid for my groceries also, rage had transformed into shock, and back into rage again. I thought I should chase after the mother and tell her what had happened, should tell her to watch her children better. I couldn't. What if I was wrong? Maybe my conversations with Laura had resulted in paranoid grocery-store delusions.

When I got home I threw the groceries into their intended destinations and sat in the living room to wait for John to come home.

How can we live in an age when it is no longer safe to take our children to the grocery store? What has happened to our culture?

Have we become so sick that one mother cannot possibly supervise four children in public and shield them from all the pedophiles that live in our neighborhoods? How are we going to repair the damage and make our world safe again when we don't know how to heal the Lauras and the Grandpa Eds?

When my husband came home he listened to what I believed I'd seen. He held me, telling me over and over that God is sovereign; He alone can make sense out of the senseless. Then we went out to pick up Chinese food for dinner.

I wasn't in a good mood the day of my next visit with Laura. I didn't want to visit "pedophile palace." I was tired and needed time for myself. But it had been several weeks since we'd talked. I didn't want to let her down.

As I walked along the pier from the dock, I noticed that we had new transportation. Once I climbed aboard, its origins were apparent. The State of Washington had purchased a tour bus from Hawaii and had it shipped over so that the staff could ride more comfortably from the dock to the institution. The bus was designed to seat about fifty people on plush, upholstered, royal-blue, flowered print. Plus there was air-conditioning, as if an island off the coast of Puget Sound ever warmed enough to need cooling. The bus was beautiful and, I presumed, also expensive.

I happened to be visiting Laura its first day on the island, and the eight SCC employees riding with me were delighted with their new transportation. The bus driver turned to face us and bask in our praise.

"Well, ladies and gentlemen," he said in an official tone of voice that sounded much like the tour guide that had once sat in that very seat. "What do you think of our new bus? Just arrived from Hawaii."

Everyone "oohed" and "aahed".

Except me. I couldn't help myself. "Wow, this sure is a beautiful bus, sir."

"Yes, ma'am, it is." He beamed.

I kind of felt sorry for him for just a moment. I knew exactly where I was going. "I'm just curious about one thing, sir."

His grin seemed to solidify slightly. I could tell he was trying to figure out what was coming. He began to guard his tone of voice in anticipation. "What might that be?"

I took a big deep breath. "As a tax payer in the State of Washington, I'd like to know how much money I spent to buy this bus and ship it here from Hawaii so that the SCC employees can sit in these very comfortable and air conditioned seats on their brief ride from the dock to the front door of the institution. Can you tell me that?"

His face immediately darkened in rage, and everyone else on the bus gasped. "No, I do not have that figure." He turned his back and started the bus with a seemingly deliberate jolt.

The passengers were silent. I stared out the window, correctly ascertaining that no one would be attempting to engage me in conversation this day. I could not for the life of me come up with a justification for the money that had been spent on this beautiful bus. The employees, their families, inmates for the prison, residents destined for the SCC, and the few families that visited sex offenders at the SCC had been riding on bumpy school buses and large, white utilitarian buses and vans for decades and no one seemed very concerned that the seats weren't soft enough.

I was sick and tired of watching my tax money being thrown at our state's failed sex offender program. The Special Commitment Center was the therapeutic equivalent of the Emperor's New Clothes. Everyone pretended they could see success, when in reality no one saw it at all. No one knew how to heal Laura and the men. No one.

Usually there is a social protocol when the bus reaches the SCC. The men wait and the women exit the bus first. On this particular day that ritual was abandoned as it applied to me. Everyone stood up. The employees stepped into the aisle, assuring that I would be the last one to exit the bus. One nice male volunteer waited and let me exit in front of him, but he didn't make eye contact with me. I had done the unforgivable. I questioned the staff's creature comforts.

When Laura and I greeted one another, her first words were, "So I thought ya' were goin' to write a letter to your grandfather and tell him how mad you still are at him." Her blue eyes were penetrating. They never missed a thing.

I immediately felt self-protective. Although I had stuffed it deep in the pocket of my raincoat, I didn't see why I needed to review it with Laura. Was my childhood really any of her business?

"I did. Did you?" I felt my lower lip beginning to protrude in a stubborn, defensive and infantile pout.

"Yeah." Laura reached into her shoe and retrieved a wrinkled, slightly damp piece of notebook paper. "You wanna go first?"

I felt myself getting angry. "Not particularly. This was your idea. Why don't you go first? In fact, don't you have a cigarette to smoke or something?"

"I quit."

"You picked a rotten time to quit!" I stood up and left her in the interview room. I didn't care that my behavior was churlish and rude. What right did Laura have to give me assignments that resembled therapy? I wasn't the sex offender. She was. I stomped outside and waited for her to join me, where we sat in silence for several minutes.

I looked at her to see if she was hurt by my bad manners. She was smiling. We both started to giggle.

"I'm sorry," I told her. "I'm afraid to read it, even now."

Laura's voice was gentle and soothing. "That's OK. Why don't ya' just tell me about it? Then I'll tell ya' about mine." She waited for me to nod. "But first, I'm goin' to go bum a couple cigarettes."

"I thought you quit."

"Yeah, well, I just started again." Laura went back inside to talk to one of the residents emptying trash.

Putting my feelings on paper had been extremely difficult. I don't remember exactly when I finally wrote to Grandpa Ed. It was in the night. It was in secret, an extremely private moment. I got out of bed and went downstairs to the living room, curled up in a blanket, and began to write the things I could not say as a child.

At first I felt afraid and timid, as though I was doing something wrong. Could Grandpa still hurt me, even now, after all these years? He'd been dead more than three decades and I was still afraid of him. I felt guilty addressing him in the dark of my own house. Instantly, I became little again and was embarrassed by how quickly the transformation occurred.

Before I could write, I had to deliberately remember. The driveway. The farmhouse. The cellar. The kitchen, dining room, living room, and their large bedroom on the first floor. I couldn't remember either bathroom. Then I climbed the stairs to the two small bedrooms. The one where I slept had a double bed and a dresser. There was an old, round, silver, metallic music box in the window sill. It was designed to hold a woman's face powder and puff. When the lid was opened the inside still smelled good, and it played the "Anniversary Waltz."

Grandpa Ed took the lid off when he was done with me. Maybe the music was my gift for not screaming.

When Laura returned, I gave her a few minutes to light up and I continued to recall the details of the farmhouse.

As a seven-year-old child, I was too afraid to speak. Something was happening that was beyond me. I was paralyzed by terror. Fear is like that in its purest, concentrated form. Forget the "fight or flight" theory. When a child is molested, the absoluteness of the horror immobilizes the mind, body, and spirit. At the time, I believed parts of me were dying and would never, ever come back to life.

What Grandpa Ed did to me was all my fault.

Later I took on his shame. It's hard to explain. To set my world back in order, it was necessary for me to somehow believe that adults were good and caring people, and that included my perpetrating grandfather. It was safer to believe that it was my fault than to believe the world was a wicked place to live. It was safer to think I should have been able to stop him, than to think he never should have touched me at all. The guilt that should have been his, became mine.

My letter was tenuous at first, but it didn't take long for me to scream through my ink pen. I told him how I felt, how frightened I had been. *You lied to me. If my mother had known, she would have killed you!*

The more I wrote, the bolder I became and the older I became. I moved from a child's fear to an adult's rage. Why me? What right did you have? Was I just a toy in your sick life? What kind of monster could destroy a child and sit down the next morning to eat pancakes like it never happened?

I let the anger go deep into my little-girl places and clean out the fear. I visualized my wrath to be "Drano" eating through the lies that were clogged deep inside me, some that he had told me and others that I had told myself just to survive.

I cried, deep wracking sobs of grief for the innocence that was stolen from me on those nights at the farm. And I cried because I was too frightened to tell my parents. I cried because I didn't know how to make him stop. And I cried because I didn't know how to grow up like other kids when it was finally over.

I cried tears from a lifetime of places that couldn't hold them anymore.

When I was done crying for myself, I cried for Laura's victims, her daughters, Annie, and the others. And then I cried for Laura, not perpetrator Laura, but for victim Laura. Deep inside her was a little girl who knew the little girl inside me.

Finally, I was empty. I'd said everything I needed to say to the man who had selfishly stolen my belief in goodness. Wrapped up in a blanket, I rocked gently back and forth in the dark, comforting myself like a child in my mother's lap.

Deep in a crevasse of my mind I could hear the faint tinkling of a music box playing the "Anniversary Waltz."

By the time I finished sharing my letter with Laura, we both wept. The cameras didn't matter. The staff that checked us every few minutes didn't matter either. The only thing important in that moment was releasing the past.

Silently we walked back inside with blotchy faces and red-rimmed eyes. Now it was Laura's turn.

Although she has courageously permitted me to tell the entirety of her story, Laura's letter was so intimate, brave and personal that I will not share it... ever. She deserves to have her fear and anger honored by my silence.

When our letters were finished, we were exhausted, but we weren't quite done.

"Laura, are you ready to forgive Daman and Gladys and all the others who let you down?"

"Yeah. I read the papers you sent me. I'm ready. I just don't know what I'm supposed to do."

"Would you like me to go first?"

Laura nodded.

I took a deep, decisive prayer breath. It was time.

"Ed Sandine, I forgive you for what you did to me, the lies you told me, and the effect you had on my life and on who I became. You have no more power over me or my life; forgiving you sets me free of our past. I don't feel kind towards you yet, but I have faith God will help me feel compassionate in time. And I pray that wherever you are, my forgiveness reaches you and gives you peace."

It was Laura's turn.

"I forgive you Daman. You too, Gladys. It don't mean what you did was right. I still carry the scars, but I forgive you just the same because it's what God wants me to do. God loves both of you just like He loves me, but now I'm free and I hope my forgiveness reaches you— wherever you are today— and gives you peace."

We were both cried out.

On the pretty Hawaiian bus driving back to the dock I thought about it all. I had been visiting the SCC for two years and I was just beginning to understand why Laura had molested the children. And why my grandfather molested me. They weren't mentally ill, stupid, evil or even categorically bad people. The answer was somewhere at the bottom of that deep hole their own abuse had carved into their souls.

My search wasn't a technical study about which any respected university would care. My search was a personal one. Compelled by a need to understand, I'd met with Laura month after month, but understanding was no longer very important. Healing was what really mattered. I was free to release my need to know.

Then I heard God speaking from a place that was at the bottom of my soul, unreachable until now. *Sylvia, you can understand or you can heal, but not at the same time. Understanding is a search by the mind. Healing is a restoration of the heart. They cannot occur at the same time. If you want to understand, get out of your heart. But if you want to heal, get out of your head. I will meet you in the places that feel broken.*

When John came home, we sat and talked for a very long time. I told him about our letters, forgiveness, and what God had spoken into my heart. Then we prayed together in thanksgiving for our God who sees and heals, for Laura's restoration, and for all the children who feel alone in that moment of their nightmares.

John admitted that since I started seeing Laura— every time I was on the island—not a moment had gone by without his prayers surrounding me.

"What did you pray for?" I asked, sitting on the sofa and resting my head in the hollow of his arm.

"I prayed you would find whatever you needed to finally be at peace."

When we were finished talking and praying, we were both flooded with emotional intimacy, the glue that has always kept our marriage together.

Chapter Twelve

FIXING WHAT'S BROKEN

Then I will sprinkle clean water on you, and you shall be clean; I will cleanse you from all your filthiness and from all your idols. I will give you a new heart and put a new spirit within you... (Ezekiel 36:25-26)

Two weeks later I saw Laura again. We walked outside. It was a pleasant, end-of-summer afternoon. The flowers had bloomed out and the grass had long since dried into hay. Air smells different when nature prepares to sleep until spring's resurrection. With each inhale, my body took in the knowledge that autumn storms were only a few weeks off shore. While Laura smoked her "hand-rolled," I breathed deliberately as I thought back to our first visit.

The silences had been uncomfortable. Now they felt gentle and companionable. We could sit without talking because there was no pretense. We didn't use them as a tool to check each other out or communicate emotional strangleholds. The spoken word has great power; the unspoken has even more. Laura and I had grown comfortable with them both.

"Laura, do you remember much about my first visit here?"

"Yeah, I guess I do. Why?"

"Did you wonder why I came?"

Laura took a gentle drag off her cigarette. "Yeah, I kinda wondered, but I kinda knew. The chaplain told me he thought I needed

221

someone to talk to, another woman, and that's why you wanted to come to see me. I was surprised you came back after that first visit."

Her admission caused me to chuckle. We'd talked about this previously, but I sensed Laura needed my reassurance again. "Why's that?"

Laura shifted her weight. The concrete bench was always uncomfortable for us both. For a moment I thought of the fancy new bus. Laura pulled me back.

"I don't know. I guess because most people don't stay in my life. They show up and then they leave. You showed up, so I figured you'd leave just like everybody else. But you didn't." Her voice became quiet, gentle. "I knew you wouldn't like me, so I waited for you to go away. I told you things *so* you would go away. If I made you go, it wouldn't hurt as bad as if you thought of it yourself."

I felt a lump grow in my throat. Laura's honesty authenticated mankind's messed up humanness.

She quietly interrupted me. "Why did you keep comin' back, Sylvia?"

I remembered the little speech I had practiced on the way over to see her that first time. On the ride back home from that visit, I had been rather miffed that she didn't ask; apparently she didn't want to hear my reason for coming. Now I knew that my original reason had been one thing, and over time God birthed more meaningful reasons.

"I suppose I started with two things. One was mostly about you and one was mostly about me."

"I wanna hear about me first," she said through the clenched teeth and a scrunched face that held her cigarette in place while she searched both pockets for another.

"In the beginning, I came because I was curious about you. I believe that every woman deserves to have one female friend. That means, it doesn't matter how bad you mess up your life, and it doesn't matter who you hurt or what mistakes you make. Every woman still deserves to have one other woman who will be her friend.

"When I heard you were being transferred here from the women's prison at Purdy, it worried me. It meant that you would be locked up here with all these sex-offender men, and the only women you would see are the ones who work here. The chaplain asked if I could come out and meet you. I said yes.

"Laura, God told me that no matter what you did, you still deserve to have someone you could talk to. I wanted to see if maybe I could be that person."

Laura took a final drag off her cigarette, used it to light the next one, and put it out on the concrete, saving the butt to take to the ash can. Her smoking etiquette had improved noticeably. She used to throw paper matches on the ground; now she politely held them for the trash receptacle.

"Could you be my friend?" she asked.

"Not in the beginning. In fact, the more you told me, the less I wanted to be close to you."

"But you came back anyway. Why?"

"Because when I imagined not coming back, God never gave me peace. What I didn't know in the beginning was that He had prepared for me an extraordinary opportunity to heal. Think about it. What are the chances that a victim of childhood sexual abuse would sit down week after week with a perpetrator of childhood sexual abuse and talk honestly about their experiences? One in a million?"

"One in ten million. You're right. You and I are rare. When chaplain talked to me about you visitin', I decided to give it a try. I didn't have any friends. Or family. You and John have become both to me." She was already searching for another cigarette.

"Most men don't understand that women need to have other women as friends," I explained. "Your chaplain is extremely wise. Women speak a language of the heart that is specifically ours. I think if we don't get to be around other women and have that part of us nurtured, healing is unlikely. I have no research to back this up; it is just one of the beliefs passed down to me from my mother. So I agreed to come out here and spend time with you."

We sat in silence again while she finished cigarette number two. She didn't ask to hear the other reason.

Laura stood up and I followed her. As we crossed the Visiting Room it occurred to me that a logical question at the time would have been, "Why is Laura Faye McCollum your business, Sylvia?

What do her problems have to do with you?" I had no answer then and I'm still not certain beyond the fact that God ordained me to be here. My initial motives may not have been overwhelmingly altruistic, but my obedience to God was overwhelmingly compelling. From the first time John came home and talked about Laura and we began to pray for her, a desire grew until it was more painful to ignore, than to follow.

I closed the door so we could talk in private.

"So you gonna tell me the other reason? The one that's mostly about you?"

I looked at Laura in a deep way that momentarily pulled me out of our rapport. I wanted to be able to see "Laura, The Pedophile" when I answered.

"I wanted you to tell me why Grandpa Ed did those things to me. I wanted you to give me just one sentence that explained it in a way that would help me forgive him and heal."

Laura looked concerned. "I didn't ever give you that one sentence, did I?"

I shook my head. "No. No you didn't. But Laura, maybe it's because there isn't just one sentence that explains it all. The whole thing is a lot more complex than one defining sentence."

"But, Sylvia, nobody knows the sentence! Nobody! That's part of the problem. I'm not going to ever get well as long as I live here! They don't know how to fix what's wrong with me. They can test me and give me stupid assignments and make me sit through hours of group therapy and all the insane, psychological babble in the world..." Laura's voice escalated in anger and frustration. Under it I could feel her raw and consuming fear.

"... but they don't know how to fix what is broken in me!"

I was glad the room was soundproof. I reached across the table and grabbed Laura's hands with both of mine. So what if the staff absurdly thought we were lesbian lovers? I didn't care what they thought anymore. I kept my voice low and even. "I know, Laura. That's true, and I think it scares you to death."

She pulled away, not as a rejection, but in a gesture of aggravation. "Of course it scares me! Wouldn't it scare you? How am I ever going to get out of here if they can't heal me? And how are they going to heal me if they can't figure out what's wrong with me?"

We sat in silence for several minutes; there were no answers to her questions. Laura had been in the mental health system for most of her life. She had been observed, analyzed, assessed, diagnosed, and medicated about as much as a human being can be. So far, all the professionals had really figured out was, if left on her own, Laura Faye McCollum would molest small children again.

I did not doubt she wanted to be healed and live a "normal" life. But Laura couldn't find a way to quit molesting. To a lesser degree I couldn't quit eating Twinkies and ice cream. The only way for me to live without sugar would be in an environment where there wasn't any. The only way for Laura to not molest children was to live in the Special Commitment Center.

For a moment, I was able to feel my inner resistance as I wrapped my brain around a concept. Throughout our visits, I was determined to see the differences between Laura and me. Although we had grown into an odd rendition of friendship, my self-esteem still depended on me being better than she was. That was the foundation on which I stood while trying to find the "why" of pedophilia. As long as I was the better person, I could comfortably continue to search.

But was that foundation limiting me? What if my arrogance prevented me from finding the truth? What if the truth was less about what she had in common with Grandpa Ed, and more about the common place she shared with me? Once we started trying to fill the empty places carved out of our souls, we neither one could restrain our addictions.

It seemed like I should be able to say to myself, "This sugar isn't making me feel better. I guess I'll try something different." It doesn't work that way. Instead I say, "Two Twinkies isn't helping so I'll try to fill the hole deeper, higher and wider with an entire box of Twinkies. That ought to do it."

Laura startled me back to our little room. "Do you have any money?"

"Huh?"

"I'd like another Dr. Pepper and Reece's if you have some money left."

When we sat back down Laura completely shocked me.

"Sylvia, I want to talk about God."

"Okay. Where do you want to begin?"

Laura thoughtfully unwrapped the chocolate and licked her fingers. She rubbed them on the purple t-shirt I'd sent her and left familiar brown smears down the front.

"You've told me God talks to you. Why doesn't He talk to me? Am I that bad?"

"Laura, God talks to everyone. You just haven't been able to hear Him very well. Why do you think that is?"

Laura looked at me, through me and far beyond me before she answered. "I think it's because I never accepted Him to be my Lord and because I was never baptized. After that, it'll just be a matter of listening better."

"Is that what you want, to accept Him as your Lord and Savior and be baptized?"

"Yes."

"We can do that right here today, the saving part at least. Baptism is something the chaplain does. Let's start by talking about what it means to confess, repent and be saved."

The next forty minutes sped by. Laura knew much more about salvation than I had expected, and she was ready to implement that knowledge and more that I gave her.

Admission of sin is usually difficult for people. Laura's was thorough, heartfelt and filled with appropriate remorse. Because I knew virtually all her story, there was no need to be guarded or minimize. She didn't fear my rejection, so she was free to be candid and honest, identifying everything that might hinder her ability to experience God's love.

By the time she was prepared to invite Jesus into her life as Lord, there was a sense of internal cleansing in Laura and profound relief to have finally reached this stage of life.

"OK, now that I know God loves me, what do I have to do to hear Him better? I can't do what He wants if I can't hear Him talk, now can I?"

We talked about the Holy Spirit and the different ways God speaks to us: scripture, prayer, circumstances, other people, and the small, direct voice that emanates from inside ourselves. And I explained that baptism is one of the vehicles that makes God easier for us to hear.

When I left we both had assignments. I needed to find Laura a Bible translation that made sense to her. All she'd ever read was King James. Because it made no sense, she didn't read it at all. My husband and I are frequently asked, "Which Bible translation is the best?" We always answer, "The one you'll pick up and read."

Second, I promised to find her a cross she could wear, something that would remind her how much God loved Laura.

Her assignment, self-generated, was to meet with the chaplain and set up her baptism.

A few days later another simple trip to the grocery store reinforced my addiction theory.

Walking from the car to the supermarket's electronic sliding door was an effort. My weight was the highest it had ever been in my life and I wondered, for the umpteenth time which part of my cardiovascular system would fail me first. Stroke? Heart Attack? I knew I could take weight off temporarily on any of about twenty different diets. Weight Watchers. Nutri System. OptiFast. Lean Cuisine. South Beach. The Grapefruit Diet. Atkins. I could go on and on. I had done diet pills in my youth, some legal and some not. There isn't any diet plan I haven't been on, no weight loss fad I haven't followed, and no weight loss product I haven't bought.

And they all worked just fine until I quit.

And I have belonged to lots of gyms, done weight training, bounced on giant balls, followed cute little aerobics instructors in tights and cropped T-shirts, jogged, and paid personal fitness gurus. Every single one of them also worked until I quit. Like Laura with her cigarettes, quitting was the easy part. Not starting again is where the real challenge was found.

On this particular day I decided to follow other women around Albertson's and see what they bought. I don't know whatever possessed me to become a grocery voyeur.

I specifically looked for a woman close to my own age, in her mid-fifties who was of average height and weight. I didn't want any marathon runners. There was a lovely lady, nicely dressed, trim, with hair just starting to gray. She had an elegant grace about her and I thought, *That is what I would like to look at in my mirror each day.*

I surreptitiously followed her around the grocery store. I stopped when she stopped. I passed her a few times and let her catch up to me, as though it were a coincidence. Each time she went by I noticed what she had placed in her shopping cart. When she finally went to check out her purchases, she had fresh fruits, fresh vegetables, chicken, fish, skim milk, eggs, shampoo, coffee, aspirin, fresh flowers and toilet paper. That's all. I looked at her cart in disbelief. There wasn't a single candy bar. No pints of ice cream. No Hostess Twinkies. What was this dear woman going to eat on the way home in the car to keep her strength up?

Instead of checking out, since I hadn't actually done much shopping, I wheeled back to the produce in the front of the store and decided to try the whole exercise again. I found another woman who appeared in her early fifties. It was now nearing dinnertime, and she was dressed as if she had just left work. She looked tired. I'd forgotten to notice if the first woman was wearing a wedding ring. This second woman was. So I followed her with great stealth, stalking her from aisle to aisle.

Cleverly I thought, *If my current career field doesn't work out, I could apply to work for the CIA as a grocery spy. I have talent.*

When woman number two had completed her shopping, my cart was also full. I scooted into line behind her at the checkout. She purchased fresh fruit, fresh vegetables, chicken, fish, and skim milk, fat free cottage cheese, paper towels, deodorant, olive oil, diet cola and a greeting card.

I looked down into my cart. Apparently, neither of the two women I followed was planning to eat a whole bag of candy in the car on the way home and hide the wrappers from their husbands— or whomever they lived with. They weren't purchasing a box of Twinkies to hide in the garage "for emergencies." And clearly, they did not need to replenish their supply of Ben and Jerry's ice cream for the basement freezer. I couldn't figure out what they did when they had nightmares and couldn't go back to sleep.

Then I began to cry... right there in the middle of the grocery store while I was waiting to checkout my groceries. There was something very wrong with me. I wasn't normal. The more I considered the hopelessness of Laura's and my respective addictions, the harder I cried.

My compulsion to eat was as powerful and compelling in my life as Laura's compulsion to molest children. In that moment I was able to see with absolute clarity that she and I were alike. If a disease could be thought of as a plant, Laura and I fed off the same root system. We were molested as children, and now we were stuck with behaviors that were frighteningly similar.

Early on in our visits I had been angry because we were both molested at about the same age. Laura became a pedophile and I didn't. Now I understood why that happened.

When Grandpa Ed molested me, abuse carved out a giant hole in my spirit. I could actually feel the hole located at the base of my rib cage. When I ate large amounts of sugar, there was always a moment when the sugar started to take effect. For a fleeting moment, the hole filled with a fluttering feeling of pleasure. That little bit of relief was enough to justify whatever it cost me in money, dignity, and health just to feel the emptiness lessen, even if it only lasted for less than a minute.

People without giant holes don't comprehend this. They stand back and say stupid things like, "Why don't you just quit?" They carry harsh judgments that shout, "You are weak. Undisciplined. The past isn't an excuse, get over it." They don't know that to a survivor of abuse, filling that hole is a life-long goal. It supersedes all other goals. It will always fight and claw its way to the top. The molestation hole is desperate and controlling to a survivor.

I would do anything to fill even a little of it, for even just a few minutes. And so would Laura.

Ice cream and Twinkies worked a little, and that was good enough for me. It didn't matter that they ruined my health and kept me from many physical and fun things I would have liked to do in my life. It didn't matter that the extra weight caused me to be the recipient of derision and scorn, especially from physically fit males. It didn't matter that I had violated my personal integrity by sneaking around the house hiding sweets from my husband. I couldn't be concerned about that. I had a screaming molestation hole to fill. That's all that mattered.

Laura's life would have gone in a completely different direction were it not for Gladys and Damon. What they did to her should have sent them to prison. The only nurturing she ever got was when Damon came to her bed. It is what she learned to identify as affection.

Throughout her whole life, she tried to fix herself by sexually violating children. In Laura's case there was one additional set-up for pedophilia. Based on her personal experience, she believed that touching children in intimate ways constituted a form of nurturing. After all, it was how *she* was nurtured. Physical arousal was perfectly consistent with her experience. In time, her molestations progressed until she was out of control. Like me with sugar, once she found something that worked, even just a little bit, Laura couldn't stop. Filling the hole is all that mattered.

We didn't put the hole in our own spirits; we had no control over its formation. The problem is, once we started throwing something or someone into that deep, deep pit of despair in a futile attempt to fill it up, neither one of us could stop. I stood there in the shopping line at Albertson's and cried because I could see the hopelessness of what Laura and I had both been doing.

I also cried because she was right. There was no known cure. We had both explored everything the therapeutic and the medical communities had to offer. Laura was locked up at the SCC and not getting any closer to a safe release. I had managed to lock myself up in a body of fat.

The problem of course, is that children are not Twinkies. The consequences of what Laura chose were considerably more horrific than my own. It would take a miracle for me to stop throwing sugar into my pit, and Laura would need a miracle before she could stop throwing children's lives into hers.

Like it or not— and I didn't— this brought me to Grandpa Ed. What happened to him as a child? I knew virtually nothing about him or his family history. I do know that all children are born innocent and loving. We are not created sexually deviant. The man who molested me became that way somewhere in his life under the influence of or exposure to someone else. I could only presume that my grandfather had his own "soul hole" and that I was one of the children he used in a futile attempt to fill it. This presumption did not bring me immediate comfort.

I didn't want to believe he and I were anything alike. Just because I'd forgiven him, didn't automatically mean I felt any compassion towards him. I didn't want to let him off the hook in any way. What he did was horrible. At the same time, I was not willing to let the horror of it build a wall so high that the truthful answer to "why" could not permeate through. It was OK for me to not like the answers as I stood there crying and unloading my unhealthy groceries onto the rolling checkout mat. Sometimes it takes time for truth to grow on me.

Because I had developed sincere compassion for Laura, I knew that over time it would gently reach back through the decades and began to soften my judgment of Grandpa Ed. He could not stop molesting children any more than I could stop eating ice cream in the night. Recognizing the wrongness of the activity had absolutely no bearing on the will to stop. Once the compulsion is ignited, it is too powerful to ignore. The bearer loses the ability to choose.

Still crying, I finally traversed the entire grocery line and paid my bill. Before she looked away, the clerk discretely commented that I must not be having a very good day.

Around this same time there were several sex crime cases in the spotlight of the national media. I followed them with the intensity of obsessed paparazzi.

Because of Laura I experienced conflict when reading the newspaper and listening to the evening news when they reported the crimes and issues. I wanted to protect her from society's judgments in the sensationalism of the reporting of the crimes, near crimes and potential crimes of sex offenders, not just in our state, but nationally. There is a near hysteria when people realize— as I did after the beer man incident at the grocery store— that our children are no longer safe doing perfectly natural activities of daily living. "Lock the perverts up and throw away the key," was the unified battle cry.

No one in the press ever mentioned that once a sex offender was civilly committed to the SCC, the process for release was so complex and subjective and controversial that it was virtually impossible to implement. Laura and over two hundred men lived in legal purgatory; the chances of them ever seeing the streets again were somewhere between slim and none, short of a change in legislation. So the tax payers of the State of Washington spent thousands of dollars per resident per year, not including purchases like the new bus, and continued to employ expensive therapists and counselors, some of whom had resumes and reputations suggesting they had a great deal in common with their clients.

Also, what about the men like DD guy who knew no life other than incarceration? Even if he really had committed a crime at some point in his youth and was now being escorted everywhere by staff, was he safe? Then there were the men who were mentally ill and probably needed to be in the state mental health hospital system. They were denied treatment because their impaired cognitive function made success impossible.

If the citizens of the State of Washington couldn't figure out what to do with sex offenders on the streets, they sure couldn't deal with Laura and her comrades.

But I personally thought the problem was much more pervasive than that. What about all the "Grandpa Eds" in the world? There are countless men and women who are child molesters and have never been identified. We share the sidewalks with them every day. They are at the grocery store, the mall, the cinema and they sit right next to us in church. Because they have never been arrested, we can't look them up on the registry. Their pictures aren't posted when they move into our neighborhoods. These pedophiles look just like the rest of us. Some of them look even better.

They are stalking our children right now. Today. That is the terrifying reality of our culture.

James Dobson of Focus on the Family did an interview with Ted Bundy right before he was executed for the sexual assault and murder of numerous women in Washington State and Florida. It was a chilling interview. Bundy was articulate and handsome right to the end. He was also honest about the origination of his perversion. He was playing in the alley one day and found a stack of pornographic magazines that a neighbor had thrown out. He took them home to look at the pictures. He was a preteen boy at the time. Those magazines were the match that lit a consuming fire inside him.

We cannot lock sex offenders up faster than they are being created. Between people's broken spirits and the excessive sexualization of movies, magazines, music, fashion and especially advertising, sex has become insipid in our culture. Maybe that is not a problem for most people. But for others it feeds compulsive disorders, personality disorders, addictions, and pedophilia. In time, some people cannot restrain themselves to movies and fantasies and self-stimulation. They require live victims in order to be stimulated at all. It is an obsession that grows and becomes insatiable and unstoppable.

When a child is abducted and molested, we as a society rise up and scream in rage and horror. Yet, we continue to deny that each one of us has a part in creating an offender's disease. We support the industries that feed the fantasies that lead to the offenses. We buy the jeans. We watch the movies. We eat the hamburgers. We wear the underwear after seeing the sexy ads. But we do not want to take any responsibility for contributing to the development of the monster that tried to snatch our neighbor's child walking home after school.

Until we quit creating pedophiles in our culture, our children will not be safe. It is that simple. And we are all— every one of us— responsible for what our society is today. If we don't like it, we can change it. We can quit supporting the sexualized advertisements by buying someone else's jeans. We can quit going to movies where women and children are objectified and sexualized. We can quit letting our teenagers dress in over-sexualized ways just because the designers tell us it's the fashion. Maybe it's time for us to tell them that good taste is always in fashion. Pants worn so low on the hips that they show pubic bones are too provocative for a thirteen-year-old at the mall. Then we wonder why men leer at our young girls. It's time to quit tempting them to that, and worse.

After hearing Laura's story and coming into a better understanding of my own childhood experience, I was ready to do my part to take back the culture. I immediately began to scrutinize the advertising. I let my shopping dollars speak for me. So what if I was only one person? So what if I couldn't change the whole world? I didn't care. There were baby steps I could take all on my own. I never did like Calvin Klein jeans and Carl's Junior hamburgers.

Two months later, John and I attended Laura's baptism. The chaplain had a portable "dunk tank" that was set up on the smoking patio and painstakingly filled using pitchers of water. Laura looked beautiful, *as radiant as any bride walking up the aisle to meet her beloved.*

When the brief ceremony concluded, I gave Laura a silver cross on a chain that wouldn't easily break. It's the first time I'd noticed she didn't wear jewelry. She laughed excitedly. "I'll wear this forever."

On the ferry ride back from the island I was overwhelmed with gratitude and humility. The full manifestation of our healing would take time for us both, but God had sent me on a remarkable journey into my worst fears, and He had walked with Laura and me to the other side.

Epilogue

WHERE ARE WE NOW?

After Laura's baptism, my role officially changed. I became her personal chaplain and we worked on discipleship for the next seven years. Like most of us, salvation was the starting place, not the finish line. Laura didn't know how to live biblical principles; some people never do. We always found discussion material. She gradually learned to recognize God's voice, and how to trust Him.

Twice, Laura improved sufficiently and was transferred to the less restrictive alternative housing. Though still on the SCC grounds she lived in a cottage with a few of the men who were also learning basic life and social skills in anticipation for eventual release. There are more privileges for residents in LRAs. One morning, Laura and I were even allowed to meet at Wal-Mart and shop together. She had GPS and two assigned staff who kept her in view at all times.

"I've never had a friend to take me shopping before," she whispered, as if the admission was shameful.

I gave her a twenty-five dollar spending limit and bought her a new pair of shoes.

Unfortunately, Laura did not do well with fewer restrictions. Both times she became an intimidating bully. One time she verbally assaulted me in a fit of uncontrollable rage. Whenever she felt judged, controlled or unloved, Laura went to a place where the remnant of her anger at Damon and Gladys lived. Then she lost control. Finally the courts had to move her back inside.

The SCC changed over the years. The administration changed many times and the line staff even more. Eventually it became a prison for the "worst of the worst," not a therapeutic place for sex offenders to heal.

The chaplain eventually retired. He taught me valuable lessons about the practical application of biblical love. I will never forget them, or him.

My husband was hired to replace him. Before he took the job, we talked about how this might affect my visits with Laura. We were assured it wouldn't. Watching him continues to bless and encourage me.

Ron, Mr. Underpants, Dave and Anthony are still there. So is DD Guy, who, as it turns out, was legally and rightly committed to be there from the very beginning.

On one visit, I noticed George was missing. No one admitted knowing the circumstances of his absence. I never saw him again.

After her baptism, Laura quit smoking—and didn't start again. Likewise, I saw my doctor, was diagnosed with diabetes, had weight-loss surgery, lost a hundred pounds, and am learning to eat like the two ladies at the grocery store. My house has no sugar hiding anywhere... well, most of the time.

Also of note, my spider imaginings left and have not returned. I still don't like the critters when I see them in real life, but I can shoo them out the door or flush them down the toilet like everybody else. Spiders hold no fear for me today.

Five months after John became the chaplain, the administration remembered I was still working with Laura. We were informed it was a violation of established, non-negotiable policy. Family of staff were not allowed to work individually with residents. The issues directly related to confidentiality and security. No visits. No phone calls. No letters. Not ever.

Laura and I weren't even allowed to say good bye.

My husband is leaving the SCC. I hope to be allowed to resume my visits with Laura, if not as a volunteer, then via her visitation list. I'm prepared that my request may be denied. No one criticizes the SCC and walks away completely unscathed.

One of the remaining issues with which I struggle is, "How can God permit innocent children to be hurt? How could He just stand there and watch what Gladys and Damon did to Laura, and what Grandpa Ed did to me?

This has occupied more sleepless nights than I care to admit, and I still don't have a definitive answer. When I attempt to figure it out with my human intellect, I can't. When I attempt to see it in my life and the lives of those I love, my search is self-limiting. When I demand God explain it to me, He doesn't.

Human suffering is not fathomable with the intellect. God is sovereign, and He sees our lives from the standpoint of eternity. He doesn't owe us an explanation for something we cannot begin to understand.

I finally realized that focusing on this issue was my way of blaming God, and subsequently holding Him responsible for the way I permitted abuse to rule my life. Recently, someone asked me if I was going to ask for an explanation when I reach heaven. No, I'm not. At that point it won't matter anymore.

People also continue to ask me three questions. Is Laura saved? Is she healed? Can she now be released into the community?

With one caveat, I want to address them here. These are my opinions, formed from my narrow exposure to Laura. I am not an expert on anyone's salvation except my own, and sex offender treatment is still in its infancy. There is certainly room for others to have different opinions.

I believe Laura is saved because I heard her profession of faith, watched her dedicated study and growth, and saw evidence of the Holy Spirit actively working in her life. She has a rare and profound gift of prophesy. After I learned to recognize and trust it, God used her to lead me in the right direction on more than one occasion.

Healing doesn't happen quickly. After forgiveness we throw off our past infirmity and learn to live without assigning blame. The behaviors we used are no longer necessary, but their root structures are sometimes deep and complex. We have to learn to walk in healthy ways without our familiar crutches and manipulative limps. That takes time.

Can Laura now be released into the community? No. Pedophilia is extremely complicated. At this time, it is not curable despite science's concentrated efforts using medications and psychotherapy modalities, and a desire for measurable outcomes. The SCC remains focused on preventing the recurrence of Laura's pedophile behaviors. It does not address the deep pain where those behaviors are rooted. Until the victim Laura is treated and healed, the perpetrator Laura will not be safe to release.

Furthermore, accepting God's forgiveness does not excuse us from the consequences of our actions. In Christ Jesus we are spiritually free, but not always free in other ways. Laura is where she needs to be.

The Holy Spirit used Laura to teach me about forgiveness, brokenness and healing. One of the lessons that shows up over and over again in my life is what God revealed to me that day so very long ago. Only when we release the need to understand, can we embrace our opportunity to heal.

My husband and I work with local churches when a known sex offender wants to worship with them. This emergent issue is the most emotionally-charged challenge facing congregations today. Do we really have the right to send anyone away who sincerely loves God and wants to experience Him with us? What about our responsibility to keep children safe? What is my church's liability if something happens after we permitted him/her to sit on my pews? So far, in every case the parishioners who are vocally against opening the door to their sanctuary have either been sexually violated in the past or are close to someone else who has. Their fear didn't reach that degree of potency just from watching the six-o'clock news.

Even when God's eternal healing is directed at our worst fear and pain, we sometimes want to flee. But as adults, if we run in the opposite direction from the sex offenders that God permits to come into our life, we will miss an extraordinary opportunity for the grace and healing that only comes through facing our nightmares. Jesus Christ is still relevant today. He will see us through to the other side. Fear does not originate with God, nor does it please Him.

One of the last things my mother said to me before she passed away was, "I want you to publish your book. It's time." I wish she could be here to read it.

After she died, my brother and I discovered that we genuinely like each other. We've become best friends. I appreciate his candor and humor and intellect. He is a treasure in my life. Sometimes, it's good to be able to talk with someone who has known you from the very beginning and still loves you.

I have had no contact with my sister since Mother's death. Our estrangement continues to cause me great sorrow.

Although pedophiles are diverse in many ways, they all share one characteristic. They are extreme narcissists. They do not have the capacity to empathize with their victims and cannot imagine they are responsible for doing harm. That's why they are able to continue committing their crimes without guilt, shame, or remorse. When we have no compassion, we lose the ability to feel bad about how our actions have affected others.

Forgiveness is difficult. While I was seeing Laura, I read several excellent books and pulled information from them all. After this epilogue is what I sent to Laura on the topic.

She coined a phrase: "Use your forgiveness muscles." When either of us encountered people we needed to forgive, Laura pointed out that they were gifts from God so that we could exercise our "forgiveness muscles." God means for us to stay fit!

Before our story went to print, Laura and I talked about any royalties there might be. As a convicted felon she cannot financially gain from telling her story. I asked what she wanted done with any money that would have been hers. There was no pause. "I want you to find someplace that helps kids who've been sexually abused. Give it to them." A portion of each book is going to the Campbell County Children's Center in LaFollette, TN because of the outstanding work they do with abused children.

During our last month together, Laura sent me the following:

"What Would You Do?"
What would you do
If you looked up and saw Jesus' face?
Would you follow the world?

Would you push him away?
What would you say?
Would you scorn him and spit?
Would you mock him and laugh?
Would you collect all his clothes
And tear them in half?
Would you gather the thorns,
Put a crown on his head?
"Save yourself, Jesus,
Or you soon will be dead."
Would you nail both his hands
To the arms of a cross?
Could you look in his eyes
And not see you are lost?
Would you push him away,
And ignore the huge cost?
What would you do
If you looked up and saw Jesus?
Would you welcome him in,
And wash his dirty, tired feet?
Would you serve your best dinner?
Would you give him your seat?
Would you offer him cold water,
Cool him off in the heat?
Would you know who he is?
Would you be able to see?
What would you do
If you looked up and saw Jesus?
Would you know he is God's only Son?
That he conquered the grave,
That he was tortured and died
So you could taste grace?
Could you really push him away?
Would you bow down before him
And fall on your face?
Would you confess him as Lord?
Would you worship with praise?
Again I ask, would you push him away?

How would you feel if he turned his back
And said, "You? I remember you not."
How would you feel if he denied you forgiveness?
If he refused to carry your sins to the cross?
What if he saw you and passed on by?
What would you say?
"Wait, Jesus! Don't go.
I'll die without your love and your grace."
Now, would you confess him as Lord?
Again I ask, or would you push him away?
He shed his own blood for your sins,
His righteousness is what he came to impart.
What would you say?
Would you give him your broken heart?
How would you feel
If you looked up and saw Jesus today?
Would you really ignore him?
And push him away?
Once more I'm asking,
What would you do?
What would you say?

I look forward to hearing more of her poetry someday when we both reach the other side.

Addendum

THE FORGIVENESS PAPERS

T his is a compilation of many author's work on forgiveness: Stanley C. Baldwin, Jerry Cook, R.T. Kendall, Leonard Shaw, Lewis B. Smedes, and others. It merits a fresh look every time the offense feels too big, the offender too evil, or the hurt so complete that I do not want to forgive.

What Forgiveness Is Not
- Forgiving someone does not mean that we must tolerate the wrong he did.
- It doesn't suggest that what happened wasn't all that bad.
- Forgiving doesn't mean that we want to- or even can- forget what happened.
- Forgiving does not mean that we excuse the person who did it.
- Forgiving does not surrender our right to justice.
- Forgiving does not mean that someone who hurt us is permitted to hurt us again.
- Finally, forgiveness does not mean that we are inviting that person back into a relationship with us.

How to Forgive
We must first rediscover the humanity of the person who has hurt us. All forgiveness begins with a decision, not a feeling of benevolence. We must be willing to see our enemy through eyes

that are not smudged by our pain, our fear and our hate. We must begin to see the real person, a mixture of good and bad traits, someone who makes mistakes but is a hodge-podge of meanness and decency, lies and truths, good as well as evil, created to be a child of God. Just like us.

The first step to forgiving is to relinquish our self-righteousness and see the person who hurt us as human and imperfect.

Secondly, we must surrender our right to get even. Vengeance will not make you feel better. They can arrest the murderer, find the body, confirm the DNA, but that doesn't get you to forgiveness. Crime victims sometimes think that "closure" will solidify into relief. It doesn't. The best it can do is point the way to forgiveness.

What makes this so hard? We confuse vengeance with justice. Vengeance is the pleasure of seeing someone who hurt us getting it back and then some. Justice is when someone pays a fair penalty for wronging another. Vengeance is personal satisfaction. Justice is moral accounting.

Finally, we must bravely and deliberately change our thoughts about the person we have decided to forgive. After we have rediscovered the humanity of our enemy and given up our right to revenge, we must allow ourselves to *feel* him differently now that we see him differently.

How Do We Know We've Really Forgiven Someone?

When we begin to feel any stirrings of benevolence inside us, any hint that it would be all right with us if some *tiniest* bit of good fortune comes our enemy's way, we can be sure that we are teamed with God in a modest miracle of forgiving. We have activated our healing.

Who Can't We Forgive?

There are four situations where we cannot forgive.

1.   We cannot forgive governments or organizations or countries. Forgiveness is personal. It happens one person at a time.

2.   We cannot forgive people for what they are. We can only forgive them for what they do. I couldn't forgive my

grandfather for being a serial pedophile. I *can* forgive him for molesting me.

3. We forgive the people who hurt us deeply. Everyone suffers little hurts while going through life. But there is a big difference between the bark of a puppy and the bite of a dog. Forgiving is for the *truly* serious wounds of life, for the inner pain and building resentment brought by deep cuts that we cannot ignore. Little scratches that heal on their own should be left alone to do just that.

4. There is pain and there is *wrongful* pain. Forgiveness is for the wrongful pains. This requires honestly on our part. A prisoner doing time for murder may feel the pain of incarceration, but that is not wrongful pain. However, the prisoner who was judged guilty based on the false testimony of a witness feels wrongful pain. At some point the witness will need to be forgiven.

SUMMARY

W hen I read the gospels and the words of Jesus, every single thing He said has to do with loving God and/or loving others. We cannot truly love unless we are willing to forgive those who have hurt us. Ask any couple who've been married longer than twenty-four hours.

The friendships I cherish most today are the ones where we have overcome conflict with forgiveness. These are the friends I trust most. Whatever happens, I am confident we will get to the other side and still love each other. Usually, we love each other even more than we did before the hurt feelings.

Through the experience of painful conflict, fear and hatred, and eventually the discipline of forgiveness, we can begin to see a little more of ourselves in God's eyes. These are the situations that remind us of His extreme love, even though we've done nothing to deserve it.

However, the decision is always ours.

END NOTES

1   Kristen Gelineau. Phillyburbs.com. March 2004.
2   Ken Schram. komotv.com. 2004.
3   Amber Smith. *The Post Standard*, Syracuse, New York. 2010.
4   2 Samuel 6:7.
5   Joseph Ciarrochi. *A Minister's Handbook of Mental Disorders*. Paulist Press. 1993.
6   Michelle Elliot. *Female Sexual Abuse of Children*. Guilford Press. 1994.
7   Jonah 1:1 – 3:10.
8   American Psychiatric Association. *The Diagnostic and Statistical Manual of Mental Disorders*. DSM-III- R. 1987.
9   M Scott Peck. *People of the Lie*. Simon & Schuster. New York. 1983.

CPSIA information can be obtained at www.ICGtesting.com
Printed in the USA
LVOW08s1819160814

399362LV00001BA/1/P